Psychosocial Aspects of Domestic Violence

Psychosocial Aspects of Domestic Violence

Major Suresh Goel (Retd)

MD PUBLICATIONS PVT LTD
NEW DELHI
www.mdppl.com

Published by :

MD Publications Pvt Ltd
"MD House", 11, Darya Ganj,
New Delhi-110 002
Phone : +91-11-41563325 (Customer Service)
+91-11-41562846 (Editorial)
E-mail (orders) : order@mdppl.com
Website : www.mdppl.com

ISBN : 978-81-7533-217-1

Published and Printed by Mr. Pranav Gupta on behalf of **MD Publications Pvt Ltd** at Printext, New Delhi.

PREFACE

Historically, in most cultures, domestic violence has been an accepted fact of life. Only in recent years has it begun to be viewed as a criminal and social problem. Domestic violence occurs in all cultures; people of all races, ethnicities, religions, sexes and classes can be perpetrators of domestic violence. Domestic violence is perpetrated by both men and women. Domestic violence occurs across the lifespan and across most cultures. Women are at a disproportionately high risk of physical, sexual and psychological violence from an intimate person such as a partner or ex-partner. Many children, too, are likely to experience violence from someone they know or be witnesses to violence within their families.

Domestic violence (also known as domestic abuse, spousal abuse, or intimate partner violence) occurs when a family member, partner or ex-partner attempts to physically or psychologically dominate another. Domestic violence often refers to violence between spouses, or spousal abuse but can also include cohabitants and non-married intimate partners.

Domestic violence has many forms, including physical violence, sexual abuse, emotional abuse, intimidation, economic deprivation, and threats of violence. Violence can be criminal and includes physical assault (hitting, pushing, shoving, etc.), sexual abuse (unwanted or forced sexual activity), and stalking. Although emotional, psychological and financial abuses are not criminal behaviors, they are forms of abuse and can lead to criminal violence.

Domestic violence may be physical, sexual or psychological, but all three can be present. Domestic violence is always characterised by the use of coercive control and psychological abuse. Victimisation is associated with alterations in the perception of the perpetrator, especially a belief in his or her omnipotence, and alterations in the victim's perception of self. Feelings of self-blame, shame and loss of self-esteem are extremely common. At the same time, psychological defenses used to cope with violence include denial of its existence and minimisation of its severity.

I am very grateful to Mr. Pranav Gupta, Director of MD Publications Pvt Ltd, New Delhi, for his kind cooperation and support for this book.

Major Suresh Goel (Retd)

CONTENTS

1

Psychosocial Aspects of Domestic Violence

An Introduction

DOMESTIC VIOLENCE

Domestic violence (also known as domestic abuse, spousal abuse, or intimate partner violence) occurs when a family member, partner or ex-partner attempts to physically or psychologically dominate another. Domestic violence often refers to violence between spouses, or spousal abuse but can also include cohabitants and non-married intimate partners. Domestic violence occurs in all cultures; people of all races, ethnicities, religions, sexes and classes can be perpetrators of domestic violence.

Domestic violence is perpetrated by both men and women. Domestic violence has many forms, including physical violence, sexual abuse, emotional abuse, intimidation, economic deprivation and threats of violence. Violence can be criminal and includes physical assault (hitting, pushing, shoving, etc.), sexual abuse (unwanted or forced sexual activity), and stalking. Although emotional, psychological and financial abuses are not criminal behaviours, they are forms of abuse and can lead to criminal violence.

There are a number of dimensions including:

- *Mode:* physical, psychological, sexual and/or social.

- *Frequency:* on/off, occasional and chronic.
- *Severity:* in terms of both psychological or physical harm and the need for treatment.
- Transitory or permanent injury: mild, moderate, severe and up to homicide.

An important component of domestic violence, often ignored is the realm of passive abuse, leading to violence. Passive abuse is covert, subtle and veiled. This includes victimisation, procrastination, forgetfulness, and ambiguity, and neglect, spiritual and intellectual abuse. Recent attention to domestic violence began in the women's movement, particularly feminism and women's rights, in the 1970s, as concern about wives being beaten by their husbands gained attention. Awareness and documentation of domestic violence differs from country to country. Estimates are that only about a third of cases of domestic violence are actually reported in the United States and the United Kingdom. According to the Centers for Disease Control, domestic violence is a serious, preventable public health problem affecting more than 32 million Americans, or more than 10% of the U.S. population.

Popular emphasis has tended to be on women as the victims of domestic violence. However, with the rise of the men's movement, and particularly masculism and men's rights, there is now advocacy for men victimized by women. In a special report on violence related injuries by the US Department of justice (in August 1997) hospital emergency room visits pertaining to domestic violence indicated that physically abused men represent just under one-sixth of the total patients admitted to hospital reporting domestic violence as the cause of their injuries. The report highlights that significantly more men than women did not disclose the identity of their attacker.

The term "intimate partner violence" (IPV) is often used synonymously. Family violence is a broader definition, often used to include child abuse, elder abuse, and other violent acts between family members. Wife abuse, wife beating, and battering are terms sometimes used, though with acknowledgment that many are not actually married to the abuser, but rather co-habiting or other arrangements. In more recent years, 'battering' or 'battered wife' has become less acceptable terminology, since abuse can take other forms than physical abuse and males are often victims of violence as well. Other forms of abuse may be constantly occurring, while physical abuse happens occasionally. These other forms of abuse have potential to lead to mental illness, self-harm, and even attempts at suicide.

The U.S. Office on Violence Against Women (OVW) defines domestic violence as a "pattern of abusive behaviour in any relationship that is used by one partner to gain or maintain power and control over another intimate partner". The definition adds that domestic violence "can happen to anyone regardless of race, age, sexual orientation, religion, or gender", and that it can take many forms, including physical abuse, sexual abuse, emotional, economic, and psychological abuse.

The Children and Family Court Advisory and Support Service in the United Kingdom in its "Domestic Violence Policy" uses *domestic violence* to refer to a range of violent and abusive behaviours, defining it as:

Patterns of behaviour characterised by the misuse of power and control by one person over another who are or have been in an intimate relationship. It can occur in mixed gender relationships and same gender relationships and has profound consequences for the lives of children, individuals, families and communities. It may be physical, sexual, emotional and/or psychological. The latter may include intimidation, harassment, and damage to property, threats and financial abuse.

In Spain, the introduction of *Ley Orgánica 1/2004, de 28 de diciembre, de Medidas de Protección Integral contra la Violencia de Género* (Organic Law 1/2004 of December 28, of Measures of Integral Protection against Gendered Violence) defined several key terms.

It defines *la violencia de género* (gendered violence) as *una violencia que se dirige sobre las mujeres por el hecho mismo de serlo, por ser consideradas, por sus agresores, carentes de los derechos mínimos de libertad, respeto y capacidad de decisión* (a violence that is directed at women for the very fact of being women and therefore being considered by their attackers as lacking the basic rights of freedom, respect, and decision making capability). The new law establishes courts titled *Juzgados de Violencia sobre la Mujer* (Courts of Violence against Women) and suspends the presumption of innocence for men accused of domestic violence. Courts are empowered to hold closed door hearings before trial and evict men from their homes; suspend parental rights, child custody, or visitation rights; and bar men from possessing weapons.

FORMS OF ABUSE

Domestic violence can take the form of physical violence, including direct physical violence ranging from unwanted physical contact to rape and murder. Indirect physical violence may include destruction of objects, striking or throwing objects near the victim, or harm to pets. In addition to physical violence, spousal abuse often includes mental or emotional abuse, including verbal threats of physical violence to the victim, the self, or others including children, ranging from explicit, detailed and impending to implicit and vague as to both content and time frame, and verbal violence, including threats, insults, put-downs, and attacks.

Nonverbal threats may include gestures, facial expressions, and body postures. Psychological abuse may also involve economic and/or social control, such as controlling the victim's money and other economic resources, preventing the victim from seeing friends and relatives, actively sabotaging the victim's social relationships, and isolating the victim from social contacts.

PHYSICAL VIOLENCE

Physical violence is the intentional use of physical force with the potential for causing injury, harm, disability, or death, for example, hitting, shoving, biting, restraint, kicking, or use of a weapon.

SEXUAL VIOLENCE

Sexual violence is divided into three categories:

1. Use of physical force to compel a person to engage in a sexual act against his or her will, whether or not the act is completed;
2. Attempted or completed sex act involving a person who is unable to understand the nature or condition of the act, unable to decline participation, or unable to communicate unwillingness to engage in the sexual act, e.g., because of underage immaturity, illness, disability, or the influence of alcohol or other drugs, or because of intimidation or pressure; and
3. Abusive sexual contact.

EMOTIONAL ABUSE

Emotional abuse (also called *psychological abuse* or *mental abuse*) can include humiliating the victim privately or publicly, controlling what the victim can and cannot do, withholding information from the victim, deliberately doing something to make the victim feel diminished or embarrassed, isolating the victim from friends and family, implicitly blackmailing the victim by harming others when the victim expresses independence or happiness, or denying the victim access to money or other basic resources and necessities.

Women who are being emotionally abused often feel as if they do not own themselves; rather, they may feel that their significant other has nearly total control over them. Women undergoing emotional abuse often suffer from depression, which puts them at increased risk for suicide, eating disorders, and drug and alcohol abuse.

ECONOMIC ABUSE

Economic abuse is when the abuser has complete control over the victim's money and other economic resources. Usually, this involves putting the victim on a strict "allowance," withholding money at will and forcing the victim to beg for the money until the abuser gives them some money. It is common for the victim to receive less money as the abuse continues. This also includes (but is not limited to) preventing the victim from finishing education or obtaining employment, or intentionally squandering or misusing communal resources.

STALKING

In addition, stalking is often included among the types of Intimate Partner Violence. Stalking generally refers to repeated behaviour that causes victims to feel a high level of fear.

VICTIMISATION

Statistics

Domestic violence occurs across the world, in various cultures, and affects people across society, irrespective of economic status. In the United States, according to the Bureau of Justice Statistics women are about six times as likely as men to experience intimate partner violence. Percent of women surveyed (national surveys) who were ever physically assaulted by an intimate partner: Barbados (30%), Canada (29%), Egypt (34%), New Zealand (35%), Switzerland (21%), United States (22%). Some surveys in specific places report figures as high as 50-70% of women surveyed who were ever physically assaulted by an intimate partner. Others, including surveys in the Philippines and Paraguay, report figures as low as 10%.

The rate of intimate partner violence in the U.S. has declined since 1993. Almost always, surveys will undercount actual numbers. Results will also vary, depending on specific wording of survey questions, how the survey is conducted, the definition of abuse or domestic violence used, the willingness or unwillingness of victims to admit that they have been abused and other factors.

Another controversy is the level of physical aggression in relationships of men versus women. For example, Martin S. Fiebert examined 219 studies on intimate partner violence and concluded that "women are as physically aggressive, or more aggressive, than men in their relationships with their spouses or male partners." Domestic violence against women in lesbian relationships is about as common as domestic violence against women in heterosexual relationships.

VIOLENCE AGAINST WOMEN

In the United States males experienced higher victimisation rates than females for all types of violent crime except rape and other sexual assault; but 20 percent of all violent crimes experienced by women in the U.S. are cases of intimate partner violence, compared to 3 percent of violent crime experienced by men. According to the U.S. Bureau of Justice Statistics "in 1994 for every 5 violent victimisations of a female by an intimate there was 1 male. Intimates committed over 900,000 victimisations of females and about 167,000 victimisations of males." There is currently limited research on the abuse of lesbian women by their lesbian partners; however an investigation by the Canadian Government saw some 19% of a survey of lesbian women respond to being victims of their partners.

DURING PREGNANCY

Domestic violence during pregnancy can be missed by medical professionals because it often presents in non-specific ways. A number of countries have been statistically analyzed to calculate the prevalence of this phenomenon:

- UK prevalence: 2.5-3.4%
- USA prevalence: 3.2-33.7%
- Ireland prevalence: 12.5%
- Rates are higher in teenagers
- Severity and frequency increase postpartum (10% antenatal vs. 19% postnatal; 21% at 3 months post partum.

There are a number of presentations that can be related to domestic violence during pregnancy: delay in seeking care for injuries; late booking, non-attenders at appointments, self-discharge; frequent attendance, vague problems; aggressive or over-solicitous partner; burns, pain, tenderness, injuries; vaginal tears, bleeding, STDs; and miscarriage.

Domestic violence can also affect the fetus, the subsequent baby, and existing children:

- Pre-birth: prematurely, Premature rupture of membranes, IUD
- Psychosocial: interference in relationship, witnessing of violence, eating and sleeping disorders, emotional neediness, withdrawn, over-compliant, clingy, aggressive, problems at school, suicidal ideation
- Legal: child protection issues, overlap with child abuse
- Long-term chronic ill-health

VIOLENCE AGAINST MEN

According to a July 2000 Centers for Disease Control report, data from the Bureau of Justice, National Crime Victimisation Survey consistently show that women are at significantly greater risk of intimate partner violence than are men, while data from the National Family Violence Survey contradict these data and consistently show that men and women are equally likely to be physically assaulted by an intimate partner. The same report, on phone interviews with 8000 men and 8000 women, reported that 7.5% of men have been raped or assaulted by an intimate at some time in their life time (compared to 25% of women), and 0.9 percent of men had been raped or assaulted in the previous 12 months (compared to 1.5% of women).

In May, 2007, researchers with the Centers for Disease Control reported on rates of self-reported violence among intimate partners using data from a 2001 study. In the study, almost one-quarter of participants reported some violence in their relationships. Half of these involved one-sided ("non-reciprocal") attacks and half involved both assaults and counter assaults ("reciprocal violence"). Women reported committing one-sided attacks more than twice as often as men (70% *versus* 29%). In all cases of intimate partner violence, women were more likely to be injured than men, but 25% of men in relationships with two-sided violence reported injury compared to 20% of women reporting injury in relationships with one-sided violence. Women were more likely to be injured in non-reciprocal violence.

While much attention has been focused on domestic violence against women, men's rights activists argue that domestic violence against men is a social problem that is also worthy of attention. Each year, 834,000 men are raped or physically assaulted by intimate partners an average 3.5 times/year, for a total of 2.9 million assaults/year (4.9 million for women). Men in intimate relationships with other men are more likely to be raped or assaulted than men in heterosexual relationships. According to the 2000 CDC/Justice study, "Approximately 23 percent of the men who had lived with a man as a couple reported being raped, physically assaulted, and/or stalked by a male cohabitant, while 7.4 percent of the men who had married or lived with a woman as a couple reported such violence by a wife or female cohabitant.

These findings, combined with those presented in the previous bullet, provide further evidence that intimate partner violence is perpetrated primarily by men, whether against male or female intimates." A 2007-2008 online non-random, self-report survey is being conducted by researchers at Clark University and Bridgewater State College, which seeks to document the experiences and health of men who have sustained partner violence in the past year. Anyone may fill out the survey.

VIOLENCE AGAINST CHILDREN

When it comes to domestic violence towards children involving physical abuse, research in the UK by the NSPCC indicated that "most violence occurred at home" (78 per cent). 40 - 60% of men and women who abuse other adults also abuse their children. Girls whose fathers batter their mothers are 6.5 times more likely to be sexually abused by their fathers than are girls from non-violent homes.

VIOLENCE AGAINST TEENS

Teen dating violence is a pattern of controlling behaviour by one teenager over another teenager who are in a dating relationship. While there are many similarities to "traditional" domestic violence there are also some differences. Teens are much more likely than adults to become isolated from their peers as the result of controlling behaviour by their boyfriend/ girlfriend. Also, for many teens the abusive relationship may be their first dating experience and have never had a "normal" dating experience with which to compare it.

2005 WORLD HEALTH ORGANISATION MULTI-COUNTRY STUDY

The World Conference on Human Rights, held in Vienna in 1993, and the Declaration on the Elimination of Violence against Women in the same year, concluded that civil society and governments have acknowledged that violence against women is a public health and human rights concern. Work in this area has resulted in the establishment of international standards, but the task of documenting the magnitude of violence against women and producing reliable, comparative data to guide policy and monitor implementation has been exceedingly difficult. The World Health Organisation Multi-country Study on Women's Health and Domestic Violence against Women 2005 is a response to this difficulty. Published in 2005 it is a groundbreaking study which analysed data from 10 countries and sheds new light on the prevalence of violence against women. It seeks to look at violence against women a public health policy perspective. The findings will be used to inform a more effective response from government, including the health, justice and social service sectors, as a step towards fulfilling the state's obligation to eliminate violence against women under international human rights laws.

Types

The form and characteristics of domestic violence and abuse may vary in other ways. Michael P. Johnson (1995, 2006b) argues for three major types of intimate partner violence. The typology is supported by subsequent research and evaluation by Johnson and his colleagues, as well as independent researchers. Distinctions need to be made regarding types of violence, motives of perpetrators, and the social and cultural context. Violence by a man against his wife or intimate partner is often done as a way for men to control "their woman". Other types of intimate partner violence also occur, including violence between gay and lesbian couples, and by women against their male partners.

Distinctions are not based on single incidents, but rather on patterns across numerous incidents and motives of the perpetrator. Types of violence identified by Johnson:

- Common couple violence (CCV) is not connected to general control behaviour, but arises in a single argument where one or both partners physically lash out at the other. Intimate terrorism is one element in a general pattern of control by one partner over the other. Intimate terrorism is more common than common couple violence, more likely to escalate over time, not as likely to be mutual, and more likely to involve serious injury.
- Intimate terrorism (IT) may also involve emotional and psychological abuse.
- Violent resistance (VR), sometimes thought of as "self-defense", is violence perpetrated usually by women against their abusive partners.
- Mutual violent control (MVC) is rare type of intimate partner violence occurs when both partners act in a violent manner, battling for control.

Another type is situational couple violence, which arises out of conflicts that escalate to arguments and then to violence. It is not connected to a general pattern of control. Although it occurs less frequently in relationships and is less serious than intimate terrorism, in some cases it can be frequent and/

or quite serious, even life-threatening. This is probably the most common type of intimate partner violence and dominates general surveys, student samples, and even marriage counseling samples. Types of male batterers identified by Holtzworth-Munroe and Stuart (1994) include "family-only", which primarily fall into the CCV type, who are generally less violent and less likely to perpetrate psychological and sexual abuse. IT batterers include two types: "Generally-violent-antisocial" and "dysphoric-borderline". The first type includes men with general psychopathic and violent tendencies. The second type of men are who are emotionally dependent on the relationship. Support for this typology has been found in subsequent evaluations. Others, such as the CDC, divide domestic violence into two types: reciprocal violence, in which both partners are violent, and non-reciprocal violence, in which one partner is violent.

Theories

There are many different theories as to the causes of domestic violence. These include psychological theories that consider personality traits and mental characteristics of the offender, as well as social theories which consider external factors in the offender's environment, such as family structure, stress, social learning. As with many phenomena regarding human experience, no single approach appears to cover all cases.

Psychological

Psychological theories focus on personality traits and mental characteristics of the offender. Personality traits include sudden bursts of anger, poor impulse control, and poor self esteem. Various theories suggest that psychopathology and other personality disorders are factors, and that abuse experienced as a child leads some people to be more violent as adults. Studies have found high incidence of psychopathy among abusers. Dutton has suggested a psychological profile of men who abuse their wives, arguing that they have borderline personalities (between psychotics and neurotics), which are developed early in life.

Gelles suggests that psychological theories are limited, and points out those other researchers have found that only 10% (or less) fit this psychological profile. He argues that social factors are important, while personality traits, mental illness, or psychopathy are lesser factors. It should be noted that Borderline Personality Disorder as used in this context is outdated. Whilst it was originally believed that a person's psychological state was between neurotic and psychotic it is now recognised that BPD is the most severe and intransigent of the personality disorders.

Social Theories

Looks at external factors in the offender's environment, such as family structure, stress, social learning, and includes rational choice theories.

Resource Theory

Resource theory was suggested by William Goode (1971). Women who are mostly dependent on the spouse for economic well being having children to take care of, should they leave the marriage, increases the financial burden and makes it all the more difficult for them to leave. Dependency means that they have fewer options and few resources to help them cope with or change their spouse's behaviour. Couples that share power equally experience lower incidence of conflict, and when conflict does arise, are less likely to resort to violence. If one spouse desires control and power in the relationship, the spouse may resort to abuse. This may include coercion and threats, intimidation, emotional abuse, economic abuse, isolation, making light of the situation and blaming the spouse, using children (threatening to take them away), and behaving as "master of the castle".

SOCIAL STRESS

Stress may be increased when a person is living in a family situation, with increased pressures. Social stresses, due to inadequate finances or other such problems in a family may further increase tensions. Violence is not always caused by stress, but may be one way that some (but not all) people respond to stress. Families and couples in poverty may be more likely to experience domestic violence, due to increased stress and conflicts about finances and other aspects.

Some speculate that poverty may hinder a man's ability to live up to his idea of "successful manhood", thus he fears losing honor and respect. Theory suggests that when he is unable to economically support his wife, and maintain control, he may turn to misogyny, substance abuse, and crime as ways to express masculinity.

SOCIAL LEARNING THEORY

Social learning theory suggests that people learn from observing and modeling after others' behaviour. With positive reinforcement, the behaviour continues. If one observes violent behaviour, one is more likely to imitate it. If there are no negative consequences (e.g. victim accepts the violence, with submission), then the behaviour will likely continue. Often, violence is transmitted from generation to generation in a cyclical manner.

POWER AND CONTROL

In some relationships, violence arises out of a perceived need for power and control, a form of bullying and social learning of abuse. Abusers' efforts to dominate their partners have been attributed to low self-esteem or feelings of inadequacy, unresolved childhood conflicts, the stress of poverty, hostility and resentment toward women (misogyny), hostility and resentment toward men (misandry), personality disorders, genetic tendencies and socio-cultural influences, among other possible causative factors. Most authorities seem to agree that abusive personalities result from a combination of several factors, to varying degrees.

A causalist view of domestic violence is that it is a strategy to gain or maintain power and control over the victim. This view is in alignment with Bancroft's "cost-benefit" theory that abuse rewards the perpetrator in ways other than, or in addition to, simply exercising power over his or her target(s). He cites evidence in support of his argument that, in most cases, abusers are quite capable of exercising control over them, but choose not to do so for various reasons. An alternative view is that abuse arises from powerlessness and externalizing/projecting this and attempting to exercise control of the victim. It is an attempt to 'gain or maintain power and control over the victim' but even in achieving this it cannot resolve the powerlessness driving it. Such behaviours have addictive aspects leading to a cycle of abuse or violence.

Mutual cycles develop when each party attempts to resolve their own powerlessness in attempting to assert control. Questions of power and control are integral to the widely utilized Duluth Domestic Abuse Intervention Project. They developed "Power and Control Wheel" to illustrate this: it has power and control at the center, surrounded by spokes (techniques used), the titles of which include:

- Coercion and threats
- Intimidation
- Emotional abuse
- Isolation
- Minimizing, denying and blaming
- Using children
- Economic abuse
- Male privilege

The model attempts to address abuse by one-sidedly challenging the misuse of power by the 'perpetrator'. Critics of this model suggest that the one-sided focus is problematic as resolution can only be achieved when all participants acknowledge their responsibilities, and identify and respect mutual purpose.

The power wheel model is not intended to assign personal

responsibility, enhance respect for mutual purpose or assist victims and perpetrators in resolving their differences. It is an informational tool designed to help individuals understand the dynamics of power operating in abusive situations and identify various methods of abuse.

ALCOHOL-RELATED AND NON-ALCOHOL RELATED VIOLENCE

Other factors associated with domestic violence include heavy alcohol consumption, mental illness, classism, various political and legal characteristics such as authoritarianism and dehumanisation.

PRESCRIPTION DRUGS

It is also important to this topic to understand the paradoxical effects of some sedative drugs. Serious complications can occur in conjunction with the use of sedatives creating the opposite effect as to that intended. Malcolm Lader at the Institute of Psychiatry in London estimates the incidence of these adverse reactions at about 5%, even in short-term use of the drugs. The paradoxical reactions may consist of depression, with or without suicidal tendencies, phobias, aggressiveness, violent behaviour and symptoms sometimes misdiagnosed as psychosis. The contribution of these reactions is one possible component.

SEX AND GENDER

Modes of abuse are stereotyped by some to be gendered, females tending to use more psychological and men more physical forms. The visibility of these differs markedly. However, experts who work with victims of domestic violence have noted that physical abuse is almost invariably preceded by psychological abuse. Police and hospital admission records indicate that a higher percentage of females than males seek treatment and report such crimes. Unless or until more men identify themselves and go on record as having been abused by female partners, and in a manner whereby the nature and extent of their injuries can be clinically assessed, men will continue to be identified as the most frequent perpetrators of physical and emotional violence.

CYCLE OF VIOLENCE

Frequently, domestic violence is used to describe specific violent and overtly abusive incidents, and legal definitions will tend to take this perspective. However, when violent and abusive behaviours happen within a relationship, the effects of those behaviours continue after these overt incidents are over. Advocates and counsellors will refer to domestic violence as a pattern of behaviours, including those listed above. Lenore Walker presented the model of a Cycle of Violence which consists of three basic phases:

Honeymoon Phase

This phase is characterized by affection, apology and apparent end of violence and during this stage when the batterer feels overwhelming feelings of remorse and sadness. Some batterers walk away from the situation, while others shower their victims with love and affection.

Tension Building Phase

This phase is characterized by poor communication, tension, fear of causing outbursts and during this stage the victims try to calm the batterer down, to avoid any major violent confrontations.

Acting-out Phase

This phase is characterized by outbursts of violent, abusive incidents and during this stage the batterer attempts to dominate his/her partner (victim), with the use of domestic violence.

Although it is easy to see the outbursts of the Acting-out Phase as abuse, even the more pleasant behaviours of the Honeymoon Phase serve to perpetuate the abuse. Many domestic violence advocates believe that the cycle of violence theory is limited and does not reflect the realities of many men and women experiencing domestic violence.

GENDER DIFFERENCES

The role of gender is a controversial topic related to the discussion of domestic violence. Erin Pizzey, the founder of an early women's shelter in Chiswick, London, has expressed her dismay at how she believes the issue has become a gender-political football, and expressed an unpopular view in her book *Prone to Violence* that some women in the refuge system had a predisposition to seek abusive relationships.

She also expressed the view that domestic violence can occur against any vulnerable intimates, regardless of their gender. A Freudian concept, repetition compulsion, has also come up in modern psychology as a possible cause of a woman who was abused in childhood seeking an abusive man (or vice versa), theoretically as a misguided way to "master" their traumatic experience.

GENDER ASPECTS OF ABUSE

There continues to be discussion about whether men are more abusive than women, whether men's abuse of women is worse than women's abuse of men, and whether abused men should be provided the same resources and shelters that years of advocacy, money-rasing, and funding has gained for women victims Sekä Carney (2007). Martin S. Fiebert of the Department of Psychology at California State University, Long Beach, provides an analysis of 219 scholarly investigations: 170 empirical studies and 49 analyses, which he believes demonstrate women are as physically aggressive, or more aggressive, than men.

In a Los Angeles Times article about male victims of domestic violence, Fiebert suggests that "...consensus in the field is that women are as likely as men to strike their partner but that - as expected - women are more likely to be injured than men. However, he noted, men are seriously injured in 38% of the cases in which "extreme aggression" is used." No statistic was given to shed light on how often "extreme aggression" occurs with women as the aggressor. The article goes on to say, "We've all learned to be wary of statistics, and Fiebert says studies abound on the subject. He notes, however, that those suggesting men are also frequent abuse victims should not be used to minimize the threat that women face from abusive boyfriends or spouses."

In a Meta-analysis, John Archer, Ph.D., from the Department of Psychology, University of Central Lancashire, UK, writes:

The present analyses indicate that men are among those who are likely to be on the receiving end of acts of physical aggression. The extent to which this involves mutual combat or the male equivalent to "battered women" is at present unresolved. Both situations are causes for concern. Straus (1997) has warned of the dangers involved – especially for women – when physical aggression becomes a routine response to relationship conflict. "Battered men" – those subjected to systematic and prolonged violence – are likely to suffer physical and psychological consequences, together with specific problems associated with a lack of recognition of their plight. Seeking to address these problems need not detract from continuing to address the problem of "battered women."

Donald G. Dutton and Tonia L. Nicholls, from the Department of Psychology at the University of British Columbia also undertook a meta-analysis of data in 2005. They concluded:

Clearly, shelter houses full of battered women demonstrate the need for their continued existence. Moreover, outside of North American and Northern Europe, gender inequality is still the norm (Archer, in press). However, within those countries that have been most progressive about women's equality, female violence has increased as male violence has decreased (Archer, in press). There is not one solution for every domestically violent situation; some require incarceration of a terrorist perpetrator, others can be dealt with through court-mandated treatment, still others may benefit from couples therapy. However, feminist inspired intervention standards that preclude therapists in many states from doing effective therapy with male batterers are one outcome of this paradigm. The failure to recognize female threat to husbands, female partners, or children is another (Straus et al., 1980 found 10% higher rates of child abuse reported by mothers than by fathers). The one size fits all policy driven by a simplistic notion that intimate violence is a recapitulation of class war does not most effectively deal with this serious problem or represent the variety of spousal violence patterns revealed by research. At some point, one has to ask whether feminists are more interested in diminishing violence within a population or promoting a political ideology. If they are interested in diminishing violence, it should be diminished for all members of a population and by the most effective and utilitarian means possible. This would mean an intervention/treatment approach based on other successful approaches from criminology and psychology. Theories that women are as violent as men have been dubbed "Gender Symmetry" theories. In the most serious violence the men do dominate for example in 1999 in the US, 1,218 women and 424 men were killed by an intimate partner, regardless of which partner started the violence and of the gender of the partner.

On the other hand, Michael Kimmel of the State University of New York at Stony Brook found that men are more violent inside and outside of the home than women. A problem in conducting studies that seek to describe violence in terms of gender is the amount of silence, fear and shame that results from abuse within families and relationships. Another is that abusive patterns can tend to seem normal to those who have lived in them for a length of time. Similarly, subtle forms of abuse can be quite transparent even as they set the stage for further abuse seeming normal. Finally, inconsistent definition of what domestic violence is makes definite conclusions difficult to reach when compiling the available studies.

Both men and women have been arrested and convicted of assaulting their partners in both heterosexual and homosexual relationships. The bulk of these arrests have been men being arrested for assaulting women. However, in the case of reciprocal violence, frequently only the male perpetrator is arrested. Determining how many instances of domestic violence actually involve male victims is difficult. Male domestic violence victims may be reluctant to get help for a number of reasons. Another study has demonstrated a high degree of acceptance by women of aggression against men. Murders of female intimate partners by men have dropped, but not nearly as dramatically. Men kill their female intimate partners at about four times the rate that women kill their male intimate partners. Research by Jacquelyn Campbell, PhD RN FAAN has found that at least two thirds of women killed by their intimate partners were battered by those men prior to the murder. She also found that when males are killed by female intimates, the women in those relationships had been abused by their male partner about 75% of the time. Some researchers have found a relationship between the availability of domestic violence services, improved laws and enforcement regarding domestic violence and increased access to divorce, and higher earnings for women with declines in intimate partner homicide. However, both men and women are far less likely to be abused when married to each other.

The bulk of injuries from domestic violence involve co-habitation or the distresses of relationship break-ups. Gender roles and expectations can and do play a role in abusive situations, and exploring these roles and expectations can be helpful in addressing abusive situations, as do factors like race, class, religion, sexuality and philosophy. None of these factors cause one to abuse or another to be abused.

SOCIAL PROGRAMMES DEALING WITH VIOLENCE

In 1997, the Canadian Advertising Foundation ruled that a National Ad campaign that featuring Nicole Brown Simpson's sister Denise with the slogan entitled, "Stop violence against Women" was in fact portraying only men as aggressors, and that it was not providing a balanced message and was in fact contributing to gender stereotyping.

DOMESTIC VIOLENCE IN SAME-SEX RELATIONSHIPS

Domestic violence also occurs in same-sex relationships. In an effort to be more inclusive, many organisations have made an effort to use gender-neutral terms when referring to perpetrator ship and victim hood. Historically domestic violence has been seen as a family issue and little interest has been directed at violence in same-sex relationships. It has not been until recently, as the gay rights movement has brought the issues of gay and lesbian people into public attention, when research has been started to conduct on same-sex relationships. Several studies have indicated that partner abuse among same-sex couples (both female and male) is relatively similar in both prevalence and dynamics to that among opposite-sex couples.

Gays and lesbians, however, face special obstacles in dealing with the issues that some researchers have labeled "the double closet". A recent Canadian study by Mark W. Lehman suggests similarities include frequency (approximately one in every four couples); manifestations (emotional, physical, financial, etc.); co-existent situations (unemployment, substance abuse, low self-esteem); victims' reactions (fear, feelings of helplessness, hyper vigilance); and reasons for staying (love, can work it out, things will change, denial). At the same time, significant differences, unique issues and deceptive myths are typically present.

Lehman points to added discrimination and fear gays and lesbians can face; dismissal by police and some social services; a lack of support from peers who would rather keep quiet about the problem in order not to attract negative attention toward the gay community; the impacts of HIV status or AIDS in keeping partners together, due to health care insurance/access, or guilt; outing used as a weapon; and encountering supportive services that are targeted and/or structured for the needs of heterosexual women and which may not meet the needs of gay men or lesbians.

DIAGNOSIS PLANNING

The American Psychiatric Association planning and research committees for the forthcoming DSM-V (2012) have canvassed a series of new Relational disorders which include *Marital Conflict Disorder Without Violence* or *Marital Abuse Disorder (Marital Conflict Disorder With Violence)*. Couples with marital disorders sometimes come to clinical attention because the couple recognises long-standing dissatisfaction with their marriage and come to the clinician on their own initiative or are referred by an astute health care professional. Secondly, there is serious violence in the marriage which is -"usually the husband battering the wife." In these cases the emergency room or a legal authority often is the first to notify the clinician. Most importantly, marital violence "is a major risk factor for serious injury and even death and women in violent marriages are at much greater risk of being seriously injured or killed (National Advisory Council on Violence Against Women 2000)."

The authors of this study add that "There is current considerable controversy over whether male-to-female marital violence is best regarded as a reflection of male psychopathology and control or whether there is an empirical base and clinical utility for conceptualizing these patterns as relational." Recommendations for clinicians making a diagnosis of *Marital Relational Disorder* should include the assessment of actual or "potential" male violence as regularly as they assess the potential for suicide in depressed patients. Further, "clinicians should not relax their vigilance after a battered wife leaves her husband, because some data suggest that the period immediately following a marital separation is the period of greatest risk for the women. Many men will stalk and batter their wives in an effort to get them to return or punish them for leaving. Initial assessments of the potential for violence in a marriage can be supplemented by standardized interviews and questionnaires, which have been reliable and valid aids in exploring marital violence more systematically."

The authors conclude with what they call "very recent information" on the course of violent marriages which suggests that "over time a husband's battering may abate somewhat, but perhaps because he has successfully intimidated his wife. The risk of violence remains strong in a marriage in which it has been a feature in the past. Thus, treatment is essential here; the clinician cannot just wait and watch." The most urgent clinical priority is the protection of the wife because she is the one most frequently at risk, and clinicians must be aware that supporting assertiveness by a battered wife may lead to more beatings or even death.

RESPONSE TO DOMESTIC VIOLENCE

The response to domestic violence is typically a combined effort between law enforcement agencies, the courts, social service agencies and corrections/probation agencies. The role of each has evolved as domestic violence has been brought more into public view. Domestic violence historically has been viewed as a private family matter that need not involve government or criminal justice intervention. Police officers were often reluctant to intervene by making an arrest, and often chose instead to simply counsel the couple and/or ask one of the parties to leave the residence for a period of time. The courts were reluctant to impose any significant sanctions on those convicted of domestic violence, largely because it was viewed as a misdemeanor offense.

Activism, initiated by victim advocacy groups and feminist groups, has led to a better understanding of the scope and effect of domestic violence on victims and families, and has brought about changes in the criminal justice system's response. Several projects have aided in filling the voids in the justice system as it pertains to the protection of victims. One such initiative, The Hope Card Project, makes an attempt to remedy several problems through the issuance of an ID card to victims of abuse. The card is used to identify both parties in a domestic violence protection order and provides additional resources to the victim through a voucher programme for services. "There is no photograph on a protection order, so a photograph is a bonus, not a necessity. There are several methods used to obtain the photograph. Some jurisdictions have a photograph taken of the offender during the first hearing while both parties are present. Another method is for officers to take a photograph in the field or retrieve a booking photograph from their local jail. In a lot of cases the victim brings a photograph and it is scanned. Lastly, the new online site has some state motor vehicle department photograph databases connected for that purpose. This is the ideal method."

MEDICAL RESPONSE

Medical professionals, who have contact with abuse victims through medical visits, have a role to play in helping domestic violence victims. Many cases of spousal abuse are handled solely by medical professionals and do not involve the police. Sometimes cases of spousal abuse are brought into the emergency room, while many other cases are handled by family physician or other primary care provider. Doctors and other medical professionals are in position to empower victims, give advice, and refer them to appropriate services. The health care professional in the United Kingdom, the United States, and elsewhere has not always met this role, been uneven in quality of care, and in many cases has been unhelpful due to misunderstandings they have about domestic violence. Myths that have prevailed in the past and influenced how a doctor approaches a case, where domestic violence may be involved, include the belief that domestic violence is rare, that women are responsible for the violence, and it is inevitable. Washaw (1993) suggests that many doctors prefer not to get involved in people's "private" lives. Clifton, Jacobs, and Tulloch (1996) found that training for general practitioners in the United States about domestic violence was very limited or they had no training.

Abbott and Williamson found that knowledge and understanding of domestic violence was very limited among health care professionals in a Midlands, United Kingdom County, and that they don't see themselves as being able to play a major role in helping women in regards to domestic violence. Furthermore, in the biomedical model of health care, injuries are often just treated and diagnosed, without regard for the causes. As well, there is substantial reluctance for victims to come forward and broach the issue with their physicians. On average, women experience 35 incidents of domestic violence before seeking treatment. A number of medications have been used for control of aggression. Good evidence exists on the efficacy of clozapine. Evidence also exists for SSRIs (selective serotonin re-uptake inhibitors), like "Prozac", hormonal anti-androgenic agents, beta-blockers, quetiapine and ariipiprazole. Lithium and anticonvulsants are widely used but their efficacy is not strongly supported.

LAW ENFORCEMENT

In the 1970s, it was widely believed that domestic disturbance calls were the most dangerous type for responding officers, who arrive to a highly emotionally charged situation. This belief was based on FBI statistics which turned out to be flawed, in that they grouped all types of disturbances together with domestic disturbances, such as brawls at a bar. Subsequent statistics and analysis have shown this belief to be false. Statistics on incidents of domestic violence, published in the late 1970s, helped raise public awareness of the problem and increase activism. A study published in 1976 by the Police Foundation found that the police had intervened at least once in the previous two years in 85 percent of spouse homicides.

In the late 1970s and early 1980s, feminists and battered women's advocacy groups were calling on police to take domestic violence more seriously and change intervention strategies. In some instances, these groups took legal action against police departments, including in Oakland, California and New York City, to get them to make arrests in domestic violence cases. They claimed that police assigned low priority to domestic disturbance calls. The Minneapolis Domestic Violence Experiment was a study done in 1981-1982, led by Lawrence W. Sherman, to evaluate the effectiveness of various police responses to domestic violence calls in Minneapolis,

Minnesota, including sending the abuser away for eight hours, giving advice and mediation for disputes, and making an arrest.

Arrest was found to be the most effective police response. The study found that arrest reduced the rate by half of re-offending against the same victim within the following six months. The results of the study received a great deal of attention from the news media, including *The New York Times* and prime-time news coverage on television. Many U.S. police departments responded to the study, adopting a mandatory arrest policy for spousal violence cases with probable cause. By 2005, 23 states and the District of Columbia had enacted mandatory arrest for domestic assault, without warrant, given that the officer has probable cause and regardless of whether or not the officer witnessed the crime. The Minneapolis study also influenced policy in other countries, including New Zealand, which adopted a pro-arrest policy for domestic violence cases. However, the study was subject of much criticism, with concerns about its methodology, as well as its conclusions. The Minneapolis study was replicated in several other cities, beginning in 1986, with some of these studies have producing different results. In the replication studies, arrest seemed to help in the short run in some cases, but those arrested experienced double the rate of violence over the course of one year. Criminologists do not fully understand the reasons why deterrent effects do not last over time. But they suggest that abusers may initially fear punishment, though many cases do not make it all the way through the criminal justice process. If the victim is uncooperative during investigation, the prosecutor may choose not to pursue the case. If the case is pursued through the criminal justice system, sometimes the resulting sentence is minor. Subsequently, any fear that the abuser has of punishment may have diminished.

DOMESTIC RESPONSE OF LAW ENFORCEMENT TODAY

Each agency and jurisdiction within the United States has its own Standard Operating Procedures (SOP) when it comes to responding and handling domestic calls. Generally, it has been accepted that if the understood victim has visible (and recent) marks of abuse, the suspect is arrested and charged with the appropriate crime. However, that is a guideline and not a rule. Like any other call, domestic abuse lies in a gray area. Law enforcement officers have several things to consider when making a warrant less arrest:

- Are there signs of physical abuse?
- Were there witnesses?
- Is it recent?
- Was the victim assaulted by the alleged suspect?
- Who is the primary aggressor?
- Could the victim be lying?
- Could the suspect be lying?

Along with protecting the victim, law enforcement officers have to ensure that the alleged abusers' rights are not violated. Many times in cases of mutual combatants, it is departmental policy that both parties be arrested and the court system can establish truth at a later date. In some areas of the nation, this mutual combatant philosophy is being replaced by the primary abuser philosophy in which case if both parties have physical injuries, the law enforcement officer determines who the primary aggressor is and only arrests that one. This philosophy started gaining momentum when different government/private agencies started researching the effects. It was found that when both parties are arrested, it had an adverse affect on the victim. The victims were less likely to call or trust law enforcement during the next incident of domestic abuse.

INTERVENTION

In 1981, the Duluth Domestic Abuse Intervention Project became the first multi-disciplinary programme designed to address the issue of domestic violence. This experiment, conducted in Duluth, MN, frequently referred to as the

"Duluth Project." It coordinated agencies dealing with domestic situations, drawing together diverse elements of the system, from police officers on the street, to shelters for battered women and probation officers supervising offenders. This programme has become a model for other jurisdictions seeking to deal more effectively with domestic violence. Corrections/probation agencies in many areas are supervising domestic violence offenders more closely, and are also paying closer attention to the victim's needs and safety issues.

There has been controversy as the Duluth framework depends on a strict "patriarchal violence" model and presumes that all violence in the home and elsewhere has a male perpetrator and female victim. Also evidence of success of the model is limited, with scholarly analysis and critique. Many victims leave their abusers, only to return. Research has shown that a major factor in helping a victim to establish lasting independence from the abusive partner is her or his ability to get legal assistance. Economists at the Brennan Center for Justice analyzed Bureau of Justice Statistics data to determine what accounted for the nationwide reduction in reported abuse.

Their findings revealed that one significant factor was the availability of legal services to assist abuse victims. Another major study by economists at Colgate University and the University of Arkansas flatly stated that the only public service that reduces domestic violence in the long term is legal aid. Legal assistance can provide essential safety planning, buttress a family's economic position through child or spousal support, allay fears planted by the batterer about loss of custody, and help victims to secure needed government benefits.

2

The Psychosocial and Cultural Issues in Domestic Violence

Cultures, histories and post-migration experiences require analysis when developing health and social welfare responses to assist refugee women affected by domestic violence. The author reflects on research undertaken into the well being of East Timorese women asylum seekers in Australia and applies human rights theory to argue that universal standards of personal safety for women should be paramount; however, understanding cultural difference, including gender roles and tolerance to domestic violence in the country of origin, is essential in the development of appropriate policies and interventions.

Additionally, the psychosocial effects of war and persecution, and various interrelated post-migration experiences, are articulated as probable causal factors. Changes in identity or perceptions of self, unemployment, isolation of women from family and social supports, insecure residency status, and increased access to alcohol and psychotropic substances are identified as factors that require consideration in the development of policies and interventions to address domestic violence affecting refugee women.

Domestic violence, or violence against women perpetrated by intimate male partners, has been articulated as one of the most concerning and prevalent public health issues in the world today. Domestic violence occurs in all countries irrespective of culture, socio-economic status or religion. Nevertheless, it has been identified that immigrant and refugee women may be at increased risk of experiencing abusive situations. The universal and specific psychosocial and cultural issues with respect to domestic violence affecting refugee women, and the development of policies and interventions in the post- migration context, are the focus of this chapter.

The issue of domestic and family violence in refugee and asylum seeker communities is a neglected area of academic inquiry, and this is particularly the case for refugees residing in western countries where generic domestic violence legislation and services are designed to support and protect survivors and to prosecute perpetrators.

A recent study into the well being of East Timorese women asylum seekers residing in Australia, focusing specifically on the effects of prolonged asylum seeker status on their well being, emphasised an interrelated issue of domestic and family violence affecting women asylum seekers. Nevertheless, it was not within the scope of the study to further explore the issue and thus it remained an identified area for further research.

This position chapter is intended to articulate and contextualise the issues of domestic and family violence as they arose briefly and yet significantly in the East Timorese women asylum seekers study and to achieve two further objectives: first, to apply human rights theory to explore secondary source material concerning the psychosocial and cultural issues of relevance to domestic violence in refugee communities generally, and secondly, to initiate discussion of social and health policy responses and interventions in the Australian context. The chapter is intended to provide impetus for future research projects to identify the extent of the problem of domestic violence and cultural variations in refugee communities in Australia, as well as to further explore the complexity of the issues and associated responses required from policy makers and practitioners.

UNDERSTANDING DOMESTIC AND FAMILY VIOLENCE AMONG REFUGEES

Domestic violence is the term used to refer to an abuse of power mainly (but not only) by men against women during or after a relationship. Domestic violence is behaviour that results in physical, sexual or psychological damage, forced social isolation, economic deprivation, or where the woman is forced to live in fear. In 2003, Queensland broadened its civil domestic violence legislation to include non-spousal intimate relationships as well as violence perpetrated against spouses. This more comprehensive legislation reflects a general move in Australia towards recognition of violence in familial and intimate relationships other than just among conjugal or de facto partners. Nevertheless, domestic violence perpetrated against women by their male partners remains the most common form of family violence in Australia and is the leading cause of female injuries around the world. It is recognised that women are targets of domestic violence primarily because of their unequal gender status in society.

Estimating the incidence of domestic violence is difficult because of the sensitive nature of the problem, the risks to women upon disclosure and the consequent underreporting. Clearly there are also variations of incidence and type, particularly across states and with the influences of culture and sub-cultural differences. Reported incidences and criminal outcomes arising from acts of domestic violence are often influenced by each state's legal and community sanctioning or prohibition, and by definitions and methodological differences between studies. The American Medical Association reported that one in three women in America are assaulted by a domestic partner in her lifetime, and another study found that 77 per cent of women with dependant immigrant status in America had been battered by a male partner. Of Australian women who had ever been married or in a de facto relationship more than 23 per cent experienced violence by a partner at some time during or following the relationship.

A recent report into violence by intimate partners found variations of incidence across countries with 27 per cent of women in Leon, Nicaragua who have ever had an intimate relationship experiencing violence from her partner, 38 per cent of currently married women in Republic of Korea and 52 per cent of currently married Palestinian women in West Bank and Gaza experiencing violence from their partner. A hallmark of domestic violence is that the perpetrator often blames his violence on the victim and her behaviour, and uses the violence to assert his perceived 'justified' control. The woman experiencing the violence can internalise her inability to avoid it, and often feels inadequate, a failure and even deserving the abuse.

Internationally, academics and service providers are framing domestic violence as a global public health issue. Furthermore it is increasingly common for domestic violence to be viewed legally as a human rights issue, highlighting contemporary concern with terrorism and the close parallel between domestic abuse and terrorist practices of violence and intimidation. The *Universal Declaration of Human Rights* states, 'no one shall be subjected to torture or to inhuman or degrading treatment or punishment'.

REFUGEES AND ASYLUM SEEKERS

The UN High Commissioner for Refugees (UNHCR) estimates that there are 19.8 million displaced persons in need of safety from persecution or serious human rights abuses. Of those, 12 million are estimated to meet UN criteria for refugee status. It is pertinent to clarify here that refugees with refugee status have undergone formal assessment and have been deemed to meet UN criteria for refugee status. In Australia, permanent protection is granted to claimants who entered the country with prior Australian government established refugee status (an offshore applicant), or with a lawful visa and a subsequent successful onshore application for refugee status. Asylum seekers are those who are yet to have their claims for refugee status assessed or proven and, as such, occupy a different and more tenuous position of legitimacy and status than that of refugees. Successful onshore refugee applicants, who originally arrived in Australia as asylum seekers without a valid visa, are provided with temporary three year protection visas.

Despite some disparity in statistics, it is widely accepted that women and children are the large majority of refugees and asylum seekers in the world today. Giles wrote that as many as 75 per cent of refugees are women and children, and in some countries women and children make up 90 per cent of the refugee population (1996, 44). Similarly, the UN High Commission for Refugees stated that 'the faces of refugees are overwhelmingly those of women and children, as they comprise up to 80 per cent of most refugee populations' (1999, 1). Refugee women are commonly affected by rape and sexual assault, dowry burning, sati or widow burning, forced marriages, compulsory abortions or sterilisations, female genital mutilation and domestic violence.

Despite the overrepresentation of women as refugees, there is an under- representation of women in claims and/or resettlement in western industrialised countries such as Australia, Canada, the Netherlands, France, Sweden, Switzerland, and the United States. As Bruce points out, industrialised countries are far from sharing the general burden of refugees worldwide, with undeveloped countries bordering refugee producing areas taking most of the refugee populations (2003).

Research into the well being of East Timorese women asylum seekers in Australia was primarily concerned with the effects of prolonged asylum seeker status on the well being of a group that had been exposed to extreme trauma in the country of origin. The term 'well being' was defined for the research as a holistic state which includes psychological, physical, spiritual, social and cultural contentment and welfare. A multi-method data collection tool included semi-structured qualitative interviewing of East Timorese women, aged between 17 years and 65 years, who were asylum seekers in

Australia and had arrived since 1990. The interview sample was a cluster sample where the cohort was selected by respected East Timorese community members or trusted professionals working with East Timorese community members.

The second method of data collection was from a questionnaire that was designed to gain information from workers within organisations providing services and support to East Timorese women in Australia. Additional information was collected from an analysis of secondary sources, particularly literature concerning the past experiences of East Timorese women living in Indonesian occupied East Timor. The research identified specific problems affecting East Timorese women asylum seekers that included ongoing retraumatisation after escaping systematic human rights abuses, unemployment, lack of access to and support for education and training, inaccessible English language skills programmes, isolation and inadequate provision of essential supports and services including subsidised pharmaceuticals and access to culturally appropriate medical care.

The research described the severe mental health risks associated with prolonged periods of insecurity and the psychological effects of fearing forcible removal from the country of sanctuary. The research found that the restrictions and lack of security associated with asylum seeker status places women asylum seekers at comparatively higher risk than refugee women, who generally do have access to resettlement services and a more secure residency status. A dominant theme was that the asylum seeker experience compounds problems and vulnerabilities which exist as a result of having previously experienced human rights abuses, including rape, torture and trauma.

In this light, the already acknowledged issues relevant to women as refugees, such as requiring specific services able to respond to the gender specific needs of women, are both shared and quite different for women asylum seekers. An analysis of the unique historical and political environment of East Timor explains the relatively prolonged period of asylum seeker status experienced by this group of people. Certainly, Australia's political relationship with the Indonesian Government, including downplaying and ignoring human rights abuses within East Timor in order to maintain good relations with Indonesia, is considered significant in understanding why the Government made repeated attempts not to process claims for refugee status. Since the 1999 vote for East Timor's independence from Indonesia the Australian Government's refusal to consider a one off special visa on humanitarian grounds for the asylum seekers appeared consistent with its harsh policies toward asylum seekers and refugees generally.

The research described the dire need for some finality to the East Timorese asylum seekers' long wait in limbo and its findings supported community and international rationale arguing that the East Timorese should be granted permanent residency in Australia. Bowing to community pressure, the Minister for Immigration has recently begun to use his discretion under s 417 of the *Migration Act 1958* to reassess unsuccessful Refugee Review Tribunal cases. The Minister has the power determine if there are humanitarian or exceptional grounds for providing residency status. To date approximately 1000 East Timorese asylum seekers have been granted permanent residency on humanitarian grounds.

DOMESTIC VIOLENCE AND EAST TIMORESE ASYLUM SEEKERS

The problem of domestic and family violence affecting East Timorese women asylum seekers was raised by professional participants and was described in the research document along with other social problems including substance abuse, incest, gambling and family conflict. The topic of domestic violence was not factored into research questionnaires, and no discussion of domestic violence arose during the interviews with East Timorese women asylum seekers. Nevertheless it was acknowledged that families and communities under stress, particularly those who have fled war and terror, are particularly vulnerable to manifestations of violence in domestic settings and that women are predominantly vulnerable to domestic abuse. In East Timorese culture family problems such as relationship issues between a husband and wife would be difficult and in fact shameful to discuss with a stranger.

Interventions to adequately respond to domestic violence affecting East Timorese women would, however, require an understanding of the history of violence and persecution in East Timor, cultural factors of relevance, and contemporary awareness of the propensity for domestic and family violence when social structures are weak or inadequate. Domestic violence is noted to be particularly prevalent in contemporary East Timor, with official statistics for December last year showing that nearly 40 per cent of all reported crimes were cases of domestic violence or violence against women, such as rape and sexual assault.

Analysis of domestic violence as a social problem in East Timor requires a cultural, socio-political and economic investigation. East Timorese women are traditionally in a subservient position to men, positioned within a patriarchal culture where women generally occupy a secondary position within the family structure. It is well accepted that where there is a clear power differential between men and women, there is a greater likelihood of abuse of that power resulting in domestic violence. Further, it has been noted that after experiencing violence and other extreme disturbances (such as fighting in a war, experiencing torture or trauma or, as this study has indicated, living as asylum seekers), the experience of violence can be turned on family members, most commonly women. The World Health Organisation also supported the hypothesis that where there is war, post-war or other social upheaval there is an increased incidence of domestic violence.

Domestic violence within East Timor has particularly increased since independence. A recent article argued that domestic violence has become a major problem with the return of the revolutionaries to their families to face new social and economic challenges, combined with the fact that women are now speaking out more than they have in the past, challenging their subservient position. Women's organisations operating at the community level in East Timor are working with a commitment to addressing domestic violence, and East Timorese men from across the country have recently established the Association of Men Against Violence. The association aims to establish and maintain a democratic, just and equal East Timorese society that is free of violence.

In the cultural, historical and contemporary context of East Timor, the concerns about domestic violence raised by the professional participants in the East Timorese asylum seeker study in Australia were significant and further consistent with existing knowledge about the compounding effects of refugee status on the functioning of families and the wellbeing of women and children.

DOMESTIC VIOLENCE AFFECTING REFUGEE WOMEN

One of the key factors in domestic violence is that of women's subservience to men, and this concept is consistent with a feminist framework based on the premise that abuse affecting women is both created and exacerbated by societal power imbalances privileging men. Unsurprisingly, male dominance is the most closely associated construct in domestic violence discourse. Violence against women is related to political, civil, and legal restrictions and inequalities for women, and where there are weak community sanctions against domestic violence. Globally, women experience various levels of restriction to fundamental rights including voting, travel, inheriting and owning property, and obtaining custody of children. Frequently women and girls have limited opportunities for education, employment, health care, and even food because of their gender.

Absence of a genuine or functioning democracy and related state persecution is a causative factor for fleeing oppressive regimes and seeking refuge. The link between oppressive state apparatus and the particular gendered oppression of women at the community and family level requires further analysis. Not surprisingly there is a higher prevalence of domestic violence in countries where there is the least state denunciation of violence. Jewkes wrote that in many countries sexual violence occurs with relative impunity compared with other crimes, and victims have fewer options for legal redress (2002). Physical, emotional and financial abuse of women perpetrated by their male partners similarly occurs in many countries where legal or community condemnation of domestic violence is absent or ineffective because of cultural, religious or patriarchal bias. The World Health Organisation statistics are consistent with the argument that countries with more effective state support for legal redress results in lower, although by no means insignificant, incidence.

It is important to stress here that even in states where domestic violence is criminalized; there is ample evidence of the widespread failure by police and courts to prosecute offenders. Lack of an adequate criminal response to domestic violence is implicated in the maintenance of societal values that either directly or indirectly condone domestic violence. In Australia, domestic violence services and academics have challenged the current application of civil responses to domestic violence through the use of civil protection orders, arguing they are being applied as a less serious alternative to the rightful criminal justice response.

HUMAN RIGHTS AND CULTURAL EXCEPTIONALISM

The application of human rights theory in the discussion of domestic violence and the way it affects refugee women is pertinent because the purpose of human rights is to define what rights are essential if all people are to live lives in a secure and healthy environment in whatever communities they belong. Quite clearly, domestic violence violates the principles that underscore this moral vision: the inherent dignity and worth of all members of the human family, the inalienable right to freedom from fear and want, and the equal rights of men and women (*Universal Declaration of Human Rights*). Nevertheless, because of the private and gendered nature of domestic violence, until recently it has been excluded from consideration as a state responsibility. O'Hare wrote that it was because of the male hegemony over public life and institutions that human rights originally came to be defined by men and in men's interests (1999).

Certainly, state sponsored violence against women has been considered a more acceptable example of a human rights violation, and violence against women occurring in the home has been more difficult to bring into the public domain as a human rights issue. Nevertheless, advocating for legal and international responses to domestic violence has been made easier with the contemporary emphasis on social and political rights. In fact, the international community has now recognised domestic violence as a human rights issue and this is articulated in the UN *Convention on the Elimination of All Forms of Discrimination Against Women* (CEDAW) and the UN *Declaration on the Elimination of Violence Against Women*. These UN instruments and the application of the UN *Convention Against Torture* have paved the way for domestic violence to be viewed as a violation of social and political rights, rather than as a private issue. Furthermore a human rights analysis extends the capacity for examination of women's experiences and rights within the context of their unique cultural and social histories and lived realities in the post-migration environment. It is critical to articulate that refugee women from war torn countries or where human rights are violated by the state do share many common experiences of gender based violence. Many experiences of gender based violence are universal for refugee women once in the country of refuge and prior to arrival. For instance, gendered forms of persecution, particularly rape and other forms of sexual assault are the most common forms of violence affecting refugee women. Once in the country of refuge, policy and practice responses to address gender based violence affecting refugee women can be inadequate. For instance, medical and welfare services sensitive to the prior experiences of women refugees are lacking. In addition, the research into East Timorese women asylum seekers supported other evidence that many women who have been raped by soldiers in the home country will again be victimised by male members of the family who feel that their personal honour and the family have been put to shame by the violations. Understanding and responding to violence against refugee women necessarily requires an understanding of why the domestic violence is occurring, and it can include very different reasons for women who have escaped trauma and persecution.

Furthermore, despite universal theories and interventions with respect to domestic violence, the unique circumstances and issues surrounding violence against women within each culture specific case should be understood and incorporated into the development of culturally relevant and sensitive interventions at the community level. Julia Perilla wrote that:

> ... If we see human beings as existing within the context of their culture, we see how all the different elements of the environment affect the manner in which they perceive and react to the world.

An analysis of culture also deepens our awareness of how a particular society impacts on the lives of people affected by domestic violence; for instance, how traditions, beliefs and social structures impact on a tolerance of violence against women. It has been argued that cultural awareness should also necessitate respect for cultural difference, and that western standards and values should not be imposed as a form of cultural imperialism. Narayan found that Indian feminists attempting to challenge domestic violence including rape and dowry murder were often condemned by sections of Indian intelligentsia as imposing irrelevant 'western' agendas. In response to this phenomenon Franck argues that 'cultural exceptionalism', where it is argued that societies are beyond universal notions of human rights because of cultural differences, only serves to support totalitarian tendencies where freedom is not concerned with culture or society, but is rather a political issue.

Additionally, domestic violence is almost universally viewed and dismissed as a private issue that occurs between men and women in marriage. However reframed as a human rights violation, domestic violence cannot be dismissed as a private issue, or an expression of cultural rights somehow exempt from international critique. Domestic violence conceptualised as a human rights issue allows the analysis to go beyond culture, to traverse the private sphere and move toward universal standards for all women. And as Chapman argued, a human rights concept is helpful because it retains the legal framework, where domestic violence should be viewed as a crime, while adding to a broader vision. In a challenge to the view that cultural specificity diminishes the credibility of human rights, Tharoor asserts that there is nothing sacrosanct about culture, which is a constantly evolving entity, influenced and shaped by both the effects of colonialism and by global interstate relations. In essence, Tharoor and others argue that where coercion or control exists, rights are violated and these violations must be condemned, whatever the traditional justification.

Nevertheless, contemporary feminist discourse with respect to human rights also supports the contention that a measure of particularity has to be incorporated into the human rights concept in order to respond adequately to the heterogeneity of the world's people. Literature pertaining to Asian women and human rights has further developed the argument for both cultural understanding and appreciation of difference, as well as universal standards of rights for women. The argument is that there should be a universal acceptance of human rights; however the key task is to develop a culturally resonant approach to the articulation of human rights. The aim of such an approach is to seek an articulation of human rights that has real meaning and relevance for the diverse groups of women at the community or grass roots level.

Tharoor agrees with this argument with respect to women within developing countries, stating that there should be an 'indigenisation' of human rights, which are asserted from within each country's traditions and history. Theoretically, the application of culturally resonant approaches to domestic violence, including a systematic analysis of cultural differences, as Ivanitz (1999) has described with respect to culturally sensitive research, should occur for refugee women both in the country of origin as part of community development action, and in the country of refuge where resettlement and generalist services are responding to domestic violence.

Certainly, in a western country of refuge, cultural difference should never be argued as an excuse for inaction with respect to the many and diverse forms of domestic violence affecting refugee communities. In fact, the unique issues and circumstances that can exacerbate or compound domestic violence need to be articulated, understood and incorporated into the development of adequate interventions for women refugees. These issues and circumstances, as described in the following section of this chapter, comprise universal as well as specific significance and are critical to the development of effective policies and best practice interventions.

IDENTITIES AND PERCEPTIONS OF SELF

Culturally determined identity and the complexity of multiple identities within the new post-migration culture are important concepts in understanding domestic violence among refugees in western countries. For instance, the roles and expectations of both men and women seeking sanctuary in developed countries can alter as part of adaptation and socialisation in the new environment, challenging previous identities and perceptions of self. It has been argued that western countries are often more socially liberal and during the process of resettlement and adjustment this can create tension and conflict. As part of an inevitable shift towards familiarisation with the dominant culture and societal opportunities, refugees often perceive an increased freedom for women in the Australian context. This was clearly found in the East Timorese women asylum seeker study where aspirations to succeed in Australia increased with knowledge about the wider society and potential opportunities, particularly in education and vocation. A report by the Refugee Council of Australia described the resettlement process as 'the point of balance where connection to the old country still exists but the refugee is able to function at the same level as a national in the community' and 'when people feel comfortable about participating in whatever community they want to'. According to resettlement literature, there is an inevitable change in cultural identity, sense of self and place in the world. For refugees originating from predominantly patriarchal cultures it is correspondingly foreseeable that the process of cultural adjustment for women in Australia could involve a challenge to gender roles, evoking a particular threat to male identity and the dominant male role.

A study that looked at domestic violence and partners' status in India found that there was a particular association between abuse and when women reported having higher levels of education or employment status than the male perpetrator. The World Health Organisation argues that violence against women by their partners will be higher in countries in transition, where women are shedding traditional gender roles, such as entering the paid workforce, and are yet to have the power and authority to challenge traditional gender expectations (2002). Translated into the resettlement environment, where opportunities for education and advancement might be greater for women than in the traditional setting, and simultaneously they remain vulnerable and without traditional social supports, the likelihood of violence is increased.

MENTAL HEALTH, CULTURE AND VIOLENCE AGAINST WOMEN

Refugees have usually escaped torture and persecution, and as a consequence can be affected by traumatic stress disorder, anxiety and depression. Difficulties with migration and adaptation can compound existing psychological problems for refugees and can make women more vulnerable to acts of domestic violence. The process of uprooting and resettlement, which is stressful for anyone, is particularly challenging when the choice to move was not an affirmative life choice. Furthermore, structural disadvantage, particularly for asylum seekers and refugees on temporary protection visas, includes limited access to support and services that are necessary for general well being, adjustment and settlement. The East Timorese women asylum seeker research identified that high levels of unemployment, exclusion from English language services exacerbating isolation, and inappropriate health services, were prevalent and caused personal and social problems in a group with existing mental health issues associated with torture and trauma experiences.

It has been argued that refugee men, with a history of experiencing trauma and persecution, tend to use violence as a means to solve problems, deal with stress, express feelings, and resume power and control in the post-migration phase. Furthermore, the use of violence to communicate anger and frustration can be perceived as more valid to men who have lived under dictatorial regimes where the use of violence and coercion are prevalent and legitimised. Evidently, the psychological effects of persecution, and trauma as a result of migration and post migration, should be considered in cases of domestic violence in refugee families.

UNEMPLOYMENT

Unemployment is high among refugees in Australia in the early phase of resettlement and correspondingly men that were the traditional breadwinner are without the capacity to earn money to financially support the family. Although it is important to stress the complexity of the issue of domestic violence and acknowledge that employed men also beat their partners, it has been identified that unemployment and stress associated with threatened male identities have been directly associated with increased levels of domestic violence in migrant families. Even 'downward mobility', where qualifications and experience are not recognised in the country of refuge, has been identified as contributing to increased pressure and violence perpetrated against female partners. Where downward mobility affects women refugees to Australia without an apparent correlating rise in violent behaviour by women against family members suggests the important interrelationship between issues of power, gender and additional stressors such as unemployment.

It is important to further note that asylum seekers and refugees on temporary protection visas are denied access to English language services, effectively rendering them isolated from many employment options. Economic independence is a protective factor for women at risk of domestic violence, and there is emerging evidence that refugee women become engaged in programmes and vocational activities more readily than male refugees. Nevertheless, refugee women and asylum seekers are commonly located in the private sphere where, because of home duties, they are further disadvantaged in accessing employment and training. Additionally, refugee women have been poorly served by many of the resettlement services developed to facilitate access to employment. Resettlement services unable to effectively assist refugee women have evolved as a result of an inadequate understanding of their particular cultural, psychological and social needs.

ALCOHOL AND SUBSTANCE ABUSE

Increased access to alcohol and other psychotropic substances in liberal western countries can lead to additional problems for refugees, adversely affecting their capacity to deal with past trauma as well as post-migration challenges. Alcohol and substance abuse are recognised as means for dealing with past trauma and abuse. The abused person often uses alcohol or psychotropic substances to self-medicate and escape traumatic memories. Nevertheless, excessive use of alcohol causes psychological and physical damage and reduces the capacity for individuals to cope or develop strategies to address problems.

Alcohol and substance abuse are recognised as

contributory factors in acts of domestic violence, where it is argued that distribution allows socially unacceptable behaviour such as aggression to occur. An American study found that nearly two-fifths of domestic violence offenders said that they had been drinking alcohol at the time the police intervened in cases of domestic violence. Easteal's research into immigrant women and domestic violence in Australia found that there was cultural variability with respect to incidence of alcohol use and domestic violence, however almost 40 per cent of participants residing in a domestic violence refuge thought that alcohol had contributed to their partner's violence and abuse.

The statistics also expose the proportion of domestic violence that occurs where alcohol is not a precipitating factor. Domestic violence occurs in a controlled environment of fear and intimidation strategically targeting one person (or family members), rather than a loss of control under the influence of alcohol or drugs and impacting on whoever happened to be present at the time. Indigenous Australians have also identified alcohol abuse as a significant factor in relation to high rates of family violence, however on the topic of family violence, indigenous representatives are quick to emphasis the complex factors impacting on indigenous family well being including loss of land, breakdown of traditional kinship systems, racism and entrenched poverty.

ISOLATION

Partner enforced social isolation from friends and family, and emotional alienation as a result of self-blame and low self esteem, commonly affect women experiencing domestic violence. Isolation is particularly acute for refugee women and requires an analysis of culture, racism, gender, economic status and psychological status. In her analysis of gender issues in resettlement Kang writes that women are known to depend more on social networks and that those social networks are often absent (1992).

Manifestations of domestic violence including physical,

emotional, sexual and economic abuse can be more extreme and more easily facilitated by a woman's isolation as a result of her refugee status.

Lack of English language skills, for instance, promotes a deficiency of knowledge about laws and domestic violence services. For East Timorese women, English language skills were found to be centrally important for attaining social inclusion, including meeting friends, accessing employment, seeking health related services, and communicating with service providers.

It is recognised that refugee women, because of their gender related responsibilities, may have fewer opportunities than men to learn English in the home country and in the country of refuge. As a result, the benefits of knowing the dominant language can be further used by perpetrators of violence as a form of power and control. Narayan found that immigrant women in the United States who were dependent spouses on an immigration visa were similarly more psychologically, economically and linguistically dependent on their spouses than wives in the general population (1997).

The relationship between lack of English language skills and social isolation was highlighted, along with a reduced capacity to negotiate any day to day issue without the husband's assistance, a scenario particularly problematic in cases of domestic violence.

ECONOMIC SECURITY

The issue of financial independence is another interrelated issue. Women living in violent relationships frequently experience strategic financial abuse, and refugee women are more vulnerable to financial deprivation because they are often unaware of government allowances and financial entitlements.

Easteal found that immigrant women had limited skills in the English language, limited knowledge of family allowance or social security payments, and their husbands took control of the finances (1996). In these cases immigrant women had limited access to money and related social inclusion and support (1996).

Certainly, refugee women encounter more significant barriers to financial well being, and this is particularly the case for those without access to all resettlement services and supports. Although there appears to be general agreement that domestic violence occurs as a result of the interplay between individual, social, situational and cultural factors, low socioeconomic status (commonly affecting asylum seekers and refugees during early resettlement in Australia) has been considered as a noteworthy feature in domestic violence.

DOMESTIC VIOLENCE INTERVENTIONS AND CULTURAL DIFFERENCE

In Australia domestic violence support services, refuges and legislation (civil and criminal) theoretically exist to protect women from domestic violence. Furthermore, community organisations, particularly women's organisations and domestic violence services, are at the forefront of making domestic violence a public issue and constructing a community intolerance of domestic violence. Nevertheless there is anecdotal evidence that refugee women affected by domestic violence seldom use mainstream services and supports.

If domestic violence services are to appeal and be responsive to refugee women they must be committed to understanding the consequences of gender specific persecution, and differences related to cultural, historical and social/structural factors.

The East Timorese are like many cultural groups where women are traditionally in a subservient position to men, have limited civil and political rights in the country of origin and where family is the defining construct. These social and cultural determinants play a part in determining whether women will have the confidence, or feel they have the right, to seek assistance for domestic violence perpetrated against them.

Additionally, it has been argued that many refugee women, with increased distrust of government and bureaucracy and a fear of deportation for those without secure status, would be less likely to consider legal options to address domestic violence despite this being a predominant Western model of domestic violence intervention.

Perilla argues that for many refugee women the family is central to their lives and the role of wife and mother is the core of their identity (2003, 3), and it is for this reason that conventional domestic violence services and responses that reframe the women as a point of centrality and importance are often not considered as an option for assistance.

Rimonte found that within many Asian communities in America the battered woman would be unwilling to seek assistance because of her commitment to saving the honour of the family from shame (1989). Perilla argues that shelters and domestic violence services need to be sensitive to the importance of family and the husband in the lives of refugee women, and to direct intervention at developing life skills and safety plans, while cautiously broadening perspectives of human rights and the responsibilities of men (2003).

A developed awareness of the effects of torture and trauma needs to be factored into interventions. Domestic violence workers might not have skills to respond adequately to severe psychological trauma, however they do need to understand manifestations of posttraumatic stress disorder and anxiety related disorders connected to both past and contemporary experiences of trauma.

Knowledge of torture and trauma experiences and the health and social consequences would aid collaborative approaches to management with mental health practitioners, as well as enhance a broader understanding of domestic violence in the context of traumatic histories, and the particular needs required to enable the best possible support.

It appears that mainstream refuges and domestic violence services in Australia do not generally have resources skills to support women in a cross-cultural context, nor do they have the expertise to support women who have experienced torture and trauma in their home country. These issues are of central importance to the experiences of women refugees and responding adequately in cases of domestic violence. Research into the wellbeing of East Timorese women asylum seekers residing in Australia indicated that domestic violence was an issue of concern. The wider experience of domestic violence affecting refugee communities generally has been exposed.

Patriarchal culture, persecution in the country of origin, post trauma and resettlement issues in the country of sanctuary are all identified as contributing factors in the development or intensification of domestic violence. Secondary literature supports the contention that refugee women are particularly vulnerable to domestic violence, and have fewer options for culturally sensitive interventions. This position chapter has described some of the predominant issues that expose refugee women to a greater risk.

The chapter has further argued that human rights theory is useful as a theoretical construct for articulating the rights of refugee women to live without violence.

The application of human rights theory, and critique of cultural exceptionalism, provides impetus and framework for understanding and appreciating cultural differences, changes and challenges exacerbating domestic violence in the post migration environment, and ultimately the development of best practice interventions to reduce domestic violence among refugee populations residing in Australia and other western countries.

3

Inter-parental Violence in Childhood and Psychosocial Adjustment in Adulthood

HEALTH ISSUES IN MEN

During screening examinations and when appropriate and other health-related visits of family physicians should be alert for signs and symptoms of common psychosocial disorders in men. Health issues of concern include alcohol and substance abuse, domestic violence, midlife crisis and depression. Alcohol remains the most abused drug in America. The highest rates of alcohol abuse are in men 25 to 39 years of age, although alcoholism is also a considerable problem after 65 years of age.

Disulfiram and the opioid antagonist naltrexone are the two medications currently labeled by the U.S. Food and Drug Administration for the treatment of chronic alcohol dependence. Like alcohol abuse, domestic violence is a sign of psychosocial distress in men. Domestic violence may be a problem in up to 16 percent of marriages. Most men move through the midlife period without difficulty. Major depressive illness occurs in about 1 percent of elderly men, whereas minor depression or sub-syndromal depression affects 13 to 27 percent of older men. Selective serotonin reuptake inhibitors have become first-line therapy for depression.

Psychologic well-being and effective social functioning are important to men of all ages. Often, men begin to have difficulties in these areas without clearly understanding that a problem is emerging. In particular, the family physician should remain alert for signs and symptoms of substance abuse, domestic violence and depression. Male patients with psychosocial dysfunction frequently mention vague complaints that do not easily fit into diagnostic categories. A compassionate, trusting physician-patient relationship can facilitate the discovery of psychosocial dysfunction and the implementation of appropriate treatments.

ALCOHOL AND OTHER SUBSTANCE ABUSE

The prevalence of drug, steroid and alcohol abuse has continued to increase at an alarming rate since the early 1990s. Recent studies indicate that 24 percent of eighth graders and 38 percent of 10th graders admit to using illegal substances in the previous year. A reported 5 percent of 12th graders use marijuana daily and from 5 to 11 percent of adolescent males report use of anabolic steroids. Alcohol remains the most commonly abused drug in America. An estimated 10 percent of the general population may have an alcohol abuse disorder, and alcohol abuse complicates medical care in as many as 20 percent of primary care and hospitalized patients. Compared with women, men are at greater risk for alcohol abuse, with the highest rates of abuse occurring in men between 25 and 39 years of age. Unfortunately, alcohol abuse and dependence are not limited to the younger male population.

Alcohol abuse is estimated to have a lifetime prevalence of 4 to 8 percent in the general population. It is a problem in 14 percent of men more than 65 years of age and in 1.5 percent of women in the same age group. Alcohol-related problems are present in approximately 14 percent of elderly patients seen in emergency departments, 20 percent of elderly patients admitted to acute care hospitals and 40 percent of elderly patients admitted to psychiatric hospitals. The rate of alcohol-related hospitalizations in the United States is comparable to the rate of myocardial infarction. These hospitalizations are responsible for more than $230 million in health care expenditures annually. In 1995, the National Institute on Alcohol Abuse and Alcoholism (NIAAA) published its definitions of moderate and at-risk adult drinking. The NIAAA defines moderate adult drinkers as persons who consume a number of drinks per day that places them at low risk for alcohol-related problems. In contrast, at-risk adult drinkers consume alcohol at a rate that puts them at risk for long-term alcohol-related complications.

Alcohol abuse and dependence are best defined in the *Diagnostic and Statistical Manual of Mental Disorders* (DSM-IV). Screening for alcohol abuse should be included in the annual health assessment. Family physicians should remain alert for signs and symptoms of substance abuse, which include vague physical complaints, relationship discord, weight gain or loss, school difficulties, depression, work difficulties, financial problems and injuries such as falls and boxer's fracture (i.e., fracture of the metacarpal neck with volar displacement of the metacarpal head caused by striking a hard object with the fist). A detailed family history regarding alcohol abuse disorders should also be obtained. Family physicians can easily incorporate the CAGE questionnaire into their medical practice as a screening test for alcohol abuse and dependence. This tool is estimated to be 85 percent sensitive and 89 percent specific in identifying patients who have an alcohol abuse disorder. However, this four-question test has not always been helpful in identifying men who are at risk for problem drinking.

Another screening tool, the Alcohol Use Disorder Identification Test (AUDIT), contains 10 questions. Three of the AUDIT questions are directed at identifying current alcohol intake. A highly useful and rapid screening tool for alcohol abuse disorders and at-risk drinking can be created by combining parts of the CAGE and AUDIT question-naires. An additional alcohol-screening test that has been validated in the geriatric population is the Michigan Alcohol Screening Test (MAST-G). Any patient with signs and symptoms of alcohol abuse or a positive screening test for alcohol abuse disorder or at-risk drinking should receive counseling and assistance appropriate for alcohol abuse. The "Four-A Model" (Ask, Advise, Assist and Arrange) is a useful approach to problems related to alcohol. Multiple treatment programmes are available, including outpatient programmes (such as the 12-step programme of Alcoholics Anonymous), day treatment programmes, programmes for hospitalized patients and residential treatment programmes. No programme has provided outcome data that indicate its clear superiority in decreasing recidivism rates for alcohol abuse.

Disulfiram (Antabuse) and naltrexone (Trexan) are the two medications currently labeled by the U.S. Food and Drug Administration for the treatment of chronic alcohol dependence. Studies indicate that naltrexone may be the more effective agent. Disulfiram interferes with the metabolism of alcohol by acting as a reversible inhibitor of the enzyme alcohol dehydrogenase. Inhibition of alcohol dehydrogenase allows the metabolite acetaldehyde to accumulate. Acetaldehyde causes tachycardia, nausea, vomiting and dyspnea.

Disulfiram promotes abstinence by acting as an aversive agent once alcohol is consumed. Unfortunately, the efficacy of this agent in preventing recidivism of alcohol use has yet to be established. One randomized, controlled trial conducted by the Department of Veterans Affairs in 605 men found no significant improvement in abstinence rates among men treated with 1 mg per day of disulfiram, 250 mg per day of disulfiram or placebo. Because disulfiram is associated with an increased incidence of hepatitis, routine monitoring of liver enzyme levels is necessary during therapy.

Naltrexone, an opioid antagonist, exerts its effect by blocking alcohol-induced release of dopamine. Through this mechanism, naltrexone reduces the pleasurable side effects of alcohol consumption and reduces cravings for alcohol. Numerous randomized, controlled trials have shown therapeutic benefits from naltrexone therapy, along with an improved abstinence rate compared with placebo. Naltrexone is usually given in a dosage of 50 mg per day for the first 90 days of abstinence, although dosages ranging from 25 to 100 mg per day have been used.

Side effects of naltrexone include nausea, headache and anxiety. In higher dosages, naltrexone can cause hepatotoxicity, but this adverse effect is uncommon when recommended lower dosages are used. Nonetheless, liver function should be monitored in patients taking naltrexone in any dosage. Although screening tools have not been established, family physicians should incorporate questions about narcotic and steroid use into their medical practice. It is helpful to have prearranged contacts (e.g., Narcotics Anonymous and other treatment programmes) within the community so that patients can be referred for counseling and treatment.

DOMESTIC VIOLENCE

Domestic violence is a major cause of morbidity, mortality and disability in the United States. A 1985 national survey found that 16 percent of married couples reported one or more episodes of physical violence in the preceding year. However, few family physicians screen patients for domestic violence or the tendency to perpetuate violence. In domestic violence episodes, the majority of assailants are men 18 to 35 years of age. Most of these men use alcohol or drugs on the day of the assault. Unemployment appears to correlate with the incidence of domestic violence. A recent study found that approximately one third of assailants were unemployed.

Because family physicians care for all members of the family, they can often recognize patterns of abuse, as well as risk factors in the assailant. Physicians should have a heightened clinical awareness for investigating and reporting possible domestic violence. In addition, they should routinely screen male patients by asking if they ever feel the urge to strike out at a family member when they are angry or frustrated. When domestic violence is discovered, interventions are directed at ensuring the immediate safety of the victim and family, providing stress management and encouraging relationship counseling. Treatment programmes exist for assailants and victims of domestic violence.

MIDLIFE CRISIS

The literature reveals very little scientific evidence for the existence of a male midlife crisis, or "male menopause." However, in the transitional period between 40 and 60 years of age, men become aware that they are aging, that life is finite and that death will occur at some point in the not too distant future. During this time, men must also deal with family changes (e.g., empty nest syndrome), retirement, physical decline, unfinished tasks and plans, and the loss of parents, friends or even a spouse. Rather than being a time of crisis, midlife should be viewed as a normal developmental change, part of an "endless circular process of beginnings, fulfillments, endings, and self-renewals that proceed as we transform and evolve."

A 1994 study of 350 men between 30 and 60 years of age found no evidence of a peaking of midlife concerns during this time period. In an earlier study, it was discovered that divorce, job disenchantment and depression occurred with approximately equal frequency throughout a man's adult years. If there is any true pathology, it is found in men who are overly neurotic, who present with low morale, high anxiety and a sense of inadequacy and resentment, and who have a diagnosis of adjustment disorder.

The authors of this chapter believe that the concept of male midlife crisis is outmoded and is not supported by behavioural science. All men make transitions psychologically and behaviourally as they age. Most men make this transition smoothly and without difficulty. However, if male patients appear to have particular difficulty with this transitional process, counseling by the family physician or a psychologist is certainly in order. Referral for psychiatric help can be beneficial for the occasional patient who is experiencing extreme difficulty.

DEPRESSION AND SUICIDE

Depression is the most common psychiatric disorder in the elderly. Approximately 1 percent of community-dwelling elderly men have major depressive illness, and from 13 to 27 percent has "minor depression" or "subsyndromal depression." The prevalence of major depressive disorders ranges from 5 to 50 percent in men and women who are institutionalized or have other medical illnesses". Depression is two to three times more common in women than in men, but men are more likely to commit suicide. Unrecognized or undertreated depression unnecessarily increases suffering and health care utilization, and decreases functioning and quality of life.

Risk factors for depression in men include previous depressive episodes, family history of depression, comorbid medical illness, medications (i.e., beta blockers, histamine H_2-receptor antagonists, methyldopa [Aldomet], benzodiazepines, reserpine [Serpasil] and barbiturates), alcohol abuse, and lack of social support, recent life stressors, single marital status and physical disability. Advancing age itself is not a risk factor. The most frequent symptoms of depression are persistent sleep disturbance, fatigue, and multiple somatic complaints, a change in bowel habits and weight gain or loss. The classic presentation of a depressed mood is less common in the elderly than in younger persons. Persistent sleep disturbance has been found to be highly associated with depression in community-dwelling elderly men and women. Office screening for depression can be conveniently performed using the Beck Depression Inventory or another depression scale.

Selective serotonin reuptake inhibitors (SSRIs) are now used as first-line therapy for depression. These agents, which include fluoxetine (Prozac), sertraline (Zoloft) and paroxetine (Paxil), are effective in 65 to 75 percent of patients with depression. The SSRIs have a wide therapeutic index and a low potential for seizures. However, a clinical response may not become apparent until an SSRI has been taken for four to eight weeks. Common side effects include nausea, agitation, insomnia and sexual dysfunction. SSRIs do not have the significant cardiovascular, anti-cholinergic and sedative side effects that can occur with tricyclic antidepressants, and they are relatively safe when consumed in overdose. Other treatment options include psychotherapy and electroconvulsive therapy. Good sleep hygiene, regular exercise, minimal alcohol and medication use, and good nutrition are other key measures in the treatment of depression. The option of psychiatric referral should be entertained if a patient has accompanying psychosis or suicidal ideation or if depression is refractory to treatment.

Early involvement of psychiatrists and other mental health experts has been shown to be cost-effective and to result in improved outcome. Because of their shorter half-lives, sertraline and paroxetine are favored over fluoxetine for the treatment of depression in elderly men. Other medications for the treatment of depression include tricyclic antidepressants, bupropion (Wellbutrin), trazodone (Desyrel), monoamine oxidase inhibitors, lithium and stimulants. Venlafaxine (Effexor) and nefazodone (Serzone) are newer antidepressants that are being used with increasing frequency in elderly patients with depression. Detailed discussions of these agents are beyond the scope of this chapter. Because most of these agents have higher side effect profiles than SSRIs, they should not be considered as first-line therapy.

Suicide is a significant concern in depressed men. In particular, elderly white men have six times the suicide rate of the general population. From 1980 to 1992, the suicide rate increased 9 percent in persons 65 years and older and increased 35 percent in persons 80 to 84 years of age.

The likelihood of a suicide attempt resulting in death is highest in the elderly, increasing from 200 attempts for every one death in young adults to four attempts for every one death in the elderly. Family physicians are in a pivotal position to identify elderly patients who are at risk for suicide. Data indicate that 75 percent of elderly suicide victims had visited their primary care physician within the month of their death, and 33 to 39 percent had seen their physician within the week before death.

The most important risk factor for suicide is an active episode of depression. If a patient also has active psychotic features, the risk is increased fivefold. Other risk factors for suicide include male gender, social isolation, alcohol abuse, chronic pain and disability, organic brain syndrome and lack of social support. Depression is an insidious and common finding in elderly men. Early recognition, diagnosis, treatment, follow-up and support are critical to a successful outcome. With early intervention, unnecessary morbidity and mortality can be prevented, and function can be improved. The opinions and assertions contained herein are the private views of the authors and are not to be construed as official or as reflecting the views of the Army Medical Department or the Army Service at large.

INTER-PARENTAL VIOLENCE

There has been continued research into the prevalence, correlates, causes and consequences of interpartner violence. One aspect of this issue that has been of concern has been the extent to which childhood exposures to inter-parental violence may have adverse effects on the children who witness this violence. There appears to be a widespread belief that children who witness violence between their parents are at greater risks of later adjustment difficulties that may include behavioural problems and mental health disorders, aggressive and antisocial behaviours, substance abuse and juvenile crime. Whilst there has been relatively little research into the specific effects of exposure to inter-parental violence on personal adjustment, there has been considerable research into the more general issue of the extent to which marital conflicts have adverse effects on the adjustment of children.

As Moffitt and Caspi (1997) observe, issues of inter-parental violence may be interpreted as being a special case of this more general literature. There is substantial evidence to suggest that children who are exposed to parental conflicts are an at risk group for a wide range of adjustment difficulties during childhood and in later life. For example, Grych and Fincham (1990) reviewed a series of 19 studies of the association between marital conflict and the adjustment of children. They found that 15 of the studies reviewed produced evidence to suggest that children exposed to parental conflict were at greater risk of adjustment difficulties. They concluded "recent research documents a modest but consistent relationship between inter-parental conflict and children's adjustment" In contrast to the literature on marital conflict and childhood adjustment, the literature on the effects of observing inter-parental violence on children has been more limited and has been based on relatively small or selected samples.

Fantuzzo and Lindquist (1989) identified 23 studies covering 1069 children that examined the linkages between inter-parental violence and childhood adjustment. This review suggested elevated rates of behavioural, emotional and other problems in children exposed to inter-parental violence. However, these authors noted that these studies were characterised by a number of limitations including: the frequent use of biased samples; inadequate control for confounding, particularly for socio-demographic influences and also for other forms of family violence e.g. child abuse; a lack of definition of the nature/extent of violence and of the child's exposure to it; the use of a limited array of measures of childhood outcomes; and a general lack of longitudinal studies of the effects of inter-parental violence. The evidence reviewed by Grych and Fincham and by Fantuzzo and Lindquist may be supplemented by a series of other studies that also have suggested that exposure to inter-parental conflict and violence is associated with increased rates of adjustment difficulties in childhood, adolescence and adulthood.

Given the weight of the accumulated evidence, there can be little doubt that children reared in families characterised by inter-parental conflicts or inter-parental violence are an at risk group for a wide range of problems of later adjustment that may include behaviour problems, mental health problems, substance use behaviours, and juvenile crime. However, while associations between inter-parental conflict and children's adjustment have been well documented, there are a number of issues that require examination. First, the majority of studies in this area have focused on the effects of generalised marital conflicts rather than the specific effects of exposure to inter-parental violence. Whilst generalised marital conflict and inter-parental violence are likely to be closely related it may be suggested that the effects of inter-parental violence on adjustment may differ from the effects of marital conflict. There is thus a need to examine the extent to which exposure to inter-parental violence per se has effects on individual adjustment.

Second, many of the studies in this general area have been based on small samples, selected samples or samples that have been studied cross-sectional or over a limited period of time. It may be suggested that a better approach to examining the effects of inter-parental violence and conflicts on adjustment is through the use of longitudinal studies that examine the linkages between exposure to parental conflict and adjustment difficulties at various stages of the life course. Third, a major threat to validity in studies of the effects of parental conflict on individual adjustment comes from potentially confounding social, family and contextual factors that may be associated with both increased rates of marital conflict and increased risks of adjustment problems. In particular, the evidence suggests that marital conflict and inter-parental violence are not uniformly distributed across the population and are more likely to occur in families characterised by social and economic disadvantage, parental separation and divorce, families facing stress and difficulties and amongst parents having adjustment difficulties.

These factors are very similar to a range of psychosocial factors that have been found to be related to a wide range of child and adolescent adjustment difficulties including behaviour problems, mental health problems, substance abuse and juvenile crime. It may be suggested therefore that, to some extent, linkages between parental conflict and children's adjustment arise because of the social and family context within which parental conflicts occur rather than from a cause and effect relationship in which exposure to parental conflict increases individual vulnerability to adjustment difficulties. This issue has been examined in a number of studies that have adjusted the associations between marital conflict and children's adjustment. In general, these studies have suggested that independently of social and family context, children exposed to parental conflicts are at an increased risk of adjustment difficulties.

These findings are clearly consistent with the view that there is a cause and effect association between exposure to parental conflict and children's adjustment. In their review of this issue, Grych and Fincham (1990) suggest that this association may arise from a series of factors and processes that lead children exposed to marital conflict to be at greater risk of adjustment difficulties.

These factors and processes include the psychosocial context within which conflict occurs, the nature and extent of the conflict, children's perceptions and interpretations of the conflict between their parents, and the child's abilities to cope with distressing and stressful family circumstances. Fourth, there is a need to examine the extent to which father initiated violence and mother initiated violence have effects on later adjustment. To date most research in this area has focused on domestic violence committed by fathers and less attention has been paid to the issue of whether exposure to mother initiated violence has harmful consequences for children. This issue is clearly of importance in the light of growing survey based evidence that suggests that males and females assault their partners at similar rates.

Against this general background this chapter reports on the results of an 18 year longitudinal study of the relationships between exposure to inter-parental violence in childhood and adjustment in early adulthood in a sample of over 1000 New Zealand children who have been studied from birth to the age of 18. The aims of this study were:

a. To document the prevalence and spectrum of inter-parental violence based on accounts of 18 year olds about the nature and extent of violent behaviours between their parents during their childhood.
b. To examine the relationship between the extent of reported inter-parental violence in childhood and rates of mental health problems, substance abuse, criminal offending and associated difficulties at age 18.
c. To examine the extent to which associations between reported childhood exposure to inter-parental violence and adjustment at age 18 could be explained by confounding social and contextual factors that were associated with exposure to inter-parental violence.
d. To examine the extent to which risks of adjustment problems at age 18 were associated with father initiated violence and mother initiated violence.

More generally, the principal aim of this analysis was to determine the extent to which varying exposures to inter-parental violence were associated with increased risks of later adjustment problems when due allowance was made for the social and family context in which this violence occurred.

METHOD

The data reported here were collected during the course of the Christchurch Health & Development Study (CHDS). The CHDS is a longitudinal study of a birth cohort of 1265 children born in the Christchurch (New Zealand) urban region during mid 1977.

These children have been studied at birth, four months, one year, and at annual intervals to the age of 16 years and again at age 18 years. An overview of the study design has been given previously. The data analysed in this report were measured in the following ways.

MEASURES OF INTER-PARENTAL VIOLENCE

At the age of 18 sample members were questioned concerning

their experience of inter-parental violence during their childhood. The questioning was based on a series of eight items derived from the Conflict Tactics Scales. The items were chosen on the basis that the behaviours could have been readily observed and reported on by the subject, and also to span the potential range of violent behaviour from verbal abuse to physical assault. Subjects were asked to rate the frequency with which they observed each behaviour on a three point scale (never, occasionally, and frequently). Separate questioning was conducted for violence initiated by the father toward the mother and for violence initiated by the mother toward the father.

Psychosocial Outcomes at Age 16-18 Years

Concurrently with the assessment of inter-parental violence, subjects were questioned on a range of measures of psychosocial outcomes during the period from 16-18 years. These measures included:

Psychiatric Disorder and Attempted Suicide- Subjects were questioned about their psychiatric symptoms over the period from 16-18 years using a questionnaire based on the Composite International Diagnostic Interview supplemented by an instrument based on the Self-Report Delinquency Inventory. The CIDI items were used to assess mood and anxiety disorders in the sample while the SRDI was used to assess conduct disorder.

Using this information DSM-IV criteria were used to construct a series of diagnoses of psychiatric disorder for each subject over the period from 16-18 years. These diagnoses included the following: i) conduct disorder; ii) major depression and; iii) anxiety disorders. A detailed account of the assessment of these disorders has been provided previously. Additionally, subjects were questioned about suicidal behaviours during the period from age 16 to age 18 years. On the basis of this information a measure was constructed reflecting whether the subject had ever made a suicide attempt during this period. These estimates were combined with reports of suicide attempts prior to age 16 to produce an estimate of suicide attempts made prior to age 18.

Substance Abuse/Dependence- At age 18 years subjects were questioned about their extent of involvement in the use of nicotine, alcohol, cannabis and other substances over the period from 16-18 years. This questioning was supplemented by items from the Composite International Diagnostic Interview (CIDI) to assess symptoms of substance abuse and dependence. Using this information DSM-IV criteria were used to construct a series of diagnoses of substance abuse/ dependence for the period from 16-18 years. These diagnoses included: i) nicotine dependence; ii) alcohol abuse/ dependence; iii) cannabis abuse/dependence; iv) other substance abuse/dependence (including solvents, prescribed drugs, hallucinogenic, other illicit drugs and plant extracts). A detailed account of the assessment of these disorders has been given previously. Criminal Offending (17-18 Years). At age 18 sample members were questioned about their offending behaviours and contact with the criminal justice system over the period from 17-18 years, based on a combination of measures including the Self Report Delinquency Inventory, supplemented by survey items concerning police contacts and the consequences of these contacts.

Using this information the following measures of the young person's offending behaviours over the period from 17-18 years were obtained. a) Violent offending. Using the young person's responses to the SRDI a measure of violent offending was created based on the sum of the number of reported violent offences including assault, fighting, physical coercion and cruelty to animals. For the purposes of this analysis a measure of repeated violent offending was created by classifying respondents who reported a total of 3 or more violent offences from 17-18 years as repeat offenders: using this definition 9.5% of the samples were classified as repeat violent offenders. b) Property offending. Using the young person's responses to the SRDI a measure of total property offending was created by summing the number of reported property offences including: damaging property, breaking and entering, vehicle conversion, shoplifting and other theft. For the purposes of this analysis a subject was classified as a repeat property offender if s/he reported 3 or more property offences from 17-18 years: using this definition 10.8% of the samples were classified as repeat property offenders.

CONFOUNDING FACTORS

To assess the extent to which the associations between exposure to inter-parental violence during childhood and outcomes in young adulthood could be explained by the effects of confounding factors a range of measures were chosen from the data base of the study for inclusion in the analysis.

These measures were selected on the following basis: a) a review of the literature identified factors which have been previously found to be associated with increased risks of domestic violence during childhood; b) previous analyses based on the CHDS cohort which have identified factors associated with the mental health, substance use and criminal offending outcomes studied in this report. The covariate factors chosen for inclusion in the analysis were as follows:

Measures of Family Socio-economic Background:

a. *Maternal age:* This was assessed at the time of the survey child's birth.
b. *Maternal education:* This was assessed at the time of the survey child's birth using a three point scale which reflected the highest level of educational achievement attained. This scale was: 1 = mother lacked formal educational qualifications (had not graduated from high school); 2 = mother had secondary level educational qualifications (had graduated from high school); 3 = mother had tertiary level qualifications (had obtained a university degree or equivalent qualification).
c. *Family socio-economic status:* This was assessed at the time of the child's birth using the Elley and Irving (1976) index of socio-economic status for New Zealand.
d. *Average family income (0-10 years):* Each year from the

survey child's birth to age 10 years estimates of gross family income were obtained from parental report. To provide an estimate of the average level of family income over this period, the annual income figures were recoded into deciles and the docile rankings then arranged to produce an average income docile rank for the family.

e. *Family living standards (0-10 years):* At each year a global assessment of the material living standards of the family was obtained by means of an interviewer rating. Ratings were made on a five point scale that ranged from "very good" to "very poor". These ratings were summed over the ten year period and divided by ten to give a measure of typical family living standards during this period.

Measures of Family Functioning:

a. *Changes of parents (0-15 years):* As part of the Study, comprehensive data were collected at annual intervals on changes of parents. This information was used to construct a measure of the number of changes of parents' experiences by the child from birth to age 15 years. A change of parents was counted if the parent left the family as a result of family breakdown or death or entered the family as a result of remarriage or reconciliation. Both natural parents and step-parents were included in this count.

b. *Parental criminality:* When sample members were aged 15 years, their parents were questioned as to whether any parent had a history of criminal offending. The young person was classified as having a parent history of criminality if one of his/her parents was reported to have a history of offending. On the basis of this classification 12.4% of the sample was classified as having a parental history of criminality.

c. *Parental history of alcoholism/alcohol problems:* When sample members were aged 15 years, their parents were questioned as to whether any parent had a history of alcoholism or alcohol problems. On the basis of this questioning 11.9% of the samples were classified as having a parental history of alcoholism/alcohol problems.

d. *Parental illicit drug use:* When sample members were aged 11 years, their parents was questioned on the extent to which they had used cannabis or other illicit drugs. On the basis of this questioning 24.4% of the samples were classified as having a parental history of illicit drug use.

e. *Childhood disadvantage score (0-3 years):* This score provides a global measure of early childhood disadvantage and is based on a weighted sum of a number of indicators of disadvantage including measures of morbidity, preventive health care, early childhood experiences, mother/child interaction patterns, family living standards and family stability assessed over the period from birth to age 3 years. A detailed account of construction of this index has been described by Fergusson, Horwood & Shannon (1981).

f. *Family life events (11-15 years):* Each year from ages 11 to 15 years parents were questioned about events occurring in the previous year using a 49 item life event checklist based on the inventory developed by Henderson, Byrne & Duncan-Jones (1981).

To measure the extent of the child's exposure to adverse family life events during the period from 11 to 15 years the number of life events reported over the five year period was computed and the resulting sum divided by five to obtain an estimate of the per annum rate of life event exposure.

Measures of Child Abuse:

a. *Childhood sexual abuse:* At age 18 years sample members were questioned about their experience of childhood sexual abuse (CSA) prior to age 16 years. Respondents who reported CSA were asked a further series of questions relating to the extent and nature of the abuse experience. On the basis of this questioning sample members were classified into four groups reflecting the extent of their experience of CSA: subjects reporting no CSA (89.8% of the sample); subjects reporting episodes of non-contact CSA (2.4% of the sample); subjects reporting episodes of contact CSA not involving intercourse or attempted intercourse (4.4% of the sample); subjects experiencing CSA involving completed or attempted oral, anal or vaginal intercourse (3.4% of the sample). A detailed account of the measurement and assessment of CSA has been given elsewhere.

b. *Parental use of physical punishment:* At age 18 years sample members were questioned about the extent to which their parent(s) used physical punishment during their childhood (prior to age 16 years). Separate ratings were obtained for both the mother figure and father figure. The ratings were then combined into a composite four point scale based on the greater level of exposure to physical punishment reported by the respondent.

   This classification was: parents never used physical punishment (10.8% of the sample); parents seldom used physical punishment (77.7% of the sample); at least one parent regularly used physical punishment (7.6% of the sample); at least one parent used physical punishment too often or too severely (3.9% of the sample). A detailed account of the construction of this measure has been given by Fergusson and Lynskey (1997).

SAMPLE SIZE

The analyses reported in this chapter were based on a sample of 1025 respondents. This sample represented 81.0% of the initial cohort of 1265 children and 92.3% of all cohort members still alive and resident in New Zealand at the age of 18 years. Losses to follow up arose from outmigration from New Zealand (56.3%), refusal to participate in the research (35.4%) and mortality (8.3%). These reports are based on responses to an 8 item checklist derived from the Conflict Tactics Scales. Two measures of inter-parental violence are considered.

a. Reports of inter-parental violence varied from the common (verbal assaults 35%) to the infrequent (choking, strangling 0.3% to 1.2%) with nearly 40% of cohort members reporting at least one violent act by at least one parent.

b. Comparison of father initiated violence and mother initiated violence suggests that rates of violent acts in which males were perpetrators were generally quite similar to rates of violent acts in which mothers were perpetrators. In general, there is a slight tendency for rates of mother initiated violence to be lower than rates of father initiated violence. However, it is clear that there are no marked gender differences in either the patterning or the rate of father initiated violence and mother initiated violence.

The results clearly suggest that there was a spectrum of inter-partner violence ranging from verbal assaults to quite severe physical assaults. To represent this spectrum, scale scores were created by summing the 8 items to produce scale scores corresponding to: a) the extent of father initiated violence; b) the extent of mother initiated violence. The resulting scales were of moderate to good reliability having internal consistency (alpha) coefficients of between.77 to.86.

The scales had a highly skewed distribution owing to the fact that in the region of 60% of the cohort reported no inter-parental violence. To address the skew in scale scores, these scores were transformed to four level ordinal variables. In this scaling those who reported no parental violence were treated as a single class and the distribution of responses for those reporting parental violence was divided into a series of class intervals based on the scale score distribution. These class intervals were: i) those whose scale scores placed them within the 61st to 90th percentiles of the distribution; ii) those whose scale scores placed them within the 91st to 95th percentiles of the distribution and iii) those whose scale scores placed them in the most violent 5% of the sample. Separate scaling were constructed for father initiated violence and mother initiated violence

The measures of father initiated violence and mother initiated violence were strongly correlated ($r = 0.68$; $p < .001$) reflecting a tendency for violence in one parent to be accompanied by violence in the other parent. In summary, the above scaling method reduced the test items to four level ordinal classifications which were of acceptable reliability and appeared to have good face validity as a measure of the extent of reported inter-parental violence. The relationships between inter-parental violence and personal adjustment at age 18.

These measures span mental health outcomes (conduct disorder, depression, anxiety, and suicide attempt), substance abuse/dependence (alcohol, nicotine, cannabis and other substance use) and criminal offending (violent crime, property crime). Each comparison is tested for statistical significance using the Mantel Haenszel chi squared test of linearity and the strength of association between inter-parental violence and the outcome is given by the phi coefficient. Furthermore, there is evidence of clear dose/response relationships in which increasing parental violence is associated with increasing outcome risks.

These results are similar for measures of father initiated violence and mother initiated violence, although associations for father initiated violence tended to be slightly higher. There is little doubt, on the basis of these comparisons, that those who reported high levels of exposure to inter-parental violence during childhood were an at risk population for a wide range of adjustment problems in young adulthood. The Social and Family Context of Inter-parental Violence shows the relationship between exposure to inter-parental violence and a series of factors that described the social and related characteristics of the family. These features include: measures of family social and economic background, parental change, parental adjustment, childhood disadvantage and exposure to child abuse.

In addition exposure to family violence is described by a composite measure based on father and mother initiated violence. Each comparison is tested for statistical significance using the chi squared test of independence and the strength of association is described by the phi coefficient. In general, families having high levels of inter-parental violence were characterised by high rates of a range of other adverse factors including social and economic disadvantage, parental divorce/

separation, parental adjustment problems, and multiple childhood disadvantages, childhood sexual and physical abuse. It is clear from these comparisons that inter-parental violence was frequently embedded in a family context that was characterised by social disadvantage, family dysfunction and child abuse.

THE EFFECT OF INTER-PARENTAL VIOLENCE ON PERSONAL ADJUSTMENT

The preceding analyses raise two issues. First, since measures of father initiated and mother initiated violence were highly correlated ($r = 0.68$) the analysis raises the issue of estimating the net effects of each type of exposure to the risks of later outcomes. Second, the findings clearly raise the possibility that the increased risks found amongst those exposed to inter-parental violence could be explained by social and contextual factors associated with inter-parental violence rather than the direct effects of this exposure on individual adjustment. To address this issue the associations between exposure to inter-parental violence and measures of adjustment at age 18 were adjusted for the effects of the contextual factors through the use of logistic regression methods. In these analyses the log odds of each outcome was modelled as a linear function of: a) exposure to father initiated and mother initiated violence and b) the social and contextual factors. The model fitted was:

$$\text{Logit } \Pr(Y_i = 1) = \beta_0 + \beta_1 X_1 + \beta_2 X_2 + \Sigma \beta_j Z_j$$

Where logit $\Pr(Y_i = 1)$ was the log odds of the ith outcome assessed at 18, X_1 and X_2 were the measures of father initiated and mother initiated violence and Z_j were the set of potentially confounding factors. In these analyses the confounding factors were not measured in the dichotomous form but in the units described in the Method section. Model fitting was conducted using forward and backward methods of variable elimination to identify the best fitting and most parsimonious model. The results of this analysis which shows estimates of the relationships between the outcomes measures and exposure to father initiated violence, mother initiated violence after adjustment for the inter correlation between these measures and relevant confounding factors. The adjusted rates for each outcome were computed by the method described by Lee (1981). The measure of father initiated violence was associated with a number of outcomes even following control for confounding and the correlation between father initiated and mother initiated violence.

These outcomes included: conduct disorder ($p<.05$); anxiety disorder ($p<.05$); and property offending ($p<.01$). However, father initiated violence was not significantly associated with other mental health outcomes, substance abuse/dependence or violent offending after covariate adjustment. These results suggest that even after control for confounding factors, exposure to father initiated violence in childhood may have been associated with small increases in risks of anxiety disorders and antisocial behaviours. The results for mother initiated violence suggest that this was largely unrelated to later outcomes when due allowance was made for confounding factors and the correlation between father initiated and mother initiated violence.

The only exception to this trend was that mother initiated violence was associated with significant ($p<.01$) increases in risks of later alcohol abuse/dependence. It should be borne in mind that reports a series of 20 significance tests involving correlated outcome measures and because of this the significance levels may be misleading. One means of taking into account the effects of multiple significance tests is to apply the Bonferroni corrected significance level. Using this criterion, none of the adjusted associations between inter-parental violence and later outcomes remain significant. At the same time, with large numbers of tests the Bonferroni significance level is likely to be highly conservative and may lead to increased risks of type II errors. These considerations suggest that the significant results should be viewed as suggesting possible associations between inter-parental violence and later outcomes.

Gender Differences in Response to Inter-parental Violence:

In the literature on the effects of parental conflict/divorce on child and adolescent adjustment it has repeatedly been suggested that gender may act as a 'modifier' of the associations between parental conflict/divorce and outcome risk, with boys and girls showing differential response to parental conflict/divorce depending on the outcomes under consideration. In the context of the present analysis this would imply that the regression parameters describing the effects of inter-parental violence on psychosocial adjustment differed for males and females. To examine this possibility, the regression models above were extended to fit a series of nested models in which the slope parameters for the effects of inter-parental violence on each outcome were permitted to be different for males and females. The fit of these models was then compared with the fit for the simple main effect gender models summarised to construct log likelihood ratio chi square tests of the extent to which the slope parameters for males and females were detectably different. The results of this analysis showed a uniform absence of any evidence to suggest that the effects of inter-parental violence varied for males and females on any of the outcomes examined. This conclusion applied to both measures of inter-parental violence (father initiated, mother initiated), suggesting that for this sample, the impact of inter-parental violence on outcome risks was similar for males and females.

In this study we have used data gathered over the course of an 18 year longitudinal study to examine the relationships between exposure to inter-parental violence in childhood and adjustment in young adulthood. The major findings and conclusions from this study are reviewed below. Childhood Exposure to Inter-parental Violence The first stage of the analysis examined the frequency with which young people reported violent behaviours between their parents. This showed that just fewer than 40% of the cohort reported some degree of inter-parental violence, with verbal assaults being most commonly reported and choking and strangling being least frequently reported.

It was, however, clear that there was a spectrum of violent

behaviours ranging from none to severe, and it was possible to develop an ordinal scaling of the responses that classified children into a series of groups having broadly similar levels of exposure to incidents of inter-parental violence. This scaling showed that children in the most violent 5% of families in this cohort had high rates of exposure to nearly all forms of inter-parental assault studied. The dimensional properties of measures of domestic violence caution against the frequent practice of reporting a single prevalence estimate of violence since it is clear that any single prevalence estimate will depend on arbitrary assumptions about the extent and nature of acts that are included in the definition of inter-parental violence and that, as a consequence, single prevalence estimates can be manipulated to either heighten or level the rate of inter-parental violence.

As with other areas of research into childhood exposure to violence, the evidence suggests the need to abandon dichotomous measures and to develop more refined measures that describe the nature and extent of the exposure to violent acts.

The study also provided an opportunity to compare the rates at which young people reported mother initiated and father initiated assaults. These comparisons showed that rates of inter-parental assault were generally very similar amongst males and females although there were small tendencies for rates of father initiated violence to be higher than rates of mother initiated violence.

These results are generally consistent with a growing body of survey based investigations that have found that rates of male initiated partner assault are no higher than rates of female initiated assaults. These findings have, however, been criticised on the grounds that survey based methods may fail to take into account the family and emotional context within which inter-partner assault occurs, the nature and severity of assault or the degree of physical harm and psychological threat occasioned by the assault. These critiques have been used to underwrite claims that domestic violence is predominantly a male problem. There may be a relatively simple resolution of the findings of survey based investigations and claims that domestic violence is a male problem. In particular, the extent to which a domestic assault is likely to be of concern or come to public attention is likely to be conditioned by the extent to which this assault leads to serious physical injury or serious psychological threat. It may be argued that because of greater male physical strength and greater male experience with physical violence, assaults by males on females are far more likely to be physically damaging or psychologically threatening than assaults on males by females.

This could lead to a situation in which, although males and females engage in partner assault at a similar rate, those assaults which cause physical injury or psychological threat are predominantly committed by males. Looked at from this perspective, claims that domestic violence is a male problem contains an element of truth and an element of distortion. The element of distortion is that it would appear that males and females show similar predispositions to assaulting their partners whereas the claim that violence is a male problem would imply that partner assault is the almost exclusive domain of males.

The element of truth in this claim may be that inter-partner assaults that lead to physical injury or psychological threat are more likely to involve assaults on females by males rather than assaults on males by females. It seems likely that whilst both gender groups assault their partners at a similar rate, the marked assaults that come to public attention and cause public concern are those committed by males because of a greater potential of male initiated violence to cause physical injury or psychological threat.

The Effects of Inter-parental Violence on the Longer Term Adjustment of Children The second stage of the analysis examined the relationships between exposure to inter-parental violence and measures of adjustment in young adulthood. This analysis showed the presence of clear dose/ response relationships between the extent of exposure to inter-parental violence and risks of mental health problems, substance abuse and juvenile crime in 18 year olds. Young people from the most violent 5% of families had rates of these outcomes that were between 1.9 to 6.1 times higher than the rates for young people who reported no exposure to inter-parental violence. These trends held for measures of father initiated violence and mother initiated violence. There seemed little doubt, on the basis of these findings, that children reared in homes characterised by inter-partner violence were at greater risk of later adjustment difficulties as young adults.

However, patterns of inter-parental violence were also found to be associated with a wide range of other social and contextual factors, with children reared in homes characterised by high rates of inter-parental violence being exposed to a range of other adversities that included social and economic disadvantage, parental separation, impaired family functioning, parental alcoholism and criminality, childhood physical and sexual abuse. In turn, these results raised the conjecture that the higher rates of adjustment difficulties amongst children exposed to inter-parental violence were more a reflection of the social and family context within which inter-parental violence occurred rather than being due to the effects of exposure to inter-parental violence on personal adjustment. Statistical modelling of the results suggested that associations between inter-parental violence and later adjustment arose by two different routes.

First, a substantial amount of this association appeared to reflect the social and familial context within which inter-parental violence occurred and adjustment for the effects of this context substantially reduced the strength of the observed associations. The effects of statistical control of family context were sufficient to explain all or most of the associations between inter-parental violence and a number of outcomes including: depression, suicide attempts, substance abuse (other than alcohol abuse), nicotine dependence and violent crime.

However, in other cases including anxiety, conduct

disorder, alcohol abuse/dependence and property crime, associations persisted between these outcomes and exposure to inter-parental violence even after control for family and social context. These findings suggest that, independently of familial and social context, children exposed to high levels of inter-parental violence during childhood may have been at increased risks of later anxiety, conduct disorder, crime and problems with alcohol.

There was also some evidence to suggest that the consequences of inter-parental violence varied with perpetrator characteristics: after correction for confounding, father initiated violence emerged as being associated with a wider range of outcomes (anxiety, conduct disorder, property crime) than mother initiated violence (alcohol abuse/ dependence).

These results suggest that inter-parental violence committed by males may have greater harmful effects on children than inter-parental violence committed by females. This conclusion is generally consistent with the conjecture offered previously that inter-parental assaults by males are more likely to have harmful consequences.

There are at least two ways in which associations between exposure to inter-parental violence and measures of depression, conduct disorder, crime or alcohol problems after control for family context can be explained. First, these results are consistent with the view that there is a cause and effect association in which exposure to parental violence increases the individual's susceptibility to longer term adjustment difficulties. Secondly, it may be suggested that these associations still could be non causal and reflect the incomplete control of confounding factors.

For example, it may be suggested that the apparent association between inter-parental violence and adjustment does not reflect the direct effects of parental violence on individual adjustment but rather reflects the parenting styles of parents prone to violent behaviour and that this source of variation may not have been fully controlled in the present analysis.

A second source of confounding that has been discussed by Moffitt and Caspi (1997) is that the association may reflect common genetic factors that are associated with both increased rates of violent behaviours in parents and increased risks of adjustment difficulties in their offspring. In general, whilst the results are consistent with the view that there is a cause and effect association between exposure to inter-parental violence (and particularly father initiated violence) and later adjustment, the possibility that this association reflects social, familial or genetic factors that were not adequately controlled in this analysis cannot be entirely ruled out. A common assertion is that boys and girls tend to exhibit differential responsivity when exposed to inter-parental conflict and violence.

This belief has its origins in a number of early studies suggesting that parental conflict/divorce was more likely to result in behaviour problems for boys than for girls. However, reviews of the research evidence for gender differences have consistently concluded that the evidence suggesting that gender acts as a modifier in response to inter-parental conflict and violence is equivocal: while boys and girls do vary in their propensity to childhood problems, with boys being more prone to externalising behaviours and girls to internalising behaviours, in general there is no consistent evidence to suggest that the ways in which girls and boys respond to inter-parental conflict and violence are different.

The present study lends strong support to this conclusion, in that there was a uniform absence of any evidence to suggest that boys and girls differed in their responsivity to inter-parental violence. This result applied to all outcomes examined and across all measures of interpersonal violence. There are two clear applied implications of the findings of this study.

First, to the extent that the present study suggests that much of the heightened risk of children who witness inter-parental violence arises from the family and social context within which this violence occurs, it is clearly important that programmes addressing issues of family violence and children take a broad perspective that considers the general social and family context in which violence occurs rather than focusing solely on the issue of inter-parental violence.

It seems likely that to reduce the risks faced by children in violent families will require broad based programmes that address a wide range of family issues rather than programmes which address family violence in isolation from its context. Conversely, the results of the present study do suggest that independently of family context, children reared in homes characterised by high levels of inter-parental violence, and particularly father initiated violence, are at greater risks of later adjustment problems. This highlights the fact that the management of family violence issues should be a component of any programme that seeks to improve the life chances of children reared in high risk family environments.

LIMITATIONS OF THE PRESENT STUDY

In this study we have assessed rates of inter-parental violence on the basis of retrospective reports made by 18 year olds about the behaviour of their parents. This approach to the measurement of inter-parental violence has both strengths and limitations.

On the one hand, it may be suggested that young people were able to provide a more objective account of their personal exposure to inter-parental violence than would be obtained from parental and other reports.

To the extent that the critical factor in linkages between parental violence and adjustment may be the extent to which children perceive their parents engaging in violent acts, the reports of young people may provide a more appropriate measure of exposure to inter-parental violence during childhood.

However, this potential strength of using young people's reports may be offset by the fact that these reports may be coloured by recall biases. In particular, it is possible that young people who develop adjustment difficulties may see the behaviour of their parents in a more negative light than those without problems and this could lead to artefactual correlations between reports of exposure to inter-parental violence and measures of adjustment.

Using the present design there is no means of establishing the extent (if any) of such a recall bias. More generally, the present study is based on report data gathered over the life of this cohort with these data being provided by parents and young people.

It would be unrealistic to expect such variables to be measured without error and to give a completely accurate picture of the individual's family life and personal adjustment. In turn this raises the issue of the extent to which errors in the reported variables may have influenced the study results.

In general, it is likely that errors of measurement in report variables will lead to an under-estimation of the associations between variables. The effect of such errors may have had two effects on the analysis: i) errors of measurement may have led to the association between exposure to family violence and later outcomes being under estimated; ii) errors in the covariates may have led to under control of this association.

Nonetheless, within the above limitations the present study suggests three major conclusions about the linkages between inter-parental violence and the adjustment of their offspring. First, children exposed to inter-parental violence are an at risk group for mental health problems, substance abuse and criminal offending.

Second, much of the elevated risk of this group arises from the family context within which inter-parental violence occurs rather than being a direct effect of this violence. Third, exposure to inter-parental violence and particularly male initiated violence may be associated with significant increases in risks of later anxiety, antisocial behaviour and alcohol abuse/dependence independently of the family context within which violence occurs.

4

Prevention and Treatment Programmes in Family Violence

The need for evidence of the effectiveness of family violence interventions arises every day in a variety of settings: in courtroom deliberations, in which judges must decide appropriate punishment and treatment for offenders; in child protection investigations, in which case workers must consider what services to recommend for their clients; and in clinical settings, in which health professionals are expected to develop an appropriate response in examining suspicious injuries of adult and child patients. Indicators of programme effectiveness are the focus of attention when programme and service budgets are under review, in public hearings in which victims and advocates seek legislation to strengthen existing services or to develop new ones, and in media reports that compare the merits of customary practice with innovative approaches to addressing child maltreatment, domestic violence, and elder abuse.

Scientific research has not been able to provide clear guidance in determining the comparative effectiveness of specific efforts. Much of the literature simply describes individual programmes rather than rigorously evaluating their outcomes. And most evaluations of family violence interventions simply describe the intervention that was provided (without providing much detail about the implementation process), estimate the number of clients served over selected time periods, review the types and costs of the services provided, or examine specific skills or knowledge obtained as the result of a training programme. These types of studies are commonly referred to as process evaluations, because they focus on the processes of the intervention rather than its results.

An emphasis on theory and outcomes has been missing in evaluations of family violence interventions: What behaviours was the intervention seeking to influence, and how do they relate to the overall problem of child maltreatment, domestic violence, or elder abuse?

Did the child, adult, or family actually improve as a result of the programme and, if so, how was this measured? Did the community experience a lower rate of family violence following the intervention?

Did changes in skills or knowledge result in modifications in behaviour among offenders or lead to new services in communities that reduced the violence and provided more safety or improved health? And are the results of a single programme or comprehensive community intervention transferable to a larger and more diverse population of clients and multiple communities?

Both public and private agencies now seek to move beyond anecdotal reports in a search for data that can guide policy and programme decisions. Yet service providers, public officials, clients, and researchers themselves are frustrated by the difficulties of measuring and assessing the impacts of treatment and prevention programmes. The enormous complexity of the phenomena, the comparatively short history with service interventions, the shifting legal and social doctrines that shape public policy, the interactive nature of the problems and the services themselves, and the demographic transformations affecting American families and communities present tremendous challenges to the use of science in this field. The urgency and magnitude of these problems and the scale of resources that our society invests in treatment and prevention efforts demand better results.

SCOPE OF THE PROBLEM

Family violence victimisation in the general population is widely regarded as a serious problem that affects large numbers of children and adults across the life span. Estimates of the scope of the problem vary according to the source of the information that provides the basis of the estimate and the definitions used in describing the nature of the problem. But although the exact dimensions of child maltreatment, domestic violence, and elder abuse are frequently disputed, conservative estimates suggest that these problems affect millions of children, women, and men in the United States. In 1996, a government survey (NIS-3) reported that 2.8 million cases of child maltreatment were known to local child protection agencies or community sources (including teachers, health care professionals, and other service providers) in 1993, when the data were collected. This estimate indicates a rate of 41.9 children per 1,000, or 1 in 24 in the U.S. child population.

No government survey has yet been published that estimates the national incidence of domestic violence in the United States. The National Crime Victimisation Survey, which collects data about incidents reported as crimes, has reported that the annual rate of physical attacks by family members for women was 9.3 per 1,000 in 1992-1993. Population-based surveys suggest that the rate of adult violence involving family members may be much higher—the National Family Violence Surveys, for example, have reported an annual rate of 116 per 1,000 women for a violent act by an intimate partner and 34 per 1,000 for "severe violence" by an intimate partner.

The rate of child deaths attributed to abuse and neglect remained relatively stable (around 2,000 per year) from 1979 through 1988. Of the 4,869 female homicide victims reported in 1993, 31 percent (1,531) were killed by intimate partners (husbands, ex-husbands, or boyfriends). No reliable statistics are kept for rates of elder abuse or deaths attributed to the maltreatment of older persons. There are no self-report surveys of elder abuse, and the surveys of elder abuse reporting and recognition are incomplete.

FRAGMENTATION OF THE FIELD

The study of family violence consists of many separate areas of research focused on the study of child maltreatment, domestic violence, and elder abuse. Each area has its own terminology, theories, experts, funding sources, data collection efforts, research instruments, and scholarly journals. Those who study domestic violence have rarely communicated with, or even read the works of, those who study child abuse.

This specialization and fragmentation, combined with a lack of methodological rigor, have contributed to a research literature that has been characterized as "extensive but not definitive". The absence of unifying theories, common measures, and datasets has discouraged efforts to draw inferences between studies of family violence and studies of other forms of criminal and violent behaviour.

Little is known, for example, about the pathways or nature of the relationship between childhood experiences with violence in the home and juvenile delinquency or adult criminal behaviour, even though research has suggested that children who experience maltreatment have an increased risk both of arrest as a juvenile or adult and of committing a violent crime. Similarly, much uncertainty exists about the extent to which men who batter their intimate partners engage in other forms of violent or criminal behaviour. The organisation of research in this field, within both academic centers and federal research bureaucracies, often isolates different forms of family violence research and discourages efforts to integrate research on violence within the family and research on violence within the community.

The fragmentation that characterizes the research field also exists in the service delivery system. As a result of history and social forces, the law enforcement, social services, and health care efforts that are focused on different aspects of family violence must address diverse policy objectives.

These goals include the punishment and rehabilitation of offenders, the protection of victims and communities, the reduction of unnecessary costs, a respect for due process and fairness (often difficult to achieve when conflicting testimony exists or physical evidence is not available), concern for the rights and developmental needs of children and vulnerable adults, the mitigation of the adverse effects of experiences with violence, and the prevention of new incidents of violence in the home. Such services are subject to enormous social and political influences in the wake of sensational cases.

The result is a patchwork of separate efforts that operate in a semiautonomous manner, although the presence or absence of one component may have direct implications for another. The basic dimensions of this loosely coupled system of treatment, prevention, and control interventions have remained ambiguous and unexamined in the research literature, and little is known about their basic character, operation, or impact.

Treatment and prevention programmes are fragmented by the focus of the interventions: some efforts are designed to respond to the needs of the victims; others deal exclusively with the offenders. Some programmes focus on children, others on adults. Some programmes seek to serve individuals; others emphasize the importance of serving their clients in the context of their relationships as parent, child, intimate partners, or members of a family unit.

Service providers and researchers are realizing that family violence is an interactive and dynamic problem that requires approaches across multiple levels of analysis and multiple service systems. This realization has profound consequences for the development of the next generation of treatment and prevention programmes as well as the design of studies of their effectiveness. The emergence of a public health response and comprehensive community initiatives focused on family violence has stimulated interest in examining collaborative approaches to multiple problems within a family.

These multiple problems may exist entirely within the context of family violence (such as the impact of witnessing spousal violence on the developmental outcomes of children) or they may co-exist within a family with a broad range of behaviours (such as poverty, family violence, and alcoholism or substance abuse).

Artificial barriers between separate programmes and institutional services still remain, but in some regions they are yielding to more integrated and inclusive approaches that focus on the need to support individuals, families, and communities as they seek to reduce the incidence of violent behaviour in families. Evaluation of these comprehensive community efforts is in its infancy, challenged by the complexities noted below as well as the difficulties of evaluating programmes that are not yet fully developed.

CHALLENGES TO EFFECTIVE EVALUATIONS

The evaluation research literature has provided limited guidance in the design of treatment and prevention interventions for family violence. Significant methodo-logical and logistical problems include difficulties in constructing and gaining access to appropriate sample sizes, limited availability of comparison and control groups, weak research measures and survey instruments, short time intervals for follow-up studies, and high attrition rates in both the interventions themselves and the evaluation studies. Some interventions that are in widespread practice have *never* been evaluated (such as the use of mandatory reporting procedures for child maltreatment cases), whereas extensive attention has focused on a few interventions in specialized settings (such as arrest policies for domestic violence, the use of home visitation services as a preventive intervention for child maltreatment, and intensive family preservation services that seek to provide family support services in crisis-oriented setting).

This imbalance between the need for knowledge in areas that are hard to measure and the availability of knowledge in discrete areas of policy and practice creates two major quandaries that this report seeks to address:

- How to review the implications of current research findings in a form that can be useful for researchers, service providers, and policy makers in various institutional settings who are concerned with discrete and multiple aspects of family violence,

- How to determine which interventions should be strong candidates for the next generation of evaluation studies. The problem of selecting interventions for evaluation will acquire increased significance as larger numbers of agencies in social services, law enforcement, and health care seek to address the complex dimensions of the problem of family violence within the loosely coupled but interactive system of services that has emerged at the national and local level.

In addition to the generic challenges to effective evaluations, studies in this specific area are complicated by a number of factors:

- Most family violence interventions have resulted from advocacy efforts in communities that focus on the specific needs of children, women, and the elderly. Many evaluations focus on a single programme rather than an overall intervention or service strategy.
- Many interventions are not fully implemented, and the status of their implementation is often missing in evaluation reports.
- The urgent emphasis on meeting the needs of victims and taking action against offenders has caused services to be developed in the absence of a knowledge base about the causes and consequences of family violence. As a result, the theoretical frameworks that guide specific interventions are often not explicit and may vary among individual programmes.

  In addition, limited attention has been paid, in either the research literature or the design of interventions, to the impact of unsubstantiated reports of family violence on the affected parties.
- Measures of the nature and scope of family violence often come from court or administrative records rather than health records or the observation of families and couples themselves.

Administrative records often include biases that distort the ability of researchers to identify key trends or risk and protective factors that may influence patterns of aggression and the outcomes of interventions:

- When evaluations are closely coupled with programme development, the research base may not have an opportunity or sufficient resources to develop an array of studies that can build on the strengths of qualitative and quantitative research.

  The programmatic emphasis on examining the results of an intervention within a short time period can inhibit efforts to learn more about the basic nature of the services that were provided and the characteristics of clients who did or did not respond to them.

- Researchers are often prevented by resource constraints as well as the nature of service systems from designing experimental studies that make use of an appropriate control group in comparing the relative effects of a selected programme. Controlled studies are especially difficult to develop when services are limited by budgetary restrictions, access to services is determined by multiple agencies within a community, and service providers are not accustomed to working with researchers. Controlled studies are also not feasible in circumstances in which random assignments cannot be made for ethical or legal reasons, such as felony violence.

- Even when it is possible to conduct rigorous evaluations, programme advocates have sometimes resisted scientific study because of concerns that the research will interfere with the basic service mission of the programme, that the researchers do not have the capacity to measure significant interactions, or that negative findings may weaken support for existing services. Researchers, as well, have sometimes displayed a lack of appreciation for the complexities of dealing with the problems of family violence and underserved populations, focusing on factors that are relatively easy to measure, such as attendance rates or length of service, rather than addressing more difficult issues, such as the capacity to change one's own or another's behaviour or consideration of the presence of multiple stressors and interactive processes that may be significant in examining the impact of policy and programmes.

- The lack of opportunities for collaboration between researchers and service providers has impeded the development of appropriate measures and study designs in assessing the impact of programmes. It has also discouraged research on the design and implementation of service interventions and the multiple pathways to services that address the causes and consequences of family violence.

These complications have hindered the development of a useful body of scientific knowledge about the impact of family violence interventions. In the absence of such knowledge, programme decisions are influenced by anecdotal reports, marketing or lobbying efforts, and the fiscal realities of budgetary politics. Proponents of law enforcement programmes may argue that stiffer penalties and mandatory sentences for offenders are effective in reducing the incidence of domestic violence and child maltreatment, but such claims lack empirical evidence. Similarly, advocates for women and children may argue that public funds should be spent on social service and public health programmes designed to meet the needs of victims of abuse and neglect, but such claims lack valid indicators of effectiveness.

CHARGE TO THE COMMITTEE

The Committee on the Assessment of Family Violence Interventions was convened by the National Research Council to undertake five primary tasks:

1. Document the impact of family violence on public- and private-sector services in the United States, especially in the area of spousal abuse. This analysis should include an assessment of what is known about the scope and

cost of service interventions, the adequacy and validity of current reporting and detection data that are used to estimate the incidence and prevalence of selected types of family violence, and areas of bias in the current reporting system that may exaggerate or underestimate estimates of service intervention costs.

2. Synthesize the relevant research literature and develop a conceptual framework for clarifying what is known about relationships among the risk and protective factors associated with family violence. This framework should make distinctions between areas in which evidence of harm is clear in the interaction of certain risk and protective factors and areas in which knowledge is limited or uncertain.
3. Characterize what is known about both prevention efforts and specific interventions in dealing with family violence, including an assessment of what has been learned about the strengths and limitations of each approach and factors to consider in designing programme evaluations.
4. Highlight successful components and, to the extent possible, identify "best practice" models of specific intervention programmes for different forms of family violence. This task includes the examination of policy and programme elements and service delivery system features that appear to contribute to or inhibit the development of effective programme responses to family violence.
5. Develop criteria and principles that can guide the development of future evaluations of family violence interventions, especially the identification of outcomes and methodological issues that are essential to rigorous evaluation efforts.

Early in the course of our deliberations, the committee recognized that the research literature associated with evaluations of family violence interventions was relatively immature and scattered across a wide range of research fields. Judging that the absence of an integrative review of this literature has discouraged efforts to understand the nature, objectives, and outcomes of interventions, the committee sought to develop a report that would describe the ways in which interventions and service strategies interact with families and communities.

Although some types of interventions have been in place for decades (for example, child protective services), they have not been subjected to rigorous evaluations to examine their impact on offenders and victims. Experience with other types of interventions is relatively new; many interventions now in place for domestic violence, for example, are not yet fully implemented and have not yet been evaluated.

The committee therefore directed its efforts toward reviewing the knowledge base associated with the array of interventions currently in place, identifying the evaluation studies that met minimal standards of scientific quality, highlighting the major challenges to evaluations of these interventions, and examining how problems such as weak design and limited study samples could be resolved in developing the next generation of evaluation studies. In developing the criteria and principles to guide future evaluations, the committee was not asked to address the nature of public policy, funding, and other critical factors that could influence whether or not these principles and criteria are actually used.

Clearly, there is a need for further consideration of the potential roles of public agencies, both federal and state, and private foundations in improving the quality of both quantitative and qualitative evaluations for family violence interventions.

The types of collaborations that might foster progress in examining the impact of the wide range of services already in place in this field also deserve attention. The committee does address the need for improved partnerships among research, practice, and policy in this report, but specific questions pertaining to the adequacy of funding for research, infrastructure, and implementation were beyond the scope of our study.

DEFINITION OF FAMILY VIOLENCE

The term *family violence* is applied to a broad range of acts whose presence or absence results in harm to individuals who share parent-child or adult intimate relationships. These relationships are often long-term and generally involve aspects of financial or physical interdependence. The definition of family violence adopted by this committee is based on one developed by the Committee on Family Violence convened by the National Institute of Mental Health.

Family violence includes child and adult abuse that occurs between family members or adult intimate partners. For children, this includes acts by others that are physically and emotionally harmful or that carry the potential to cause physical harm.

Abuse of children may include sexual exploitation or molestation, threats to kill or abandon, or a lack of the emotional or physical support necessary for normal development. For adults, family or intimate violence may include acts that are physically and emotionally harmful or that carry the potential to cause physical harm. Abuse of adult partners may include sexual coercion or assaults, physical intimidation, threats to kill or to harm, restraint of normal activities or freedom, and denial of access to resources.

Despite progress in identifying the characteristics of family violence, serious problems remain in defining the severity of the injury or threat, the amount of harm, and the extent of the consequences associated with its occurrence. The question of what constitutes a family relationship is also complicated by the diversity of intimate or dependent care giving relationships in home environments. Furthermore, uncertainty remains about the strength of the relationship among the different forms of family violence. This report examines opportunities for interactions among child maltreatment, domestic violence, and elder abuse in terms of both research and service. These relationships are important because the forms of family violence may share common risk factors or may represent a developmental continuum, such as the case of an abused child who becomes either a batterer or a victim of domestic violence.

They are also important because opportunities may exist in the service delivery system to combine or integrate services and to reinforce individual programme goals by adopting common strategies.

The report does not address the issues of sibling violence or violence among same sex intimate adults, primarily because research in these fields is less well developed and the committee did not identify evaluations of interventions for these forms of family violence that met the selection criteria for the study. Although the report often emphasizes the interactions among different forms of family violence, it is important to maintain diverse approaches in examining the array of programmes, services, and interventions.

In some situations, the origins of domestic violence may have stronger theoretical links to other forms of violence against women, such as rape and sexual harassment, than to other forms of family violence. Similarly, some forms of child maltreatment may have stronger theoretical links to interpersonal violence, such as pedophilia, assault, and homicide, than to other forms of family violence. The complexity of the field is daunting to scientific study; theory building remains in an early stage of development.

Levels of Attention

In formulating its approach, the committee developed distinctions among strategies, interventions, and programmes. Although these terms are often used interchangeably in discussions of programme effectiveness, they are not synonymous.

By *strategies*, the committee refers to a general course of treatment, control, or prevention that is designed to achieve a broad social goal, such as the prevention of family violence, the identification and protection of victims, and the punishment or deterrence of offenders. The term *interventions* refer to the array of services and policies used to implement strategies at the individual, family, and community levels. Examples of interventions include parenting education programmes for child maltreatment cases, treatment services for batterers, and universal screening for pregnant women to enhance the access to services of victims of domestic violence. Interventions include not only organized services but also legal, judicial, and regulatory policies and procedures, such as protective orders and mandatory reporting systems, some of which have been evaluated in the research literature. *Programmes* are community-specific examples of particular interventions. Batterer treatment interventions, for example, may be voluntary or mandatory, depending on the setting and context of a particular programme.

Some interventions consist solely of a single community's programme; other interventions may be composed of several programmes that share a common theoretical framework but rely on different approaches in achieving their goals. These programme variations often are regarded as the same intervention. The home visitation intervention, for example, consists of several models, some of which rely on public health nurses who establish contact with mothers during their pregnancy and provide frequent visits after birth; others rely on paraprofessionals who meet with the mother after her discharge from a hospital. The home visitation intervention is part of a broader child abuse prevention strategy designed to detect risk factors for child maltreatment and to strengthen parenting skills through public health and family support services.

This report focuses primarily on interventions rather than individual programmes or broad strategies. Specific programme examples are used when they illustrate community efforts to implement a particular intervention or when they have served as the subject of an evaluation study.

APPROACH TO THE EVIDENCE

The committee has identified interventions that have been

evaluated in the literature, as well as key interventions worthy of study because of their perceived value to victims and communities in responding to family violence. Some evaluations that did not meet the committee's criteria for inclusion nonetheless are discussed in the report because they offer insights concerning outcome measurement and programme implementation. The literature review covers scientific journals, federal research reports, national research databases, state agency reports, and foundation studies. In our search we identified and reviewed over 2,000 studies to determine if they included evaluations that relied on a scientific design that included the use of a control or comparison group. The use of a control group is critical to good evaluation research, because it allows the researcher to compare the relative effects of the intervention under study to what might be expected in its absence.

In selecting evaluation studies for detailed analysis, the committee relied on the following criteria:

- The evaluation involved a programme intervention that was designed to treat or prevent some aspect of child maltreatment, domestic violence, or elder abuse;
- The evaluation was conducted between 1980 and 1996 (this time period was selected to provide a contemporary history of the evaluation research literature while maintaining manageable limits on the scope of the evidence considered by the committee);
- The evaluation used an experimental or quasi-experimental design and included measurement tools and outcomes related to family violence; and
- The evaluation included a comparison group as part of the study design.

A total of 114 evaluation studies were identified that met this standard. Most of the studies reviewed by the committee have been published in the peer-reviewed literature, although some state agency reports, foundation reports, and studies in progress are included in the research base for this report. In addition, the committee relied on 35 research review chapters that include detailed analyses of independent research studies, even though the individual studies within each review chapter may not be consistent with the selection criteria outlined above.

The committee initiated its search with a review of the relevant on-line databases that include evaluation studies of family violence interventions. We also contacted several public and private national clearinghouses, which aided in identifying unpublished materials that were included in the literature review. In addition, we learned of a small number of evaluation studies that meet our criteria but have recently been completed or exist only as state agency reports and have not been included in the literature or national clearinghouse collections. It is important to note that the range of evaluation studies presented in this report does not reflect the current range of treatment and prevention interventions. The research literature is primarily focused on small or innovative programmes that provide an opportunity for research study.

Science-based evaluations are rarely conducted on major existing interventions, such as foster care, domestic violence shelters, adult protective services, health care provider training programmes, and court procedures, because research samples and appropriate measures are not available to assess the intervention, the intervention was already in place prior to the development of evaluation methods, the organisational setting is not conducive to evaluation, or policy and programme sponsors are not prepared to provide funds to examine the impact of the intervention. As noted later in this report, rigorous evaluations are focused primarily on social service interventions in the area of child maltreatment and legal interventions for domestic violence. Experimental evaluations of interventions for elder abuse are almost nonexistent.

THE COMMITTEE'S PERSPECTIVE

The committee considered several different conceptual schemes in considering how to organize the material reviewed in this report. We could have presented this material in terms of the life spans of victims and offenders: child, adult, and elder. We could have sought to distinguish between victims and perpetrators and between treatment, prevention, and enforcement interventions by focusing chapters on each approach. However, we decided that an approach that divides the targets of the interventions would perpetuate the fragmentation that has characterized this area of research, policy, and practice.

The committee decided that the intended audience of this report, which includes researchers, service providers, and policy makers from distinct institutional settings, would be best served by a synthesis of research that brings the relevant knowledge to bear on specific services and policies within their own organisational service system. At this stage in the development of family violence interventions, the institutional settings of the interventions exercise a major influence on their objectives, resources, and method of implementation.

This choice of a categorical structure for the report, however, was disturbing to several committee members, who would prefer to see a more holistic approach that builds on the needs of children, adults, and the elderly. In our analysis of cross-cutting themes, we highlight key issues that cut across these institutional sectors. We also highlight, examples of interventions that experiment with comprehensive community approaches and that seek to replace bureaucratic structures with service systems focused on the developmental and multiple needs of clients and communities rather than the convenience of the service provider. These approaches, while not yet evaluated, represent an important dimension in the design of family violence interventions that requires further examination.

In the decades ahead, research will provide more powerful insights that can lead to improved services, policy, and practice. But the integration of research knowledge and the development of interventions will require consistent and explicit attention to the ways in which the domains of science, law, health care, and social services interact.

The absence or presence of interventions in one setting—such as shelters for battered women—may directly influence the operation and effectiveness of services in another domain—such as arrest policies for batterers. This interactive process is often missed in current assessments of family violence interventions, although it is often intrinsic to the experience of service providers.

The interactions among service systems add a new level of complexity to the design of both interventions and evaluations. Addressing this complexity will require collaborative partnerships between researchers and service providers to develop approaches that are consistent with the needs of the scientific process, that can be implemented in large systems of ongoing services as well as smaller innovative programmes, and that can provide guidance in determining what works, for whom, and under what conditions. An integrated research foundation, the development of reliable measures and large datasets, careful descriptions of the goals of an intervention and the characteristics of clients, and documentation of the services that were actually provided all provide important opportunities for such partnerships.

Through such efforts, the institutions and agencies that have supported the development of the interventions themselves can acquire the capacity to look closely at what they have achieved and to translate this knowledge into improved efforts to address the problem of family violence.

FAMILY VIOLENCE INTERVENTIONS

In the 1960s, physical child abuse and child neglect were recognized as significant problems that required identification and intervention. In the 1970s, similar attention was called to domestic violence. In the 1980s, child sexual abuse and elder abuse gained attention. Each type of family violence developed its own set of definitions, research, and interventions.

In recent years, researchers have begun to examine family

violence across the life span, seeking commonalities among various forms of child maltreatment, domestic violence, and elder abuse. Although the very nature of family relationships makes it reasonable to look for common risk and protective factors and interactions among the forms of family violence, debate continues about what determines the appropriate unit of analysis: the individuals who perpetrate or are victims of violent behaviour, the family, the community, or broader social-cultural norms.

How the nature of family violence is conceptualized has an important implication for the ways in which interventions are structured and outcomes are measured in evaluating them. This chapter examines similarities and differences in research on child maltreatment, domestic violence, and elder abuse in definitions, measurement, risk factors, and interventions.

Each area has developed its own approach to the problems under study, resulting in tremendous variation in theoretical frameworks, research instrumentation, scholarly journals, and funding sources. Although studies of the field of family violence are now emerging, research in this area has traditionally been fragmented into separate areas of inquiry.

How family violence is measured and studied and who is identified to receive interventions depend on its definition. The multiple dimensions of family violence make definition tasks both difficult and controversial, and definitions have evolved somewhat differently for child maltreatment, domestic violence, and elder abuse. Although precise definitions are required for research and data collection, the situational context of many cases of family violence often challenges efforts to establish consistent criteria that can govern case reporting and selection decisions.

The types of cases deemed appropriate for intervention may differ by service sector as well as within service settings. Despite these differences, common concerns have emerged that influence efforts to define family violence: a trend toward broadening the set of behaviours that are viewed as abuse or neglect, the role of cultural norms, the role of intentionality, the balance of power in the offender-victim relationship, and the influence of service-sector resources on definitions.

BROADENING OF DEFINITIONS

Early definitions of child maltreatment were narrowly focused on issues of physical harm and endangerment. They were often based on a medical diagnostic approach, emphasizing the more serious forms of physical abuse and neglect that can result in physical injury and poor health. More recent definitions focus on the impact of maltreatment on development, expanding the category of abuse and neglect to include actions viewed as harmful to children, such as emotional abuse or educational or medical neglect, even though they are not necessarily associated with immediate physical injury. The negative impacts of exposure to domestic violence on children have recently been recognized. Some perpetrators of domestic violence have been charged not only with assault of their wives, but also reported as child abusers for exposing their children to their violent behaviour. The National Center on Child Abuse and Neglect (1988) recognizes six major types of child maltreatment: physical abuse, sexual abuse, emotional abuse, physical neglect, educational neglect, and emotional neglect.

Similarly, initial definitions of domestic violence focused on acts of physical violence directed toward women by their spouses or partners. Survey research found women also committed acts of physical violence against their husbands, suggesting that the initial definition might be too restrictive. Further research broadened the definition to include sexual violence, marital rape, and acts of emotional or psychological abuse. Feminist scholars conceptualize domestic violence as coercive control of women by their partners; the coercion can be physical, emotional, or sexual. The recognition of elder abuse through adult protective services has led to definitions similar to those of child maltreatment. Elder abuse is generally defined to include physical and sexual violence, psychological abuse, and neglect. However, elder abuse definitions frequently go beyond those of child maltreatment to include financial abuse or exploitation. Elder abuse may also be a continuation of domestic violence in the relationship, in which case the issue of coercive control is pertinent.

Definitions of family violence have also broadened with respect to who is considered family. For domestic violence, the trend is to include all intimate relationships, such as cohabiting couples, same-sex couples, and ex-spouses, as well as currently married couples. Dating couples and ex-boyfriends/girlfriends may also be included. For child maltreatment, a distinction is made between abuse and neglect; the definition of neglect is generally limited to acts by a child's parents or legal caregiver. For child physical and sexual abuse, no consensus exists as to how broadly the set of potential abusers should be defined, although, in the context of family violence, strangers are not included. For elder abuse, family members as well as legal or informal caregivers can be involved, and self-neglect has sometimes been counted in elder abuse data. In addition, violence between siblings and violence by children directed at their parents may be included in family violence.

The broadening of definitions of the various forms of family violence has been criticized by some on the grounds that it leads to a diffusion of effort within service agencies that have limited resources. Others have noted, however, that because emotional abuse and emotional neglect are often associated with other forms of maltreatment, the broader definitions create opportunities for early interventions that may be successful in preventing more serious and lethal forms of violence.

How broadly or narrowly family violence is defined has an obvious impact on its prevalence. Wyatt and Peters (1986) demonstrated empirically the impact of variations in definitions of sexual abuse on the estimated prevalence rates reported in a number of studies. Physical violence is the most commonly measured form of maltreatment of adults and is second only to neglect in the maltreatment of children. Although clinical reports suggest that emotional abuse (such as yelling, criticism, ridicule, and threats) may be pervasive and central components of family violence, no rigorous measures currently exist to assess the extent of this type of behaviour.

THE ROLE OF CULTURE

Definitions of family violence vary not only over time, but also across cultures. Behaviour that may be considered the norm by some groups may be considered abusive by others. Debate continues over the extent to which definitions of family violence can accommodate cultural variability without promoting different thresholds for intervention on the basis of race, ethnicity, or socioeconomic status. Agreement across cultural groups may be easy to reach on severe forms of family violence, such as beating a family member to death. Less severe behaviours are more subject to cultural differences. For example, a number of child advocates, researchers, and some parent groups believe that corporal punishment is abusive and harmful to children and should be illegal. In contrast, many working-class parents believe in strict child discipline practices and favor its use. Role expectations derived from traditional family relationships (which commonly viewed children and wives as property of the head of the household) can also contribute to conflict and violence when major changes occur in the status of women and children within a society. Pervasive gender inequality may be embedded in cultural norms and may influence patterns and rates of victimisation.

As U.S. society becomes more diverse, cultural practices such as "coining" (a curing ritual that involves the forceful pressing of coins on a child's body, resulting in bruises) among Vietnamese populations and female genital mutilation among some African and Middle Eastern populations will increasingly be the focus of debate. Although such practices may meet criteria for abuse in the United States, it is important to understand their social and cultural contexts, at least in the perceptions of the families involved, in order to influence behavioural changes. American society lacks a clear definition of caregiver responsibility for elders comparable to parental responsibilities for children, and conflicts may arise in certain cultures, classes, and social groups as to what types of arrangements constitute maltreatment. Recently, some researchers have questioned the legal and clinical definitions of elder abuse, suggesting that it is the older person's perception of particular behaviour, influenced by culture and tradition that should be the salient factor in identification and intervention.

THE ROLE OF INTENTIONALITY

Although some definitions of family violence require that acts be intentional, recent trends in research definitions have been to focus on acts that are harmful or potentially harmful rather than on intent. Although intent is often difficult to determine, it is often important in determining the type of intervention necessary when decisions are made to investigate a family. Neglect of children and the elderly may result from ignorance or lack of resources rather than malevolence. Parental knowledge of children's developmental abilities (especially feeding and toilet training), parental abilities to supervise young children, and parental expectations regarding the needs and behaviour of young children have been identified as key areas in which significant variation exists within neighborhoods and between social classes and cultures.

These discrepancies may be particularly difficult to resolve in identifying cases of maltreatment that occur in settings characterized by extreme poverty, substance abuse, community violence, and transience (including immigration and homelessness). Elder abuse may also be unintentional because of the caregiver/perpetrator's ignorance of the needs of the elderly or because of his or her own infirmity. The lack of a clear definition of caregiver responsibility for elders also makes determining intentional withholding of care difficult. Whether behaviour is labeled as abusive or neglectful may depend on its frequency, duration, intensity, severity, and consequences.

DEPENDENCE AND POWER

Running through discussions of child maltreatment, domestic

violence, and elder abuse is the idea of unequal power in the relationship between abuser and victim. In all three domains, abusers may use violence to control the victim. It is expected that children are dependent and that parents have more power than their children and will exert control over them. However, if the parent abdicates responsibility for caring for the child, neglect can occur. If the parent uses excessive physical force in exerting control, abuse can occur. For the incapacitated elderly, it is also expected that they are dependent on family or a caregiver; the typical elder abuse victim was thought to be frail and dependent. Although some research has found that elder abuse may be more likely when an adult child remains financially dependent on his or her parent rather than when the elderly parent has become dependent, the adult child may still have power over the elderly parent by virtue of size, strength, and mobility.

The feminist analysis of domestic violence posits that physical violence is but one tactic used by abusers to exert control over their partners. In this paradigm, physical violence, emotional abuse, sexual violence, social isolation, and withholding of financial resources all serve to undermine a woman's autonomy and limit her power in the relationship. Feminist theory focused on gender inequalities offers a framework for a broad set of interventions designed to expose the pattern of male dominance and control in violent relationships and the ways in which society tolerates and legitimizes social inequalities that can contribute to entrapment.

INFLUENCE OF THE SERVICE SECTOR ON DEFINITIONS

There is interplay between the conceptualization of the types of family violence and the service sector in which interventions take place. For example, the identification of the "battered child syndrome" in the health care system at first focused the definitions of child maltreatment on physical injury. As the legal and social service systems became involved and the emphasis in services became that of protecting the child, acts that threatened the child's well-being became a relevant factor in defining maltreatment; the definitions were subsequently broadened to include emotional abuse, sexual abuse, and neglect. It is important to note that legal definitions encompass stringent standards in each category of abuse focused on thresholds for legal intervention that may not be useful in other service systems.

Similarly, the emphasis in domestic violence was first on physical injury. Even the term "battered wife" echoed the earlier use of "battered child," and much attention was focused and continues to be focused on the identification and documentation of physical injury in medical settings. Also for domestic violence, an emphasis on physical injury carried over to early legal interventions. For example, evidence of physical injury was often deemed necessary before an arrest was made. As a result of research studies and programmes to change community attitudes toward the needs of battered women, definitions broadened beyond physical injury to include sexual and emotional abuse and threats of harm. Recent legislation now recognizes the stalking of estranged or former partners as domestic violence.

The recognition of elder abuse grew out of adult protective services—that is, services for adults who, for whatever reason, are unable to care for themselves. The similarity to child protective services heavily influenced definitions of elder abuse. It has been suggested that there has been an over reliance on the child abuse model. Recent findings suggest that domestic violence may be a more useful framework for study and intervention, since the individuals involved are legally independent adults. To some health researchers, however, the family violence paradigm is also not suitable. They recommend that elder abuse be considered from the perspective of "inadequate care," since it is easier to measure unmet needs than inappropriate behaviour.

MEASUREMENT ISSUES

Even if there were consensus on definitions, estimates of the scope of family violence would vary because of the different methods used to measure its incidence and prevalence.

Detailed discussions of measuring the scope of family violence are available elsewhere. Data on family violence are available from clinical data, administrative data, and social surveys. Each type of data has its own strengths and weaknesses and is useful for different purposes. Clinical studies, carried out by psychiatrists, psychologists, and counselors, continue to be a frequent source of data on family violence. This is primarily due to the fact that these investigators have the most direct access to cases of family violence. The clinical or agency setting (including hospital emergency departments and battered women's shelters) provides access to extensive in-depth information about particular cases of violence. Studies of violence toward women have relied heavily on samples of women who seek help at battered women's shelters.

Such samples are important because they are often the only way of obtaining detailed data on severely battered women. Such data are also necessary to study the impact of intervention programmes. However, because they are based on small, non-representative samples, such data cannot be used to estimate the incidence and prevalence of domestic violence. Administrative data collected from official sources, such as child protective services, police departments, and adult protective services, provide the bulk of the information from which estimates of the incidence and prevalence of family violence are made. There are a number of factors that influence how well these data accurately reflect true incidence and prevalence. First, the quality and amount of these data vary by type of violence.

All states now mandate reporting of child maltreatment and most states mandate reporting of elder abuse, although the definitions of reportable abuse differ from state to state. Even with mandatory reporting laws, it is widely acknowledged that abuse is underreported. One study found that only 44 percent of cases known to community professionals were officially known to child protective services agencies. This discrepancy may be based on the unwillingness of professionals to report, contradictory community standards regarding maltreatment definitions, or screening practices in child protective services agencies. Furthermore, the number of substantiated cases may vary with the amount of resources devoted to case investigation. There is no administrative data source for domestic violence that is comparable to the state child and elder abuse datasets, and surveillance efforts are often challenged by concerns about victim safety and confidentiality.

Second, segments of the population at risk are subject to different levels of surveillance. Families who, because of their demographic characteristics (e.g., poverty, unemployment, single parenthood), have more frequent contact with public-sector services (e.g., welfare, housing) are more often exposed to mandated reporters and get closer scrutiny. Consequently, children who are poor or members of minority groups are more likely to be identified as maltreated than are more affluent white children.

To remedy underreporting, national incidence studies of child maltreatment include official reports supplemented by surveys of other professionals about suspected cases of child abuse that have not been reported. The most recent National Incidence Study of Child Abuse and Neglect (NIS-3) found 2.8 million cases of child maltreatment, a significant increase over the 1.4 million cases known by the agencies surveyed in 1986. An unknown part of this increase may be due to broader definitions and broader sampling frames in the survey sample. Based on the NIS methodology, the National Center on Elder Abuse has launched a similar incident study of elder abuse, scheduled to be completed in 1997.

Researchers often turn to survey research to overcome the problems associated with administrative data. Surveys often find higher rates of violence than do administrative data; however, surveys have their own drawbacks. They are constrained by the low base rate of most forms of abuse and violence in families, as well as the sensitive and taboo nature of the topic. Some investigators cope with the problem of the low base rate by employing purposive or non-representative sampling techniques to identify cases.

Another approach has been to use large groups of

available subjects. For example, investigators of courtship violence have made extensive use of survey research techniques using college students as subjects. Other sources of bias in social survey data on family violence include inaccurate recall, differential interpretation of questions, and intended and unintended response error.

Survey results may also vary by question wording and context. For example, when the National Crime Victimisation Survey revised its questionnaire to stress, among other things, that they wanted to know about incidents involving relatives and family members as well as acts committed by strangers, the reported violent attacks by family members nearly doubled from 5.4 per 1,000 for women in 1987-1991 to 9.3 per 1,000 in 1992-1993. This change most likely reflects the change in the survey and not a sudden increase in the rate of violence against women. The rates for domestic violence are lower than the rates found in other surveys that did not rely solely on crime reports. The 1985 National Family Violence Survey found much higher rates of domestic violence: 116 per 1,000 women reported experiencing violence during the past year; 34 per 1,000 women reported severe violence; and 12 per 1,000 reported marital rape. In the 1993 Commonwealth Fund Survey of Women's Health, 70 per 1,000 women reported physical violence by an intimate partner.

The source of data has an impact not only on measures of incidence and prevalence of family violence, but also on what factors and variables are identified as risk and protective factors. In an analysis based on clinical data or official report data, risk and protective factors are confounded with factors such as labeling bias and agency or clinical setting catchments area. Researchers have long noted that certain individuals and families are more likely to be correctly and incorrectly labeled as offenders or victims of family violence. Social survey data are not immune to confounding problems either, as social or demographic factors may be related to willingness to participate in a self-report survey and a tendency toward providing socially desirable responses.

RISK FACTORS

Researchers have looked, unsuccessfully for the most part, for traits that predispose children or adults to being victims of family violence. Much of the early retrospective research lacked comparison groups and confounded traits that preceded abuse with those that resulted from it. Research next focused on the traits of perpetrators. Although there appears to be a relatively high incidence of psychological and emotional problems among perpetrators of family violence, no characteristic profile of a child abuser, batterer, or elder abuser has emerged.

It appears that no single factor can explain family violence. Rather it seems most likely that the complex interaction of personal history, personality traits, and demographic factors with social and environmental influences leads to violence in the family. Understanding better the particular factors that are relevant in a given family, and the sequence in which they emerge, may be important for choosing the most appropriate intervention.

In the sections that follow we review the most widely discussed risk factors in the study of family violence and, when appropriate, identify for which forms of violence and which types of relationships the factors are relevant. To overcome the limitations of studies of single factors, interactive models of risk and protective factors may further understanding of the etiology of family violence.

However, the complexity of analysis associated with these models and the difficulty of distinguishing causal effects from observational data have inhibited their testing and application. Hence, research often focuses on risk factors that appear to be subject to change as a result of intervention or that are helpful in identifying at-risk populations.

In research on domestic violence, several reviews of case-comparison studies have noted that potential risk markers are highly correlated with each other (e.g., family socioeconomic status and husband's occupational status, witnessing and experiencing violence as a child). This conceptual and statistical redundancy requires careful attention to disentangle risk factors that are directly related to the use of violence from other confounding factors.

RISK FACTORS FOR PERPETRATORS

Age

One of the most consistent risk factors for perpetration is age. As in violence between non-intimates, family violence is most likely to be perpetrated by those between ages 18 and 30. For child abuse, the age of the mother at the birth of the abused child has been found to be related to rates of physical abuse, with younger mothers exhibiting higher rates of abuse. An analysis of data from the 1985 National Family Violence Survey found young men significantly more likely to abuse their spouses. Over 20 percent of men between ages 18 and 25 and 16.9 percent of men between ages 26 and 35 committed at least one act of domestic violence in the past year. Violence was reported by 7.2 percent of men ages 36 to 50 and 4.5 percent of those over 50. Youth has not been found to be a risk factor for elder abuse perpetration, although the rate of elder abuse is lower than the rate of other forms of family violence.

Gender

Men are the most likely offenders in acts of intimate as well as non-intimate violence. However, the differences in the rates of offending between men and women are much smaller for family violence than for violence outside the home. Men and women have comparable rates of child homicide. Although women have been regarded as more likely to be offenders when the child victim is young (under 3 years of age) because of their traditional roles as primary caregivers for infants and toddlers, recent research suggests that extremely stressed or enraged male adults (including birth fathers, stepfathers, and boyfriends) are more often the cause of physical abuse fatalities involving an infant or small child. In cases of child deaths from neglect, including bathtub drowning, fires started by unsupervised children, dehydration, and starvation, mothers are most often held responsible.

The extent of male victimisation is controversial in the field of family violence. The earliest studies of spousal violence reported violence by women toward their husbands. The two National Family Violence Surveys also found a higher than expected incidence of violence toward men—the rate of violence was the same or even higher than that reported toward women. In addition, women initiated violence about as often as men did. However, the researchers qualified their findings by noting that much of the female violence appeared to be in self-defense and that women, because of their size and strength, appeared to inflict less injury than male attackers. In contrast to the National Family Violence Surveys, the National Crime Victimisation Survey found women reporting much higher rates of victimisation by partners or ex-partners than men reported. In 1992-1993, the average rate of physical and sexual violence by an intimate was 9.4 per 1,000 for women, but only 1.4 per 1,000 for men.

These differences may be accounted for by the fact that the National Crime Victimisation Surveys included only victimisation serious enough to be considered a crime by the respondents. Rates of disclosure of experience with violent incidents are thought to be susceptible to several factors, including the wording of the questions, the context in which questions are asked about sexual or intimate partner violence, and the extent of convergence or difference between interviewers and survey participants. Although some research has suggested that women are likely to be more forthcoming about their experiences with violent victimisation when interviewed by women who share their ethnic heritage, the impact of interviewer-respondent characteristics on survey responses has not been deeply investigated. Studies have found that female partner victimisation is more likely to be accompanied by sexual and emotional abuse. Female victims of intimate violence also suffer more physical injuries and emotional and psychological consequences than do men.

Income

A series of research studies over the past decades has found consistent evidence of strong relationships between poverty and the reported occurrence and severity of child maltreatment, especially neglect.

Although child maltreatment may occur in families in high income brackets, abuse and neglect seem to be concentrated among the poorest of the poor. Pelton (1994) has estimated that more than 90 percent of all reported incidents of child maltreatment occur in families below the median income (estimated at $40,611 in 1995); 40 to 50 percent of all incidents occur within families whose incomes fall above the poverty level (estimated at $15,569) but below the median income.

The absence of experimental research that can examine the impact of different forms of material and income supports on the reduction of poverty and child maltreatment rates makes it difficult to identify the pathways by which low income influences parenting behaviours and interactions with children. Stress is thought to be the dominant variable associated with the relationship between low income and care giving behaviours, but research attention has recently focused on other factors as well, including material hardships, housing, coping and care giving strategies, and dangerous environments.

Severe violence toward children is more likely in poor families who have fewer economic and social resources to help with child care responsibilities, especially among those who are least able to cope with the material hardships of poverty. Although most poor people do not use violence toward intimates, self-report surveys and official report data find that the rates of all forms of family violence, except child sexual abuse, are higher for those whose family income is below the poverty line.

As noted above, poor families are more likely to be in contact with social service agencies and hence be under greater scrutiny, thereby increasing the likelihood that they will be reported for abuse or neglect. Nonetheless, the association between child maltreatment and poverty persists in self-report data as well as in official data.

In their review of studies of risk markers for domestic violence, Hotaling and Sugarman (1990) report that, although wife assault occurs across all occupational, educational, and income groups, it is more common and more severe in families with lower socioeconomic status.

In addition, higher-socioeconomic-status women seem to be just as likely as lower-socioeconomic-status women to report being verbally assaulted and just as likely to have experienced minor physical violence (i.e., having something thrown at them, being pushed, shoved, slapped, or grabbed). But the frequency and severity of serious assaults appear to be linked to socio-economic status. Pillemer and Finkelhor (1988) found no difference in elder abuse rates based on economic status.

Race

The two National Family Violence Surveys, however, found stronger relationships between race/ethnicity and both violence between partners and violence toward children. Although in the first National Family Violence Survey, the difference in rates between blacks and whites disappeared when income was controlled; an analysis of the larger dataset from the Second National Family Violence Survey found that some differences persisted even when income was controlled. The second survey also found significantly higher rates of domestic violence and child physical abuse among Hispanics than among non-Hispanic whites.

When income, place of residence (urban/non urban), and age were controlled, the differences disappeared for domestic violence but remained for severe physical abuse of children. The picture is less clear on race. Both official report data and self-report survey data often report that child abuse and violence toward women are overrepresented among minorities. Data from the National Crime Victimisation Survey indicate that the rate of domestic violence is essentially the same for whites (5.4 per 1,000), blacks (5.8 per 1,000), and Hispanics (5.5 per 1,000). All three National Incidence Studies of Child Abuse and Neglect found no significant relationships between the incidence of maltreatment and the child's race or ethnicity.

SITUATIONAL AND ENVIRONMENTAL FACTORS

Personality Characteristics

Researchers have searched for personality characteristics or psychiatric disorders to explain the behaviour of family violence perpetrators. Only a small percentage of parents involved in child maltreatment are diagnosed with a psychiatric disorder. Although no consistent pattern has emerged, identification of psychiatric disorders in perpetrators, when present, is important in determining appropriate intervention strategies, especially in cases involving depression or schizophrenia. Although a consistent profile of parental psychopathology or a significant level of parental mental disturbance has not been supported, a set of personality characteristics associated with child maltreatment has emerged with sufficient frequency to warrant attention. These characteristics include low self-esteem, external locus of control, poor impulse control, depression, anxiety, and antisocial behaviour.

A number of studies have found a high incidence of psychopathology and personality disorders, most frequently antisocial personality disorder, borderline personality organisation, and post-traumatic stress disorder among men who assault intimate partners. Nonetheless, batterers appear to be a heterogeneous group, a finding that has led some researchers to develop typologies to represent different subgroups. In some cases, the psychological needs of perpetrators can reflect socially constructed role expectations, especially when cultural norms can provide social permission for males to terrorize and control their partners. A high incidence of psychological or emotional problems among those who physically abuse an elderly relative has also been reported.

STRESS AND MARITAL CONFLICT

A number of stressful life events, such as unemployment, financial problems, and sickness or death in the family have been identified as possibly related to violence. For example, an association between unemployment and child maltreatment has been documented by a number of researchers. In another analysis, high levels of marital conflict and low socioeconomic status emerged as the primary predictors of increased likelihood and severity of wife assault.

The relationship among stressful life events, the personalities of the people affected by them, and the role of stress as a factor in marital conflict and family violence remains poorly understood. For example, it is not certain whether individuals in violent relationships lack specific skills that can improve their ability to negotiate and compromise and eliminate the use of violence as a strategy to resolve conflict, or whether the sources of marital conflict in seriously or frequently violent relationships are different from those that characterize other relationships. Conflict over heavy drinking by husbands, often exacerbated by their employment or status insecurity (such as having less education than their wives) illustrates the type of interaction that may increase the use of violence as a conflict resolution strategy.

SOCIAL ISOLATION AND SOCIAL SUPPORT

The data on social isolation are somewhat less consistent than are the data for the previously discussed correlates. First, because so much of the research on family violence is cross-sectional, it is not clear whether social isolation precedes violence in the home or is a consequence of it. Second, social isolation has been crudely measured, and the purported correlation may be more anecdotal than statistical. Nevertheless, researchers often agree that people who are socially isolated from neighbors and relatives are more likely to be violent in the home. Social support appears to be an important protective factor. One major source of social support is the availability of friends and family for help, aid, and assistance. The more a family is integrated into the community and the more groups and associations they belong to, the less likely they are to be violent.

INTERGENERATIONAL TRANSMISSION OF VIOLENCE

The notion that abused children grows up to be abusing parents and violent adults have been widely expressed in the family violence literature. One review that examined self-reports of the intergenerational transmission of violence toward children concluded that the best estimate of the rate of intergenerational transmission is 30 percent. Although a rate of 30 percent is substantially less than the majority of abused children, it is considerably more than the rate of 2 to 4 percent found in the general population. A study that examined continuity and discontinuity of abuse in a longitudinal study of high-risk mothers and their children found that mothers who had been abused as children were less likely to abuse their own children if they had emotionally supportive parents, partners, or friends.

In addition, the abused mothers who did not abuse their children were described as "middle class" and "upwardly mobile," suggesting that they were able to draw on economic resources that may not have been available to the abused mothers who did abuse their children. A study that looked prospectively at the cycle of violence hypothesis found that physically abused and neglected children are at risk of becoming violent offenders when they grow up, compared with matched controls of the same age, sex, race, and approximate social class. Evidence from studies of parental and marital violence indicates that, although witnessing or experiencing violence by caregivers in one's family of origin is often correlated with later violent behaviour, such experience is not the sole determining factor. When the intergenerational transmission of violence occurs, it is probably the result of a complex set of social and psychological processes and confounded with other, more discriminating risk markers, such as marital conflict and socioeconomic status. Some studies have examined childhood sexual abuse as a risk factor for committing sex crimes as an adult. A review of 23 retrospective and 2 prospective studies concluded that experiencing childhood sexual abuse is neither a necessary nor a sufficient cause of adult sexual offending. However, one of the prospective studies did find a significant correlation between being sexually abused as a child and being arrested for prostitution as an adult. Although experiencing and witnessing violence is believed to be an important risk factor, the actual mechanism by which violence is transmitted from generation to generation is not well understood. The role of the media, for example, may have a powerful influence in transmitting sex-role expectations, conflict resolution strategies, and images of family interactions.

ALCOHOL AND DRUG USE

The use of alcohol is often associated with aggression, suggesting that it may be a risk factor for family violence, but the associations among alcoholism, drug use, and family violence are poorly understood. Results of studies on alcoholism and child maltreatment have been contradictory, with some studies finding a significant relationship and others not. Estimates of the extent of alcoholism among abusive parents range from 18 to 38 percent, compared with estimates of 6 to 16 percent for the general population.

Alcohol use has been reported in 25 to 85 percent of incidents of domestic violence. Although alcohol consumption patterns are associated with other variables related to violence (such as witnessing violence in one's home), the positive relationship of men's drinking to domestic violence persists even after socio-demographic variables, hostility, and marital satisfaction are statistically controlled. Men's drinking patterns, particularly binge drinking, are associated with domestic violence across all ethnic and social classes. Alcohol abuse is also present in a large proportion of elder abuse cases.

GENDER INEQUALITY AND SEX-ROLE EXPECTATIONS

An important risk factor for violence against women appears to be gender inequality. Individual, aggregate, and cross-cultural data find that the greater the degree of gender inequality in a relationship, community, and society, the higher are the rates of violence toward women. One review of 52 case-comparison studies did not find significant differences in measures of sex role inequality between violent and nonviolent couples.

In a later analysis, the authors observe that expectations about division of labor in the household were one of four markers associated with a risk factor that they labeled "marital conflict." The other three markers were marital conflict, frequency of husband's drinking, and educational incompatibility.

PRESENCE OF OTHER VIOLENCE

A final general risk factor is that the presence of violence in one family relationship increases the risk that there will be violence in others. For example, children in homes in which there are violence between their parents are more likely to experience violence than are children who grow up in homes where there is no such violence. Moreover, children who witness and experienced violence are more likely to use violence toward their parents and siblings than are children who do not experience or see violence in their homes.

RISK FACTORS FOR VICTIMS

Early research in domestic violence and child maltreatment looked for factors that differentiated victims from non victims. It was suggested that personality or other personal traits of victims could provoke anger or aggression. Much of this research has been criticized on methodological grounds, and it has been suggested that personality traits of victims identified in some early studies were the result rather than the cause of the violence. Compared with research on offenders, there has been somewhat less recent research on victims of family violence that focuses on factors that increase or reduce the risk of victimisation. Most research on victims examines the consequences of victimisation (e.g., depression, psychological distress, suicide attempts, and symptoms of post-traumatic stress syndrome) and the effectiveness of various intervention efforts.

CHILDREN

Early research suggested that a number of factors raise the risk of a child's is abused. Low-birth weight babies, premature babies, and children with developmental or other disabilities were all described as being at greater risk of being abused by their parents or caregivers. However, a review of such studies calls into question many of these findings. One major problem is that few investigators used matched comparison groups. More recent studies did not find premature babies or children with disabilities as being at higher risk for abuse. The very youngest children appear to be at the greatest risk of abuse, especially the most dangerous and potentially lethal forms of violence. Not only are young children physically more fragile and thus more susceptible to injury, but also their vulnerability makes them more likely to be reported and diagnosed as abused when injured. Older children are most likely to be underreported as victims of abuse.

MARITAL PARTNERS

Being female is the most consistent risk factor for being a victim of domestic violence. Early studies unsuccessfully attempted to find a psychological profile that put a woman at risk of being battered. Early descriptive and clinical accounts described battered women as dependent, having low esteem, and feeling inadequate and helpless and reported a high incidence of depression and anxiety among clinical samples. Later studies have questioned whether these victim characteristics were present before the women were battered or are the result of the victimisation. Clinical studies often use small and selective samples and fail to have comparison groups.

A comprehensive review of risk factors found that the only one consistently associated with being a victim of physical abuse was having witnessed parental violence as a child. As noted earlier, this finding was modified in a later review, and the authors attribute this modification to the use of multivariate analysis that can distinguish between minor and severe violence, marital conflict, and the use of violence in the home.

ELDERS

Research on elder abuse is divided on whether elder victims are more likely to be physically, socially, and emotionally dependent on their caregivers or whether it is the offender's dependence on the victim that increases the risk of elder abuse. Conventional wisdom suggests that it is the oldest, sickest, most debilitated, and dependent elders who are prone to the full range of mistreatment by their caregivers. However, Pillemer and Suitor (1992) have found that the victim's dependence was not as powerful a risk factor as perceived by clinicians, the public, and some researchers. A history of violence, particularly between spouses, may be predictive of elder abuse in later life.

INTERVENTIONS

A broad set of public and private initiatives at the national, state, and local levels has generated a complex array of institutions to address the consequences and the origins of family violence, but the dimensions of this effort are difficult to observe or measure. The large majority of legal, health, and social service interventions and programmes rely extensively on community resources that reflect both regional strengths and limitations. In some cases, such efforts have emerged in the absence of national legislation to determine eligibility criteria or accountability standards as a basis for federal funding, and activities have evolved in health, social service, and legal settings (such as home visitations programmes and adult protective services) that were not designed with the treatment or prevention of family violence as a primary goal.

In other cases, federal and congressional initiatives sought to influence the design of interventions by establishing eligibility criteria, funding direct services, and specifying key elements of programme design (such as the Family Violence

Prevention and Services Act, the Child Abuse Prevention and Treatment Act, and the Violence Against Women legislation). As a result, the overall "system" of family violence interventions is highly disjointed, loosely structured, and often lacks central coordinating offices or comprehensive service delivery systems.

FRAGMENTATION OF SERVICES

The fragmented nature of the categorical services involved in addressing different aspects of family violence has inhibited the development of a detailed picture and integrated datasets in this field. The fragmentation of services discourages research and cost analyses in assessing the impact and outcomes of family violence; it is therefore difficult to determine whether sufficient services exist in selected settings, the ways in which services address selected goals (such as identification, prevention, protection, or treatment), or the conditions under which persons in need of services do not have access to appropriate care.

Victims of domestic violence, for example, may be seen by emergency department personnel, other health care providers, court officials, and battered women's shelter staff, but rarely do these service or agency staff members have an opportunity to collaborate, review, or understand the full dimensions of the victim's needs and experiences. Children who have been assaulted by relatives in their homes may have also witnessed incidents of violence between their parents, but the social service agency and law enforcement personnel who respond to cases of child maltreatment may not be in a position to address other forms of violent behaviour in the home.

The fragmentation of the field has led some observers to question whether there is, in fact, a unified body of research and knowledge that can inform and integrate the different dimensions of this social problem. This complicated terrain has also discouraged and impeded efforts to determine the scope of federal, state, or local treatment and prevention programmes, many of which are authorized and funded through a series of statutes that lack a coherent framework or strategy. Yet the broad array of services and resources, while poorly integrated, serves an extensive population. The lack of evidence and analysis about the effectiveness of the system of interventions as a whole does not mean that individual services are not doing an adequate job in addressing the needs of individual clients and communities. But the absence of coherence in the system of family violence interventions makes it difficult to observe or understand ways in which discrete parts of this system may interact, complement, or conflict with each other.

In some cases, federal programmes have provided resources to assist with organizing services, technical assistance, and data collection requirements that have helped to standardize a developing programme or set of activities. Yet federal efforts lack a set of common goals or comprehensive strategy and often reflect administrative desires to meet the needs of child or adult victims in the context of existing service systems rather than initiating broad reforms focused explicitly on family violence. Furthermore, the role of the federal government has in large part been designed to strengthen and support local or state initiatives that reflect an enormous array of policy and programme strategies, often through unrestricted block grants. The inherent flexibility in these types of funding mechanisms inhibits national or regional efforts to collect data on the clients, programme outcomes, and measures of effectiveness.

The broad scope and desegregated nature of federal efforts in the area of family violence interventions are reflected in a 1986 report prepared by the Office of the Assistant Secretary for Planning and Evaluation in the U.S. Department of Health and Human Services (DHHS). It is the last known federal interdepartmental review of programmes focused on child abuse and neglect, domestic violence, and elder abuse; it identifies nine federal departments and three independent agencies that provide services or sponsor research relevant to family violence. The 1986 report was preceded by a detailed review of DHHS services for victims of domestic violence undertaken in 1979, when legislation for a categorical programme of financial assistance for the provision of services to victims of domestic violence was being considered by the Congress.

The 1981 report noted that no information on services for domestic violence victims had been routinely collected in prior years, because no programmes within DHHS had a specific mandate to serve these victims. This report describes ways in which 13 separate DHHS service programmes had been used to provide assistance to victims of domestic violence, although the vast majority of the eligibility requirements for these programmes did not include domestic violence. For example, through the Social Services (Title XX) programme, states receive federal funding for their child protective services programmes, which provide social services designed to protect children from abuse, neglect, and exploitation.

Service providers who participated in the survey that was part of the 1981 DHHS report indicated that they refer victims of spouse abuse to other service providers (such as shelters or adult protective services programmes) for direct help with the problem of domestic violence. As a result, multiple agencies may become involved in meeting the needs of one family, and problems of coordination and integration of services become increasingly important with the emergence of specialized services.

IMPACTS AND COSTS

The costs associated with family violence include two key components:

- Direct costs, those of providing treatment and services, and
- Indirect costs, such as reduced productivity, diminished quality of life (including pain and suffering), and decreased ability to care for oneself or others. It is extremely difficult to estimate the range of these costs. Efforts to collect data on the dimensions of the programmes and

services are impeded by their desegregated nature and their reliance on different reporting measures and units of analysis.

Yet it is known that the injuries and mental health problems that occur in the wake of family violence have imposed a heavy burden on a broad range of service providers, including women's shelters, schools, hospitals, mental health clinics, police stations, and district attorney's offices. Responses to reports of domestic violence or the endangerment of children, for example, involve time-consuming and costly investigations to determine programme eligibility by a broad range of social service programmes, including child protective services, children and family resource programmes, child welfare, and foster care offices. In cases in which injury has occurred and the victim or caregivers seek medical assistance, a wide range of health resources may be used, such as emergency department and trauma centers; various medical services, including pediatric, obstetric, and gynecological services; mental health services; oral health and nursing facilities; orthopedic, neurological, and radiological treatment programmes; and community health centers.

One recent study of the cost implications of treating children in a pediatric intensive care unit, for example, reported that children rendered critically ill from abuse differ markedly from other critically ill children in terms of age, severity of injury, mortality, and expenses for acute medical care. This study further indicated that, despite the resource-intensive nature of their cases, children whose caregivers sought medical treatment for abuse-related injuries in an intensive care unit were at greater risk of death and severe residual morbidity, often because of irreversible brain injury, than the general patient population in the same unit within the time period of the study. The legal system has been profoundly affected by the problem of family violence, especially in handling cases involving decisions about child placement, termination of parental rights, and abuse by intimate partners.

Massachusetts state courts, for example, issued almost 100,000 restraining orders during the period 1992-1994; on average, once every 10 minutes in Massachusetts a victim of domestic violence seeks a restraining order against an abusive defendant. The documentation and treatment of reports of family violence, especially abuse by intimate partners, presents a significant burden on local police agencies and state and municipal courts, including the criminal, family, and juvenile justice systems.

More recently, a broad range of voluntary and quasi-public programmes have emerged to deal with the aftermath and prevention of family violence, including battered women's shelter programmes, child fatality review teams, children's trust fund organisations, family preservation services, and local and state coordinating councils. The true range of costs associated with the immediate impact of family violence is simply unknown, but conservative estimates would suggest that the costs are quite large. Estimates vary widely depending on the definitions applied, the measurement of both extent and service utilization, and assumptions about the cost of service utilization. The expenses of treatment programmes for child maltreatment have been estimated to cost more than $500 million annually (U.S. General Accounting Office, 1991a); these costs cover only direct services (such as medical treatment, short-term foster care, and specialized education) and do not include mental health or educational services that may be required as a long-term consequence of child abuse or neglect.

The General Accounting Office estimate also does not include additional costs associated with juvenile courts, longer-term foster care, drug or alcohol treatment, adult criminal activities, foregone future earnings, and potential welfare dependence, which have been acknowledged as consequences of child maltreatment but not quantified.

Recent estimates place the annual cost of domestic violence in the United States at between $1.7 billion and $140 billion. The variation among cost estimates stems from differences in the variables selected to generate cost figures; for example, Miller's estimate includes a high set of indirect costs associated with pain and suffering, which were not included in the Straus estimates. Another major source of difference is the definition used to determine the size of the victimized population.

Depending on what prevalence estimates are used, the number of cases for which costs are estimated is affected. And the larger the prevalence rate used, the higher the annual estimate of total cost. One way to narrow the wide range of cost estimates would be to generate a national estimate of the prevalence or incidence of specific types of family violence.

The Centers for Disease Control and Prevention, for example, is involved in an effort to define intimate violence in a form that could be used to establish national baseline rates. An interagency task force on child abuse and neglect is conducting a similar effort to define child maltreatment so that common data elements could be established in research studies in this field.

The consequences of victimisation are another variable that can generate vastly differing total costs. Cost estimates can include mental as well as physical health, long- as well as short-term treatment costs, family or social costs (such as lower productivity, absenteeism, high rates of turnover, and loss of earnings) as well as personal costs, indirect as well as direct costs, and costs of services for perpetrators as well as for victims. A model that includes emergency room costs only will generate a smaller total cost estimate than one that includes the cost of long-term mental health services to victims, which may not be accrued until months or years after an abusive incident.

Once it has been determined how many cases of family violence should be counted and what costs will be measured, the source of cost data can affect total cost estimates. Conservative estimates may rely on cost data that are relatively easy to obtain, such as the cost of medical treatment; such estimates may thus be limited to expenses directly associated with service fees. In contrast, comprehensive cost estimates may include indirect costs for which no reliable estimate is available, such as the cost of diminished productivity and the costs incurred by the need to provide volunteer advocacy services. Large differences between total cost figures associated with estimating the impact of the problem of family violence can result from the inclusion or elimination of such indirect costs.

The size of indirect cost measurements can be influenced by various estimating factors, such as the use of econometric forecasting techniques, including discount rates and future productivity costs. Applying annual productivity increase rates and discount rates will affect the total cost and result in a more sophisticated, and theoretically more accurate, estimate. The techniques used to estimate loss of productivity, usually human capital or willingness-to-pay approaches, also affect indirect cost measurements. The more comprehensive the model, the greater the cost estimate it yields.

One comprehensive model for estimating the annual cost of domestic violence includes direct costs, such as health care costs, social service costs, and criminal justice costs, as well as indirect costs, such as morbidity and mortality costs, which measure lost output when a victim is incapacitated or killed. Several assumptions are implicit in the model that direct cost components can be estimated with available data on charges and expenditures for goods and services; that a discount rate of 4 percent and an average annual increase in productivity of 1 percent are appropriate in generating future costs, and that certain other costs of health and social services, such as moral support and advocacy for victims, should be excluded. The costs of these may be significant, but no reliable data exist from which to estimate them.

A cost estimate for child maltreatment for the year 1983 was developed by calculating the number of child abuse reports received, what percentage were substantiated, and what percentage actually received various types of services, including foster care. It estimated that the immediate cost of hospitalizing abused and neglected children was $20 million annually, rehabilitation and special education cost $7 million annually, and foster care costs were $460 million annually.

Additional short-term costs include education, juvenile court and detention costs, $646 million for long-term foster care, and future lost earnings of abused and neglected children of between $658 and $1.3 billion. Extrapolating Daro's costs for 1994, Westman (1995) included estimates for hospitalization, rehabilitation and special education, foster care, social services case management, and court expenses. His cost estimate was between $8.4 and $32.3 billion each year, based on a range of $12,174 to $46,870 per maltreated child per year. Miller et al. (1994) estimate that personal crime costs Americans $105 billion each year. Including pain and suffering, the cost rises to $450 billion. Violent crime accounts for $426 billion of the total. The authors estimate that child abuse costs $67,000 per incident, sexual abuse $99,000, and emotional abuse $27,000 for an average of $60,000 per incident of child abuse.

The authors estimated that child neglect costs $9,700 per incident. Thus, the total cost of child abuse and neglect per year is estimated to be $56 billion. Miller et al. (1994) do not include in their estimate the cost for sibling violence, non criminal violence toward parents, or non criminal elder abuse. Thus, their cost estimate of $77 billion for child abuse and domestic violence still underestimates the total costs of family violence each year. What is also unknown in reviewing these cost estimates is the extent to which existing expenses associated with health, social services, and legal services could be reduced if effective preventive interventions were in place. Reducing the scope of family violence and mitigating its consequences would have some impact on existing service expenses, most of which are borne by individuals or public agencies, but the size of that impact remains uncertain.

5

The Lasting Effects of Domestic Violence on Women and Children

Warning: perils ahead. That's life: lightning strikes, fires, accidents and injuries, family crises, food poisoning and falls, cancer and heart attacks. Risk is inherent in life, and we learn to protect ourselves and control what we can. When tragedy strikes and we fall victim to forces outside of our control or from lifestyle choices, we can find comfort from the support of others. Social workers are specifically trained to help people regain their equilibrium following an illness, family challenges, and accidents. Keeping yourself and your family safe and healthy should be a high priority. And when disaster happens, seeking help just makes good sense.

Violence in the home touches the lives of people from all races, educational backgrounds, and socioeconomic groups, often causing devastating consequences for women, children, and families. Domestic violence, also known interpersonal partner violence or family violence, is the single largest cause of injury to women between the ages of 15 and 44, more than muggings, car accidents, and rapes combined. As many as 4 million women are abused and 2,000 die from their injuries every year, according to the American College of Emergency Physicians.

Studies have found that batterers are most commonly males who use violence to control a wife or girlfriend. They may use physical violence, such as punching, kicking, slapping, or strangulation, or sexual violence. Another form of abuse is psychological; the abuser may threaten to hurt other family members or pets, may use insults, criticism and name-calling, and intimidation. Domestic violence also includes abuse against older adults (elder abuse), and dating violence against teenagers.

The damaging effects of violence in the home can be far-reaching and long-term. Women with a history of domestic violence have higher rates of all health problems than other women, according to the Centers for Disease Control and Prevention (CDC). They also report long-lasting health conditions, such as chronic pain and gastrointestinal disorders. Abused women are often depressed and anxious. Growing up in a violent home can be traumatic for children, even if they are not the victims. Children who witness their parents' domestic violence are more likely than their peers to experience depression and anxiety, to abuse drugs and alcohol, run away from home, commit sexual assault crimes, and attempt suicide.

Children exposed to domestic violence are more likely to exhibit increased levels of aggression and anti-social behaviour, unhealthy peer relationships, and poor school performance. Victims of domestic abuse often fear their partner's retribution if they try to get help. Still, community services are available to protect women and children from abuse. Social workers can refer clients to residential shelters, support groups, assertiveness classes, and services that provide legal assistance. The National Domestic Violence Hotline (800-799-7233) provides crisis intervention and is available 24 hours a day.

CHILD ABUSE AND CHILD PROTECTIVE SERVICES

Like domestic abuse, child abuse can be a dangerous family secret that is underreported to authorities. In 2002, 906,000 U.S. children had been abused, according to child protective service agencies. Of these, 61 percent had been neglected, 19 percent were physically abused, 10 percent were sexually abused, and 5 percent were psychologically abused. An estimated 1,500 children died from abuse that year, according to CDC. The effects of child maltreatment can last a lifetime. The stress of chronic abuse in infancy or early childhood can slow or alter brain development, leading to sleep disturbances, panic disorder, attention-deficit disorder, and other problems later in life. Child abuse has also been linked to long-term health problems, such as heart disease, cancer, and lung and liver disease. Children who have been abused by a parent often do not form an emotional bond with them, which can later lead to difficulties in forming attachments with other adults and with peers. Abused teenagers have a higher risk of experiencing teen pregnancy, low academic achievement, and mental health problems.

Social workers play an active role in protecting children through the child welfare system and they are in a position to provide early intervention. The child welfare system is comprised of many community organisations that collaborate to promote child safety. These organisations include public agencies, such as departments of social services, and private child welfare agencies and organisations. They often collaborate with the schools, health and mental health agencies, and other community-based organisations to meet the needs of children and families.

This network investigates reports of possible child abuse, provides services to families to assist with protecting children, and arranges for foster care or permanent adoptive homes for children who are not safe at home. Child protective service workers follow up on child abuse reports if the report meets the state's legal definition of abuse or neglect. After talking with the parents, teachers, childcare providers, and others, child protective service workers may move a child who is believed to be in immediate danger to a shelter, foster care home, or to the home of a relative. In some states, when the risk to a child appears to be minimal, the child protective service worker may identify family problems and offer needed services. For example, he or she might counsel the family. The parents' attendance at a mental health or alcohol abuse treatment programme may be recommended. The child protective service worker can also make regular visits to the family where there is a risk of child abuse or neglect.

In abuse cases that meet the state's definition of child abuse or neglect, child protective service workers will offer voluntary, in-home services to help the family resolve the conflicts that led to the abuse. If services are refused, court intervention may be necessary.

The child welfare system provides an array of prevention and intervention services to children and families; particularly to children who have been or are at risk of abuse or neglect. This system's role is to promote the safety and well being of children. Part of this role is to teach adults parenting skills and offer services that will help to minimize future risk to children.

CAREGIVER ABUSE AND NEGLECT

Caring for another person is a rewarding and challenging job. Often caregivers take care of others while neglecting themselves. Stress can build leading to actions that would not normally occur. Abuse refers to any willful act or omission of a caregiver or any other person which results in physical injury, mental anguish, unreasonable confinement, sexual abuse or exploitation, or financial exploitation to or of a vulnerable adult.

Signs of Physical Abuse:

- Multiple bruising, not consistent with a fall
- Black eyes, slap marks, kick marks, grasp marks, finger tip bruising and other bruises
- Burns such as cigarette burns, dunking burns (hands/ feet being immersed in boiling hot water)
- Fractures not consistent with falls
- Stench of urine or feces
- Indications of malnutrition or over-feeding
- Administration of inappropriate drugs

Neglect is failure of a caregiver to provide essential services necessary to maintain the physical and/or mental health of a vulnerable adult.

Signs of Neglect:

- Lack of basic care
- Abandonment
- Not providing proper food or fluids
- Failure to provide proper health care
- Lack of personal care
- Not dressing someone (for example, from the waist down because the person is incontinent
- Not dressing someone appropriately (such as wearing thin clothes in the winter)
- Refusing to buy new clothes for someone who has gained or lost weight
- Being left to sit in urine/feces
- Absence of mobility aids so the person's movements are restricted
- Absence of necessary medication
- Improperly fitting or damaged dentures
- Nonfunctioning hearing aids, including lack of batteries
- Isolation (for example, the person may be locked in a room or confined space with only basic necessities)
- No social contact or stimulation

How to Get Help

Highly trained social workers are available to help you identify options to alleviate elder abuse. Social workers can identify state and local human service centers that offer mental health services. These services are often available on a sliding fee scale that is affordable to everyone. Also, social workers can refer you to crisis centers, private counselors, and others who can help.

Safe Home Environment

Home may be where the heart is, but there are also potential hazards that threaten the safety and welfare of children.

Unintentional injuries are the leading cause of death among children ages 14 and under in the United States. Each year, more than 4.5 million children are treated in hospital emergency centers for injuries incurred specifically in the home, according to the National Safe Kids Campaign. Children most at risk are those age 4 and under, males, minorities, and children living in poverty. Low-income families often must live in a hazardous environment where there is overcrowded housing, inadequate supervision, and a lack of safe play areas for children. Parents can't protect children from every hazard, but they can consider safety an important issue and take precautions. An estimated 90 percent of unintentional injuries can be prevented. Never leave your toddler unattended.

Preventing Drowning, Falls, and Lead Poisoning:

- Drowning is the leading cause of injury-related death among children ages 1 to 4. Prevention is a matter of carefully watching children while they are in the bathtub and around swimming pools and ponds. Flotation devices in swimming pools should not be a substitute for supervision. Empty large buckets when they are not in use. Also, learn child first aid and CPR. In many places, the local Red Cross will offer CPR training sessions.
- Falls can be prevented by keeping young children away from heights, such as high porches or balconies; strapping children into high chairs and strollers; securing rugs with double-sided tape or a rubber pad; using a rubber mat in the bathtub; and keeping windows closed and locked when children are around. Insect screens are not sturdy enough to protect children from falling out of windows.
- Lead poisoning can cause irreversible brain damage and may impair mental functioning. Infants and young children are especially vulnerable to the effects of lead. Homes built before 1960 may contain lead-based paint that can be either removed or covered. Take advantage of community lead screening programmes to have children tested for lead poisoning.

Additional Safety Precautions:

- Safety proofs your home.
- Store medicines and cleaning products on high shelves.
- Make sure toys are age appropriate to avoid choking.
- Make sure your child's car safety seat is age and weight appropriate.

For more safety information, contact local health agencies and social services organisations. Discuss health, safety, and family issues with helping professionals in your community.

PSYCHOSOCIAL CORRELATES OF DATING VIOLENCE VICTIMISATION

A growing literature attests to the fact that dating violence is an important public health problem. Risk Behaviour Survey of high school students indicate that approximately 10% had been hit, slapped or hurt on purpose by their boyfriend or girlfriend over the previous year. Available national data also suggest a clustering of problem behaviours and other risk indicators among adolescents who experience dating violence; that is, adolescents who report sad/hopeless or depressed feelings, poorer self-esteem, substance use, multiple sex partners, and unprotected sex are more likely to report being a victim of dating violence. Elsewhere, among largely urban minority youth, Howard et al. found religious service attendance and perceptions of high parental monitoring to be associated with fewer reports of dating violence.

When national data are examined by ethnicity, Hispanic girls appear more likely to report dating violence victimisation than their peers. Despite this, there is little information on the experience of dating violence victimisation among Latino youth. Clearly, more needs to be learned about the correlates of dating violence among various ethnic groups in order to support the development of culturally sensitive prevention and intervention efforts. There is also a great deal to learn about the correlates of dating violence among male and female Latino youth. In addition to the correlates they share in common, there may be important gender differences in the risk profiles associated with dating violence. Among U.S. girls, dating violence has been associated with binge drinking and cocaine or inhalant use, whereas among boys, attempted suicide and fighting is linked to dating violence.

There were several primary aims of the present study. First, we examined whether there was a clustering of problem behaviours among Latino youth who reported dating violence. It was hypothesized that Latino youth who reported engagement in a host of risk behaviours would be more likely to report being a victim of physical dating violence. Second, the study assessed whether certain personal and familial factors were associated with decreased likelihood of dating violence. It was hypothesized that youth who had a good sense of self, were engaged in religious or community activities, and perceived strong parental monitoring or family connectedness would be less likely to report dating violence.

Finally, the study examined whether there were gender differences in the risk profiles of Latino youth who reported dating violence. While most research and intervention efforts to date have focused on girls as victims, the experience of physical dating violence among boys may be a more serious problem than has previously been recognized. If indeed, dating during adolescence is preparation for adult relationships and the patterns learned early become habituated, then such investigations must begin now. Further, as argued by Foshee (1996), the traditional approach to dating violence prevention, which focuses on males as perpetrators and females as victims may be not only inappropriate but also lacking in conceptual clarity. Thus, the stratified analyses were expected to provide useful information for tailoring preventive interventions.

Study Design and Sample Selection

The study was a cross-sectional, anonymous, self-administered survey of Latino adolescents (n = 446) residing in a suburban area outside of Washington, DC. After receiving IRB approval from the University of Maryland, trained Latino interviewers' recruited Latino youth through direct invitation using a central location intercept strategy. There were no restrictions on eligibility based on gender, sexual orientation, socioeconomic status, school enrollment status, or English speaking and reading proficiency.

Recruitment sites included school areas (off school property), athletic and social events, and malls. Respondents were reimbursed for their time with a movie ticket or a gift certificate to McDonald's. In addition, youth were provided with resources about Identity, Inc, a Latino youth-serving community-based organisation, local health service agencies, and relevant hotlines. The survey was administered in either Spanish or English depending on the preference of the respondent. Adolescent informed consent was utilized. Given the nature of the recruitment methodology, the difficulty in contacting parents, and the anonymity of this survey, parental consent was not required. There were no privacy concerns reported by respondents in the obtained sample. Further details on recruitment and sampling methods can be found elsewhere.

A total of 476 surveys were collected; however, only 446 were usable due to missing data and other inaccuracies that rendered them invalid. While it was not possible to precisely determine the refusal rate, estimates across interviewers ranged from as low as 5% to as high as 25%.

SURVEY AND MEASURES

The survey used in this study was the Identity Positive Youth Development Survey for Latino Youth. It is a comprehensive, 2-part, 10-page questionnaire that takes approximately 30 minutes to complete. The survey was constructed after a rigorous development process that included an extensive literature review, feedback by a team of experts, cognitive testing (a formal process of review and feedback by members of the target population), and pilot testing with 110 male and female Latino adolescents. Part I of the survey included questions regarding a variety of social indicators of youth well-being, such as prosocial behaviour, family connectedness, and academic support and encouragement. Part II of the survey concentrated on a developmentally appropriate risk assessment, including use of a variety of licit and illicit substances, violence-related behaviours, sexual practices, and emotional states such as depression and suicide ideation. The survey also included questions pertaining to the socio-demographic characteristics of respondents and their parents/guardians, such as age, gender, country of origin, length of U.S. residence, and parent/guardian education level.

The dependent variable was physical dating violence. Five sub-domains of psychosocial factors were examined in relation to dating violence: other violence engagement, substance use, emotional well-being, prosocial behaviours, and parent and other family factors. In addition, demographic variables (grade and gender) were included.

DATA ANALYSIS

All statistical analyses were performed using the statistical software SPSS 11.5 for Windows. Initially, frequency distributions were examined for each item to determine coding of variables. Due to the small number of victims (n = 39), dating violence was collapsed to an "ever" versus "never" binary variable. Based on the frequencies in response categories and the appropriateness for statistical analysis, most independent variables were also recoded as dichotomous variables. In such cases, a coding of "1" indicated "ever" use while "0" indicated "never" use. A previously developed algorithm was utilized to distinguish the most frequently monitored adolescents from those less frequently monitored. Adolescents who reported that their parent/guardian engaged in each of the six monitoring behaviours "most" or "all of the time" were considered the frequently monitored group (n = 91, 20.5%), while youth who reported more infrequent monitoring were considered the less frequently monitored group.

The data were first analyzed using univariate logistic models between the dependent variable (physical dating violence) and each domain of the independent variable (violence, substance use, emotional state, protective behaviours, parental/familial factors and demographics) to examine their relationship. Analyses were performed on the entire sample and separately by gender. The unadjusted odds ratios (OR) and 95% confidence intervals (CI) as well as [chi square] tests were examined. To identify the most significant variables in relation to physical dating violence, multivariate logistic regression was used to include all significant independent variables from the univariate analyses in the models. Adjusted OR and 95% CI were examined to assess the significance of the relationships.

SAMPLE CHARACTERISTICS

The age range of respondents was 14-19 years, with a mean age of 16.1 years. The sample was comprised of slightly more males (51.6%) than females (48.2%). The majority of youth reported living in a two-parent household (60.3%). More than half the sample was born outside the U.S. (56.3%); the majority were from El Salvador (19.1%), Mexico (7.8%), and other Central American countries (11.7%).

PREVALENCE OF DATING VIOLENCE VICTIMISATION

Approximately 9% of Latino adolescents reported experiencing physical dating violence in the previous year. There were non significant differences in dating violence by gender; that is, roughly 8.9% of the girls and 8.8% of the boys reported being a victim of dating violence.

For the overall sample, dating violence victimisation was positively associated with engagement in a host of risk behaviours and inversely related to sense of self and family connectedness; that is, adolescents who were engaged in violence-related behaviours, such as weapon carrying, fighting, or gang involvement, or used substances (binge drinking or cocaine use) were more likely to report dating violence victimisation. Depression and suicidal ideation were also positively associated with dating violence. Neither parental monitoring nor religious involvement, two factors often seen to be protective against adolescent risk behaviour, were significantly related to victimisation. Similarly, volunteerism and grade in school were non significant. With respect to monitoring, the odds ratio was, however, in the expected direction. Furthermore, being at a party without parental supervision was significantly related to dating violence victimisation.

A similar pattern was exhibited for both adolescent females and males with several noteworthy exceptions. Girls who reported a stronger sense of self and higher family connectedness were less likely to report dating violence. This relationship was not evident for the males. Rather, boys who reported spending at least one hour each week with a mentor or caring adult other than a family member were more likely to report dating violence. For females, engagement in gang-related activities, but not gang membership, was significantly related to victimisation, whereas both were highly significant for males. Among males, the odds of dating violence were lower if they were actual members of a gang rather than simply being involved in gang-related activities.

In most instances, the magnitude of the association between risk behaviour and dating violence victimisation was much greater for males than females. The most dramatic gender differences were seen for "being at an unsupervised party over the weekend." Compared to girls who never went to weekend unsupervised parties, those who did were almost twice as likely to have experienced victimisation. Among boys, this behaviour was associated with a ten-fold increase in victimisation.

In order to detect risk factors that were uniquely associated with physical dating violence victimisation, multivariate logistic regression analyses, including all significant variables from the univariate models, were performed. Overall, youth who reported carrying a gun, involvement in physical fights, and who had considered suicide were at greater odds of also reporting being slapped or physically hit on purpose by a boyfriend or girlfriend. Important differences emerged when analyses were stratified by gender.

Among females, fighting was the sole risk behaviour associated with the dating of violence victimisation. At the same time, girls who reported a stronger sense of self were less likely to report dating violence. Among the males, gun carrying, but not physical fighting, and having considered suicide were uniquely associated with dating violence. Furthermore, spending time each week with a mentor was also significantly associated with dating violence.

Findings from this study substantiate what has been documented elsewhere regarding the reach of dating violence into the world of adolescents and are in accord with estimates of its prevalence.

Almost one in ten Latino youth reported physical dating violence experiences during the past year. While no systematic pattern emerged by grade, prevalence data clearly suggest that attention needs to be focused on psychosocial dynamics in dating relationships among mid-adolescents. The risk profile of adolescents who were victims of dating violence adds further evidence that such victimisation may fit the framework of Problem Behaviour Theory.

That is, there appears to be a subset of vulnerable Latino adolescents who are prone to multiple problem behaviours in tandem, and this syndrome may derive from personal and socio-environmental antecedent factors. In this sample, dating violence clustered with other violence-related behaviour. Regardless of the motive for carrying a weapon, youth who possessed a gun were seven times as likely to have also been a victim of dating violence. The odds that physical fighting would correlate with physical dating violence was of a similar magnitude. Youth who had considered suicide were also more likely to report dating violence, though the strength of this relationship was less than that for overt, actual acts of violence. Arguably, suicide can be seen as an act of violence directed inward, rather than externalized.

The relationship between suicidal thoughts and dating violence was essentially a dynamic among the males. Indeed, boys who reported having thoughts about suicide were almost six times as likely to report dating violence during the past year than did those without such thoughts. The despair these boys report experiencing appears to be linked to their dating violence experience. It is unclear, however, whether these feelings lead to increased vulnerability to being physically mistreated, or whether having experienced physicality in a dating relationship may lead to extreme psychological distress. In addition, some third unidentified factor may actually explain both of these observed relationships. Substance use behaviour did not remain significant once the relationship of all risk factors were jointly accounted for. Considered individually, such behaviour may represent important risk factors; however, its relationship to dating violence victimisation may have been eclipsed by the violence-related behaviours.

We did not find evidence that familial factors were associated with a decreased likelihood of dating violence. Parent monitoring and religious involvement were not found to be significantly associated with physical dating violence victimisation among these youth. This runs counter to the work of Howard et al. among a population of predominantly African American youth.

Measurement differences cannot explain these differences since both studies used the same parental monitoring scale, operationalised in a similar way. Since the process by which parental monitoring exerts its effect on youth behaviour is not fully clear, it is possible that other aspects of this dynamic may be more pivotal for Latino youth. Perhaps it is not the youths' perception that their parents know where they are, who they are with, and what they are doing after school hours, but that factors such as honest disclosure and communication translate into protection from harm or reduced exposure to risk. Also, power insufficiency may have made this relationship difficult to detect.

While the prevalence of dating violence was similar for females and males, important gender differences were found among correlates. For girls, a strong sense of self seemed to decrease the odds of being physically abused in a dating relationship.

Again, due to the cross-sectional nature of the data, it is not possible to determine the direction of effects. It could be argued that a strong sense of self makes it less likely that a girl would find herself in or tolerate a physical dating violence situation. It is also plausible that if a girl has been abused, her sense of self would be diminished.

An unexpected finding was that boys who spent more than one hour each week with a mentor (i.e., a caring adult outside one's family) were approximately ten times as likely as those without such contact to report physical dating violence. One would want to know whether boys who are victims of dating violence more actively seek time with a mentor for comfort and coping or whether it is some dynamic of these relationships that actually poses physical harm to the boys. The study also did not afford an opportunity to examine the extent to which boys' reports of physical dating violence reflect behaviour within heterosexual or same-sex relationships. Such information would be critically important in directing intervention efforts.

Limitations

Clearly, cross-sectional studies, while allowing for determination of the prevalence of health behaviours and conditions, limit the investigator's ability to clarify temporal relationships. Nor was the sample size sufficient to allow examination of correlates of dating violence by age. Measurement of physical dating violence by a single-item, self-report question is subject to bias, and self reports of dating experiences (as constituting intent of harm or purposeful force) are highly subjective.

Indeed, the context of dating violence victimisation may differ for males and females; that is, it is not clear whether male victimisation occurs at the hands of females who are acting in self defense. Important background information regarding the dynamics that preceded the violence, including who initiated use of force, was lacking. Without such information we cannot disentangle perpetration from victimisation. While the potential for physical harm is greater for females who are victims of dating violence, the psychological effects of dating violence on both males and females may affect their subsequent relationships in very consequential ways.

These findings, while addressing some dimensions of the familial and parenting dynamics, do not shed light on other aspects of the home, family, and school setting that might provide important insight into the factors associated with dating violence.

Finally, the data did not afford the opportunity to examine the profile of perpetrators of dating violence, an area that warrants further attention with regard to dating violence prevention and intervention efforts. Physical dating violence appears to affect a small but significant number of Latino youth. The correlates of dating violence provide further evidence of a clustering of problem behaviours among certain vulnerable adolescents. Both the antecedents and consequences of dating violence victimisation deserve further study.

6

Reintegration in an Environment of Disintegration

The psychological and social, or psychosocial consequences of war on the lives of adolescents last long beyond its end, and as long as war persists they involve an ongoing and simultaneous process of disintegration and reintegration. As young people bear and cope with physical and emotional upheaval, they are continually coping in an ongoing process of recovery.

As the principal targets of war in northern Uganda, adolescents are under constant attack; their spirits depleted and their healthy development short-circuited by violence and insecurity. Surviving adolescents face drastically altered social relationships that often include physical and emotional abuse from families and communities. Violence has spread from warring parties to families and neighbors, where domestic violence and sexual abuse are on the rise. Adolescents named child abuse as one of their top five concerns.

Feeling hopeless and alone, young people are desperate for support and protection. They also protect themselves against their own vulnerability with defensive, aggressive or detached, often anti-social behaviours. Yet they are proactively surviving and continually strive to improve their lives in many creative and constructive ways. Young people are both hindered and helped along their path to recovery by a community that views them with alternating and simultaneous suspicion and sympathy. The conflict has altered young people's lives and their roles in the community at an accelerated rate. They are seen increasingly as "immoral" and disrespectful, and their role as perpetrators as well as victims in the conflict has invoked confusion and fear in the hearts and minds of their families and communities.

A huge gulf is emerging between the generations as local traditions and war-related stresses discourage young people from open discussions with adults, including public officials and teachers, about their situation and changing roles. Some adults and several local organisations are, however, working to support the needs and strengths of adolescents, although most of them address the urgent and immediate needs of those returning from captivity. Support for the countless other adolescents living in dire circumstances is also urgent, but less forthcoming. Psychosocial and reintegration interventions should maximize young people's direct involvement in decision-making and implementation, and there should be continuous follow-up on their circumstances and progress.

RETURNING HOME WITH MYRIAD PSYCHOSOCIAL BURDENS

Former abductees carry to freedom the memories and emotions of agonizing experiences, symbolic reminders of the heavy burdens they were forced to carry during captivity. Many remain haunted by the acts of violence they have suffered and have been forced to commit. Some experience nightmares, emotional disconnections, acting out, even violence and other symptoms of what in Western medicine is called Post Traumatic Stress Disorder (PTSD). Too many young people, these dreams and experiences reflect spiritual distress, where they are troubled by the spirits of those they have harmed, and they feel wracked with guilt. Formerly abducted young people also know that they are among the most vulnerable to LRA attack. If re-abducted and recognized, they are likely to be killed immediately.

Many escapees have been pursued by rebels and killed.

Relatives and friends of those who escape may also pay a similar price. Many formerly abducted young people stated that they are so afraid of re-abduction by the LRA, that each night they sleep in the bush instead of in their huts, believing they are less likely to be found there should the LRA attack their homes and villages. Like dozens of others, one former abductees from Omiya Anyima told the Women's Commission: "We don't sleep at home. We are very vulnerable to re-abduction, and our huts are dangerous to stay in at night."

Formerly abducted young people are haunted by many other worries: that they will not find or then be accepted by their families and peers; that they will be stigmatized as killers and thieves, or in the case of sexually abused girls, especially those with children, tainted and shamed; that they are infected with HIV/AIDS and will not live long. Will they be able to catch up or even return to school? Will they find employment? In addition to these weighty emotional burdens, formerly abducted young people have lost much trust in a world that has failed to protect them, and even betrayed them. Adolescents said that these fears and anxieties are further reinforced by LRA indoctrination. The rebels warn them repeatedly that despite promises of amnesty, the UPDF will punish torture and kill them rather than allow them to return home.

The rape and sexual enslavement of girls, many of whom have borne children, has been used as a deliberate attempt to tarnish their virtue in the eyes of their community and make it more difficult for them to return. This in turn can undermine the value of formerly abducted girls to society and make them the potential objects of ridicule, humiliation or further sexual violence. Sexual violence also serves to stigmatize girls returning to their communities as potentially diseased, including with HIV/AIDS. Such mistrust and rejection can turn into self-fulfilling prophecies, where young people become more rebellious, violent, uncaring or anti-social, pushing away the adults whose support and love they most need but which they are not getting. At the same time, the majority of adolescents are constructively coping with their circumstances.

YOUTH AND VIOLENCE

Little data exists on increased violence committed by returned and other youth within their communities, but it is much discussed. Many adolescents stated that desperate poverty is driving orphans and other young people to steal and that some former abductees are turning to crime out of difficulty in readjusting to civilian life and finding jobs. Others blame the pervasive culture of violence within the LRA from which it is hard to break free. Unconfirmed reports from juvenile justice experts in recent months have included reports of violent acts of banditry committed by bands of youth, sometimes pretending to be LRA or UPDF soldiers. In IDP camp settings and in the Achol Pii refugee settlement adolescent boys are raping adolescent girls, as discussed earlier in this report.

While anecdotal evidence indicates an increase in such adolescent crimes, there is no supporting information or statistics. In fact, reports from people working to help reintegrate formally abducted children and young adults observe the opposite - that few to no formerly abducted young people commit crimes after their return home. A telling and complex twist on youth violence has been reported by the Kitgum Concerned Women's Association (KICWA), a center for returning abductees in Kitgum District. KICWA reports that it has received cases of adolescent boys who claim to be formerly abducted and who have committed crimes. They are then turned over to the center for rehabilitation. KICWA finds out eventually, however, that these youths are adolescents from the community pretending to be escapees out of desperation for help. Additional research is needed on the extent to which young people are turning to violence and crime, and the social, economic, political, psychological and cultural factors that surround these activities.

CHALLENGES TO OVERCOME

Young people who manage to escape the LRA return to communities that are in turmoil and which bear the weight of insecurity, displacement and poverty. The LRA are well aware that the atrocities to which they have subjected adolescents are likely to demonize them in the eyes of their communities. Creating an image of youth as irrevocably corrupted has further blurred the lines for their communities in distinguishing them as perpetrators or victims, or both. Often preoccupied with their own concerns and unsupported themselves, families and communities have limited energy or patience to give to the returning adolescents. Young people reported that many adults face the return of young abductees with confusion and ambivalence that range from anger to compassion, fear to protection.

Moreover, families and communities often expect the returning adolescents to behave like adults while still having the authority to treat them like children. Despite the numerous obstacles in the way of healing and reintegration, communities have worked hard to welcome and accept the young people. They struggle to face many difficult conflicts. For example, parents of abducted girls wonder what they might do if their daughters return home pregnant or with a child. While they would rejoice in seeing their daughter, they question how they would feel about a child whose father is a rebel and how that child would be treated by the community. In general, communities are also willing to offer forgiveness and support amnesty for the LRA. Adults said that they try to remember that the young people abducted by the LRA were not there by choice, but under the threat of death.

Community groups also recognize that reintegration is about far more than curing medical ills. They understand that healing is a long process for young people and their families, which requires determined and ongoing follow-up, even in the face of frustration, discouragement and other setbacks. Communities also understand that education and livelihood activities are particularly important to young people, giving them some hope for the future and helping to provide for the whole family. They know that the authority and responsibility their children may have had while in the LRA is hard to let go once they are back to civilian life, especially if there is nothing else to occupy or make them feel good about themselves. They believe that if young people know they can begin to lead productive lives post-abduction, they will be less likely to return to the LRA should they be overwhelmed or disappointed by life outside captivity.

COMMUNITY GROUPS AID REINTEGRATION

A number of community groups have formed to help these young people and their families. Most notable is the CPA, which supports families of abducted children, helps to reintegrate the former abductees and prepares them and the wider community for their return home.

CPA helps parents and other community members confront fears about their children's transformation and develop the support they need to give to the young people upon their return. Programmes by KICWA, GUSCO and the World Vision Children of War Center in Gulu help adolescents find their families and reintegrate into their communities. They believe that music, drawing and other creative and sports activities have a powerful healing impact. Young people in all the centers are engaged in chores that serve the whole group, such as helping to prepare meals or cleaning up.

These organisations also work with the young people afterwards to follow up on their integration, and provide skills training and other educational opportunities that the former abductees overwhelmingly want and need. They also work to minimize the time young people spend in the custody of the UPDF following their escape and ensure that while in custody they are treated with full care and protection. Each center also does its best to create a safe and secure environment for the young people, and to this end, each center is placed in the relatively safe town centers of Gulu and Kitgum.

DEBATE OVER APPROACHES TO REINTEGRATION

There is debate among organisations over the best approach

to reintegration. Some argue that the process should avoid institutionalization, which is believed to contribute to the further stigmatization of young people. They also believe that young people should return home as swiftly as possible, where the most critical part of the healing and recovery process takes place. These organisations provide shelter in traditional structures known as "ot lums," or grass houses, which are familiar to the former abductees and to which they will be returning. They build the capacity and skills of local community members, including parents, to work with the returnees, rather than leaving the challenge of reintegration to outsiders or those with formal education. A different approach assumes that successful transition to community life requires more extended rehabilitation time in a center, including longer periods of exposure to Western-oriented individual counselling.

This approach also involves a more dormitory-like atmosphere for the young people. Despite these differences, the majority of former abductees interviewed reported having had good, helpful experiences under each set of circumstances. However, none of the rehabilitation programmes make sufficient use of the capabilities of young people who have already been successfully reintegrated, who should be made an integral part of helping new arrivals. With further training and by involving them in decision-making, these young people could work with and inspire confidence in the new arrivals and would likely create ways to further improve the process of return and reintegration. It would also offer all formerly abducted young people opportunities to continue to build networks of solidarity and support and expand the reach of the organisations to conduct follow-up.

RELIGION AND RITUAL

Many young people find solace in traditional rituals and by attending the Christian churches that flourish in the north. Churches provide spaces for prayer and an offer of forgiveness from God and the community. Many young people rely on churches and their belief in God for strength and to create a bridge to full community acceptance. In the case of KICWA, support is also provided to families who choose to perform traditional Acholi rituals to cleanse and renew the young person who has returned.

Often until such a ritual is performed, neither the community nor the young person will be at rest. In such a poor region, however, the necessary materials to perform these rituals are often out of reach without assistance. In most cases, such activities provide enormous relief to all involved and help the healing and community acceptance process of the young person.

Coordination has improved in recent months between local and international reintegration organisations and the UPDF's Fourth Division, responsible for the war-affected region and often the first to come in contact with escapees. Together, NGOs and the UPDF have decreased the amount of time former abductees spend in UPDF custody. Improved communication and cooperation have increased the speed at which young people can return to their communities. Save the Children Denmark has assisted the UPDF in this process with children's rights training for soldiers in the Fourth Division's Child Protection Unit. These improvements help to strengthen the climate for peace-building and bolster work being done by community-based organisations to prepare families and communities to welcome the returnees.

IOM, UNICEF and the governments of Sudan and Uganda have also increased cooperation to secure the safe repatriation of former abductees who managed to escape the LRA within Sudan and wished to return home to Uganda. In September 2000, a Joint Communiqué on Immediate Action on Abducted Children was signed by the governments of Uganda and Sudan. The Sudanese government in Khartoum subsequently established a center in Juba, in Southern Sudan to receive and process young people who have escaped the LRA inside Sudan. These young people had been abducted by the LRA in northern Uganda between 1990 and 1999. While the three reintegration centers in Gulu and Kitgum are poised and eager to assist all new returnees, should the number of returns accelerate rapidly, they will require immediate increased resources to be sure to adequately assist each person. Cooperation among internat-ional organisations and community groups in northern Uganda could be further improved in order to minimize unnecessary problems for the young people and their families. For example, the Women's Commission encountered former abductees who had been transferred from one site to another without warning and without notifying their families. Better communication and coordination between agencies is needed, as is consistent vigilance in each case in order to avoid stressful delays.

RECOGNISING THE COUNTLESS OTHER ADOLESCENTS

Several thousand formerly abducted adolescents in northern Uganda are coping with enormous assaults on their psychosocial well-being; they are also the recipients of most of the support for adolescents in the region. But they are still a small percentage of the countless tens of thousands, who have not been abducted but are living with the same insecurity and deprivation. All adolescents are suffering from hunger and poverty, fear of abduction and the destruction of traditional values that used to protect children.

They are also victimized by an increase in domestic violence and child abuse, as the adult community fails to cope well with the effects of the conflict. Thousands are orphaned heads of household or refugees who are unaccompanied or separated from their families and who are fending for themselves. All of these young people are actively coping with their situation in ways that require increased support from within and outside their communities.

Some of the adolescents hardest hit by the conflict are the many thousands who have lost one or both parents due to war, HIV/AIDS and other diseases, including Ebola, and those who are refugees, separated and unaccompanied minors. Left to fend for themselves, they are especially vulnerable to all of the violations of protection previously described. At the same time, forced to take on enormous responsibilities, they are among the most resourceful young people.

ORPHANS

Estimates place the number of orphaned children in Uganda at up to 1.8 million. One NGO report has estimated that nearly one in six children in northern Uganda has been orphaned by HIV/AIDS and another government report asserts that 16 percent of children up to the age of 17 are orphans in Acholiland. Once orphaned, adolescents are left without parental guidance and are vulnerable to extreme poverty. There are increased numbers of child- and adolescent-headed households, most of which lack access to education, livelihood sources, healthcare services, psychosocial support and protection. The growing number of orphans and lack of services that respond to their needs are also viewed as among the primary reasons behind a rising number of street children and the purported increase in adolescent crime.

Focus groups conducted at an orphanage with adolescent girls revealed their primary concerns to be psychological and physical abuse of the girls by teaching and supervisory staff. "We don't have any sanitary napkins," said some, while others were very concerned that if they don't do well enough in school to go on to secondary school, they will not be allowed to stay in the orphanage. When asked where they would go, many started crying, as they had nowhere to go.

Most adolescents expressed special empathy for AIDS and war orphans, and recommended that the Ugandan government provide free schooling for orphans. Others suggested that the Ugandan government, NGOs, religious groups and international donors provide educational sponsorships to orphans, help pay for their school fees and construct more schools. Furthermore, adolescents suggested that these same groups ensure a stable place for orphans to live with adult supervision, and that they provide food, clothing and other basic necessities to enhance their living conditions.

REFUGEE UNACCOMPANIED MINORS AND SEPARATED ADOLESCENTS

In the Achol Pii refugee settlement, as of March 2001, some 197 unaccompanied minors and 251 separated children were registered. Many of them live in Block 14, which is located in a section of the settlement that is relatively far from UPDF installations, schools and the market center. These young people stated that they are faced with the constant fear of attack. Their section of the settlement had been the site of a particularly gruesome, lethal attack by the LRA and continues to be used sporadically as a transit point for LRA groups. Although not sinister, the atmosphere in Block 14 is reminiscent of that in the book Lord of the Flies, where young people are left mostly to their own devices and have established their own system of group protection. Some of these young people have relocated to other, more central sections of the settlement, but many remain situated there.

With limited adult support, they must take full responsibility for all aspects of their lives, including collecting; preparing and rationing out their monthly food supply, pumping water from bore holes and getting themselves to school and to medical facilities as needed. With extremely limited possibilities for cultivation and frequently late food distributions, these young people complained of severe hunger. Even when the food supplies are not late and food is available, rationing is very difficult and young people said they find it hard to save the food for a later date. The issue of non-food items was also of great concern to the young people. All refugees, including unaccompanied minors and separated children, are given a supply of household materials, such as a pot for cooking, soap and a blanket.

If they are lost, stolen or destroyed in the harsh conditions of the camp, the only way to get more is to purchase them from local shops in the settlement, which few refugees can afford. One 11-year-old unaccompanied minor told the Women's Commission that even if he had food he would not be able to prepare or cook it because he had no pot and would have trouble making the fire with limited fuel. He said, "I sold my pot to an adult. He told me it was a good idea to sell it so I could buy food. I was very hungry." The young people deal with many of these problems by helping each other in small groups. They guard each other's belongings, take turns preparing food and share the remaining non-food items.

At times they feel very alone, and some told the Women's Commission that they miss their families and struggle over decisions about whether or not they should try to go back to Sudan and find family members. Many stay because they feel there are more educational opportunities in the settlement and they would like to finish their schooling. At the same time, adolescents said few make it to school regularly and those that do find it hard to concentrate because of their persistent hunger. While community services staff and volunteers work closely with the unaccompanied minors and separated children in the settlement, limited resources prohibit comprehensive assistance for their needs. Their protection must be monitored, to prevent forced recruitment into the SPLA, sexual violence against girls and other abuse.

DOMESTIC VIOLENCE AND CHILD ABUSE

Young people named "child abuse" their number five concern overall in the survey. According to the focus group discussions and case study interviews, this category appears to be a "catch-all" phrase for a number of abuses they suffer. It includes physical abuse in school and in domestic settings. It also includes psychological abuse, where young people feel they are demeaned and demoralized, devalued and ignored. No full statistics are available on the nature and prevalence of domestic violence, including sexual violence. However, testimonies from young people and health professionals depict it as very widespread and perpetrated mainly by adult males against women, children and adolescents. On one occasion when the Women's Commission was conducting interviews in the Achol Pii refugee settlement, a woman who had been beaten by her husband was carried to the medical dispensary.

Medical and other staff said such cases are common.

Young people reported widespread alcoholism among adults and smaller numbers of adolescents, particularly boys. They said that mostly women and girls make the "local brew," which is alcohol distilled from local plants and vegetables. The men, whose traditional roles as farmers and providers have been undermined and who feel they have little else to do, sit together in small communal drinking areas and get drunk regularly. Young people said that when men get drunk, they often return home and become violent against women, girls and boys, beating them, threatening them and at times raping the women and girls. IDP and refugee adolescents also said that violence in their homes and among community residents are on the rise because of the restricted living quarters in the camps, which have increased tension.

Sexual violence has resulted in an increase in unwanted pregnancies and the loss of education for girls, who are then forced to drop out of school. Fights are not uncommon among adult and adolescent males, and some boys described conflict with their fathers, who were being abusive, dictatorial and unsupportive, mostly due to alcoholism. Adolescents also reported the use of corporal punishment in schools and orphanages. They said that it was extremely painful to be hit with sticks, for example, as a punishment for not following the rules or getting answers incorrect in school. Apart from stating that drinking alcohol should be discouraged, the young people were not fully sure how domestic violence and child abuse should be stopped. The authority of adult males is highly traditional in the culture, as is the permission for these males to abuse their wives and children. The concept of rape within marriage is discussed little and given little credence. Nevertheless, young people's ability to name the symptoms of and discuss the issues of domestic violence, not knowing the terms themselves, was impressive.

TRADITIONAL PROTECTIONS FOR CHILDREN AND ADOLESCENTS

According to many adults interviewed, the decimation of Acholi culture has resulted in the loss of traditional practices and beliefs that served to protect children, adolescents and other people considered vulnerable within the society. Under the code of beliefs known as "Lapir," for example, clan elders must carefully consider the reasons for going to war with another clan and must be satisfied that there is a just cause for such a conflict. To go to war without such a just cause would be to call evil upon the community. In this setting, children and women were exempted as targets of war, which was conducted entirely by males. Today, this traditional practice has been turned on its head as the LRA wages war on the Acholi people with children as direct targets. In a culture where compensation and guilt are borne by the whole community, the compounding evil accrued by the misdoings of those fighting in this war affects everyone.

Other traditional practices, such as parents providing their children a piece of land to farm themselves, have been so undermined that young people have lost a level of financial independence and an opportunity for learning and achievement. Adolescents and adults say that the disappearance of parental mentoring and guidance has led some to turn to violence or prostitution because they cannot fend for, or support them. Despite this, the Acholi tradition of storytelling has survived through organized drama and music groups, and some sing about the troubles facing their communities. Women's Commission staff watched performances by young people for their community in Padibe IDP camp. Through song, dance and theater, the performers dramatized the war between the LRA and the Ugandan government and enacted the government's lack of attention to the problems of the Acholi people.

Often with humor, they described family problems such as drunkenness, abuse and neglect. Some stories told of the spiritual causes behind tribal conflicts that they believe have led to the war. These traditional processes should be used as a resource by the local, national and international community and should be incorporated into peace-building activities. In addition, the Acholi people must continue to create spaces for community discussion about the destruction of values that protect children and adolescents with an eye to considering courses of action for constructive change.

Unlike the situation for formerly abducted adolescents, there are few NGOs or community groups focused on addressing the wide range of problems facing young people and their communities in northern Uganda. The international NGO AVSI, with support from UNICEF and in collaboration with the Kitgum District Community Development Office, has taken action to fill this gap through psychosocial programmes in the Kitgum District. Their efforts have aimed to address the many social stresses that are tearing families and communities apart, including excessive drinking, family violence, and sexual abuse and increasing school drop-outs.

AVSI's approach has involved recruiting and training a corps of 300 Community Volunteer Counselors (CVCs), who, based on their own understanding and experience, came together around their own trauma and coping to reach out to others in their community. CVCs facilitate and support communities in a variety of ways, from helping people to identify small loans, to identifying disabled children and adolescents among the population and assisting them with access to services. The District also helps to support and coordinate their work, which includes awareness-raising in schools with students, teachers and parents about welcoming formerly abducted young people back to their communities. While their efforts have not wholly focused on adolescents and youth alone, their issues have been incorporated into their work and provide a basis for further community organizing around youth concerns. A strong model moving forward involves training equivalent adolescent and youth CVCs, who can help to reach out to their peers and find constructive solutions to their concerns.

ADOLESCENT COPING AND RESILIENCE

Adolescents in northern Uganda and southern Sudan have shown enormous strength in coping with situations of crisis. Some of the skills they have developed have helped them survive armed combat, extreme poverty and deprivation.

They are incredibly resilient and have attempted to weather each new crisis as it has arisen. Some of the coping mechanisms they employ are highly constructive, while others are more destructive. Each, however, serves a purpose in getting them through a process of recovery. Adolescents are called to continually adjust and recreate their coping skills, but despite all they have done to keep their lives together, most adolescents hardly even recognize that they have strengths and capacities, and their abilities go largely unsupported.

Adolescents must recognize the skills they have developed in the process of surviving the conflict as extremely impressive and valuable. In so doing, they need international and local support during the long process of changing their knowledge and their attitudes about themselves, so that they can identify and gain confidence in their abilities. At the same time, they must also find ways to transform destructive coping strategies into more constructive outlets for promoting their ongoing recovery. Young people can and should begin to pool their resources and talents to improve their lives and their communities as leaders, not just survivors. Given the magnitude of what they are up against, however, they can only be fully successful if they are involved in serious, collaborative efforts by government and other community members to end insecurity and reduce poverty and the spread of disease.

DESTRUCTIVE COPING SKILLS PURPOSE

Surviving adolescence is difficult in the best of times, let alone during the assaults of armed conflict, when adolescents are the deliberate targets of war. Research participants identified concerns about what they believed an increase in bad behaviour among adolescents, calling some of their activities "immoral" or unhealthy. What community members are not necessarily seeing, however, is that these behaviours are really about young people's process of surviving the conflict. By their own acknowledgement, young people have stated that they often "act out," as known in Western terms. They are at times rebellious, refusing to follow the instructions of authority figures. Some go to traditional dances or discos against the will of their parents. Some engage in casual sex, which is frowned upon by society and which may expose them to STIs, including HIV/AIDS, or lead to pregnancy.

Many are considered to be disrespectful and stubborn. Some steal in order to get money for drink, food or other reasons. Others have been drawn into prostitution, as a means of survival. Some have learned to be manipulative and to lie in order to get what they need. They might pretend to be a former abductees in order to get care in a rehabilitation center or they might lie to refugee settlement officials so they can receive an extra set of non-food items and sell them on for a profit. And while it would not be considered particularly good for their health under other circumstances, many young people also continue to sleep in the bush at night to avoid LRA attacks on their huts. While these behaviours may seem highly negative, they serve a purpose for adolescents, as means to an end. In some cases, acting out helps them avoid difficult emotions they may be feeling about their experiences or current circumstances.

Casual sex may bring them the connection or affection they feel they need; it may provide an element of risk-taking that allows adolescents to feel as if they are free from the constraints of their world; and it may reflect a loss of self-esteem. Manipulation and lying sometimes lead to concrete solutions for getting help. Prostitution may seem like the only option for many girls, who need to make ends meet, have few other avenues of support and feel a low level of self-worth. These behaviours are condemned within the community, but they should be recognized as part of a process of coping, recovery and survival so that they can be discussed and dealt with openly with young people.

CONSTRUCTIVE COPING SKILLS

Despite the enormous responsibilities and stresses that the conflict has placed on their shoulders, many young people are engaged in very constructive actions and have developed many skills for their survival and recovery. These skills range from those developed in the process of trying to stay alive in the bush, foraging for food, lighting fires and building shelters, to attempting to simultaneously find work, stay in school and care for siblings. All of the skills and activities described below provide a huge reservoir of hope for the future of northern Uganda and southern Sudan. These adolescents are resilient and dedicated, not just to their own survival but also to a better future. Their ideas, strengths and abilities will form the basis for continued community recovery.

Toward their recovery, adolescents:

Ask for help - It is a sign that a community is in the process of healing when its members make demands for assistance. While young people in northern Uganda may have few opportunities to influence community decision-making, many are actively asking for help from the adults around them, despite frequently being turned away or disappointed. In perhaps one of the most stirring examples of desperation and tenacity facing adolescents in asking for help, a 15-year-old boy saw Women's Commission researchers on the street in Gulu and randomly said hello. Not even knowing their names, he later traveled over 80 kilometers along a dangerous road to Kitgum to find them again and ask for help. Like countless others, he was an orphan with many brothers and sisters to care for, with no one to help pay for his schooling or other needs.

Attempt to learn new things, including by staying in school - Young people's commitment to education, in school and elsewhere, is overwhelming.

They cling to the possibility of an education with great hope, and do whatever they can to be able to finish their schooling. If they cannot go to school, adolescents still desire to, and do, participate in non-formal education and learning activities. All of these provide enormous stability to their lives and a sense of purpose and self-esteem.

Care for others and themselves and take responsibility - Young people go to great lengths to support themselves and others, particularly orphaned adolescent heads of household. Very young teenagers frequently make enormous personal sacrifices in order to work to support their siblings. Girls especially work very long, exhausting days, accomplishing many tasks.

Keeping busy with this work provides a needed sense of structure and regularity for some, and while the tasks are exhausting and often create barriers to doing other things, many young people say that they enjoy them and enjoy the responsibility.

Form clubs, associations and organisations - Many young people have initiated and joined dozens of activity and recreational groups, which provide them with constructive and creative activities. Such involvement increases their self-esteem and their sense of accomplishment, gives them hope and is a source of fun. Refugee young people have formed a peace club in Achol Pii, for example, and countless other young people are involved in recreational and creative groups that play sports and engage in artistic activities.

Go to church, practice religion - Many young people turn to a belief in God or the spirit world for strength. The process of prayer, community acceptance, forgiveness and serenity that comes from religious practice assists many young people. Traditional cleansing rituals also help formerly abducted adolescents recover from their experiences in captivity.

Undertake group income-generation activities - In order to find a solution to the poverty they are facing, many young people have formed cooperative income-generation projects. These creative activities provide young people with opportunities to earn money teach them about working with others and give them a sense of purpose and accomplishment even if they do not produce enormous profit. They also provide opportunities for young people to come together to talk and find support and companionship. Raise adolescent and community concerns through art, music and drama - Many young people are engaged in creative groups. At times, these groups perform for their communities and even enter competitions with one another. In so doing, they provide entertainment and relaxation for others, but they also use the opportunities to address important community issues.

In Padibe IDP camp, for example, Kitgum District and AVSI sponsored a competition for youth drama, music and dance groups around the theme "Living Happily amid Difficulties." The young people revived the storytelling tradition through depictions of the problem of alcoholism in families and its effects on youth, as well as the problems of orphans and Ebola.

Socialize - Many young people cope with their circumstances by spending time with their peers, talking, laughing and having fun when possible. For example, girls stated that although the work is hard, they enjoy talking to others at the bore-holes when they go for water and when they "dig" together. Peer support and opportunities for recreation are important ways that young people take their minds off their worries and find care. Form support groups for the formerly abducted - Some former abductees, including boys in the village of Omiya Animya and Awer IDP camp, have formed their own support groups. They said that sometimes a group of former abductees will get together to plan a project, or they will just sit together, talk and pass the time. These meetings help them to feel supported and give them confidence. While former abductees do very much interact with other young people, they tend to look to one another for solace and support. As fewer girls have escaped than boys, it is not clear that they have opportunities for mutual support to a similar extent.

Help other refugees who are more "vulnerable" - One way that young people cope with their own problems is to help others. In Achol Pii unaccompanied minors are helping others who are even more "vulnerable" than they are. One group is building new huts for other "vulnerables" in the camp in exchange for an allotment of blankets, which they will then decide how to distribute to others in need. This project allows them to feel good as they help others and focus less on their own problems.

TURNING SURVIVAL SKILLS INTO LEADERSHIP

Few of the young people interviewed appear to recognize their strengths and abilities or see themselves as valuable to their communities. Few expressed any sense of personal agency or ability to make positive changes in their situation or community. The reliance on humanitarian assistance and the inability of the governments of Uganda and Sudan and the international community to end the war have contributed to a growing sense of dependency among young people, and almost every single solution put forth by the young people for the concerns they raised was something that had to come from outside their world to help them.

The level of need facing them daily has moved many young people beyond any level of realistic expectation, to a point where they are hoping for miracles to change their circumstances. Young people cling to religious beliefs in the hope that their problems may suddenly be solved through a deus ex machina ending.

Young people may not recognize their own abilities in part because they are so preoccupied with survival and feel so vulnerable to attack that they feel completely powerless. They also lack encouragement and support from adults, who in general do not affirm their abilities or provide them with opportunities to share their opinions or participate in community decision-making. Yet the sheer magnitude of the strength involved in surviving in the bush or finding food and getting to school without adult support, is what is going to make a better future and provide hope for northern Uganda and a peaceful Uganda as a whole.

Young people's strengths and coping must increasingly be transformed into leadership. Young people must find ways to recognize how their survival skills can be built upon to increase youth-led organizing and activism in ways that constructively and democratically address key adolescent and community issues.

Support for young people's capacities and involvement in decision-making is urgent, and it must be balanced with protection, humanitarian and development assistance that addresses their immediate needs for security, food, education and health care.

7

Scope and Nature of Violence

The problem of violence against women has gained increasing attention in recent years, but the scope and magnitude of the problem are the subjects of on-going debates. For example, studies of how many women experience rape in their lifetimes have reported as few as 2 percent and as many as 50 percent; most estimates fall between 13 and 25 percent. There are similar debates about the number of battered women. Similar wide discrepancies are reported for women who experience violence by an intimate partner: annual rates range from 9.3 per 1,000 women to 220 per 1,000 women. The most often cited figures come from the National Family Violence Surveys, which found a rate of 116 per 1,000 women for a violent act by an intimate partner during the preceding year and 34 per 1,000 for "severe violence" by an intimate partner.

The debates about scope and magnitude sometimes overshadow and divert attention from the discussion of the actual problem of violence against women, its consequences, and what can be done to prevent it. This chapter highlights what is known about the extent of violence against women. It first reviews the data on the most extreme violence, that which ends in death. For non fatal violence, the chapter considers information gathered from representative sample surveys and official data sources and discusses reasons for discrepancies in study findings. It also discusses gaps in the data, uses for data, and offers recommendations for improving the information about both the extent and nature of violence against women.

FATAL VIOLENCE

Data on homicides in the United States are collected by two sources—the Federal Bureau of Investigation (FBI) and the National Center for Health Statistics (NCHS). The FBI's Uniform Crime Reports (UCR) system collects basic information on serious crimes from participating police agencies and records supplemental information about the circumstances of homicides. The NCHS collects and tabulates data on causes of death, including homicide, from death certificates. The NCHS data provides detail on causes of death by homicide, by age, sex, and race, but it does not provide information on the offender-victim relationship. Although U.S. homicide rates are substantially higher for men than for women—16.2 and 4.1 per 100,000, respectively—homicide ranks similarly as a cause of death for both men and women. Homicide is the second leading cause of death for those aged 15-24 and the fourth leading cause for those aged 10-14 and 25-34.

However, the pattern of offender-victim relationship for homicides has changed since the 1960s for men, but not for women. Today, men are more likely to be killed by a stranger or an unidentified assailant, while women are still substantially more likely to be killed by a male intimate or an acquaintance. In 1993, of the 4,869 female homicide victims (aged 10 and over), 1,531 (31 percent) were killed by husbands, ex-husbands, or boyfriends; of the 17,457 male homicide victims (aged 10 and over), only 591 (3 percent) were killed by wives, ex-wives, or girlfriends. The rate of homicide by an intimate has remained remarkably stable for women, but not for men. The rate for women was between 1.5 and 1.7 per 100,000 from 1977 to 1992. For men, however, the rate dropped from 1.5 per 100,000 in 1977 to 0.7 per 100,000 in 1992. It has been suggested that the availability of services for battered women, which began in the late 1970s, may have played a role in the decrease in males killed by intimates by offering women alternative means of escaping violent situations.

Women, like men, are most likely to be murdered with a firearm: 70 percent of all homicides in the United States in 1993 were committed with a firearm (Federal Bureau of Investigation, 1993). The risk of homicide in the home by a family member or intimate for both women and men is 7.8 times higher if a gun is kept in the home.

Thus, laws that allow judges to require persons against whom temporary restraining orders (known also as protection-from-abuse orders) have been issued to relinquish firearms in their possession may help reduce the lethality of violence against women; the question has not yet been directly studied. U.S. homicide rates are significantly higher for women of color than for white women: 10.7 per 100,000 for all women of color; 13.1 per 100,000 for African American women; 2.8 per 100,000 for white women. The same pattern holds for homicides by intimates. In 1992, the rate of intimate homicide of African American women aged 18 to 34 was 6 per 100,000; for whites in that age group the rate was 1.4 per 100,000.

The overall homicide rate in the United States is 9.3 per 100,000 persons, far higher than that of most other developed nations. For example, in Canada, a country that classifies most criminal offenses under rules similar to those in the United States, the 1993 homicide rate was slightly over 2 per 100,000. Interestingly, the homicide rate for Canadian women killed by their spouses is comparable to that in the United States, averaging 1.3 per 100,000 women each year; however, Canadian men are killed by their spouses at a rate of 0.4 per 100,000, about half the rate in the United States.

NON FATAL VIOLENCE

Information on the scope of non fatal violence against women comes from both official records and survey data. Thirty-five states collect some statistical information on domestic violence, and 30 states collect statistical data on sexual assaults. However, the source and nature of the data vary greatly from state to state. Some states collect data from health or social service sources, such as hospital emergency rooms, other health care providers, or victim service provider records, but most of the data collected come from the criminal justice system, particularly from law enforcement agencies. The Bureau of Justice Statistics of the Department of Justice and the Centers for Disease Control and Prevention of the Department of Health and Human Services have each funded demonstration projects to attempt to integrate data from the various sources to create a comprehensive data set on violence against women.

While such data sets could be of great value to researchers and policy makers, concerns about confidentiality and the use of the data must be taken into account. For example, recording of domestic violence in women's medical records has resulted in some women being denied health insurance because domestic violence was classified as a preexisting condition. The most consistently collected and commonly used official data set is the UCR. Because the FBI has been collecting and annually tabulating UCR data since 1930, they provide long-term, national trends. But the UCR includes only incidents that are considered crimes and that have been reported to the police. Based on comparisons with national survey data, it is estimated that only 40 to 50 percent of crimes become known to police, and that percentages may be much lower for violent crimes against women.

For example, a major survey of family violence found that only 6.7 percent of women assaulted by an intimate had reported the incident to police. UCR rates further depend on the recording of reported incidents by the police as crimes. What is recorded may vary because of differences in state statutes (for example, marital rape would not be counted in those states in which it is not a crime), as well as by differences in policies among jurisdictions and the discretionary judgments of individual police officers. Furthermore, the UCR contains little information about non fatal crimes other than race, age, and sex of arrested offenders; offender-victim relationship is not recorded. In order to overcome the limitations inherent in official data, researchers have turned to surveys to gain a fuller picture of violence against women.

Standard measures in survey research include incidence and prevalence. *Incidence* is the number of new cases within a specified time period (often, a year). *Prevalence* is the rate of established cases within a specified time period. Most of the surveys on violence against women measure either annual prevalence or lifetime prevalence (or both). Annual prevalence rates are important for looking at trends in the rate of violence over time; lifetime prevalence rates give an indication of the number of women who will be affected in the course of their lifetimes. The primary sources for national data on violence against women are the two waves of the National Family Violence Survey, the on-going National Crime Victimisation Survey, and, for sexual assault, the National Women's Study. A number of other studies have addressed a distinct subpopulation or specific topic.

Many of the studies on sexual assault were funded by the National Center for the Prevention and Control of Rape, which was located in the National Institute of Mental Health from 1976 until its termination in 1987. Currently, both foundation and federal government funding sources emphasize ameliorating the aftereffects rather than assessing the nature and scope of violence against women. Overall, there have been few survey studies on violence against women, and methodological constraints have precluded direct comparison across investigations, yet few resources in either the public or private sector are currently available for such work.

The more than 20 years of survey research on violence against women show a number of consistent patterns. The most common assailant is a man known to the woman, often her male intimate. This holds true for both sexual and physical assault. It also holds true for African Americans, Mexican Americans, and whites and for both urban and rural populations. The highest rates of violence are experienced by young women.

The average annual rate of victimisation is 74.6 per 1,000 for women aged 12-18 and 63.7 per 1,000 for women aged 19-29; in comparison, the average annual rate for all women is 36.1. Although the actual rates may vary, the age trend is similar for homicides, sexual assaults, and intimate partner violence. Women self-report violent actions toward their male partners at rates similar to or higher than men self-report violent actions toward their female partners. However, men consistently have been found to report their own use of violence as less frequent and less severe than their female partners report it to be.

Furthermore, rates do not provide information on the outcome of the act or whether the violent act was one of self-defense or attack, so the meaning of this finding is unclear. Both survey findings and health and crime data do indicate, however, that women are more frequently and more seriously injured by intimates than are men. Differences in study findings are primarily ones of magnitude rather than substance. For example, although risk characteristics (e.g., being young) and assault characteristics (e.g., by a known man) are fairly consistent across studies, estimates of the lifetime prevalence of sexual assault range from 2 percent to 50 percent with most estimates hovering around 20 percent.

There have been so few representative sample investigations of physical violence against women that cross-study comparisons are necessarily limited. The 1992-1993 National Crime Victimisation Survey (NCVS) found 34.7 of every 1,000 women had been victims of assault in a year: 8 per 1,000 for aggravated assault and 26.7 per 1,000 for simple assault, with 7.6 per 1,000 being assaults by intimates. In contrast, in the 1985 National Family Violence Survey (NFVS) 116 women per 1,000 reported being victims of violence by an intimate. The huge difference between the NFVS and the NCVS rates of assaults on women by intimates—the NFVS rate is 15 times higher—has been attributed to the difference in contexts of the two surveys: the NCVS questions relate to crimes; women may not view assaults by intimates as criminal, hence fail to report them in this context.

Few data are available to determine how violence against women has changed over time or how it is related to overall rates of violence. In the United States, the rate of reported violent crime has increased dramatically in the past 20 years, from 46.1 per 1,000 in 1974 to 74.6 per 1,000 in 1993—a 61.8 percent increase. In that same time span, the rate of forcible rape reported to police increased 54.9 percent, but is not known how much of that increase may reflect increased willingness of women to report rape to the police and how much is an actual increase in the rate of rape. From 1973 to 1991, the rate of overall violence against women remained relatively constant at about 23 per 1,000. The NCVS did not specifically ask about sexual assaults or violence by intimates prior to 1992; after changes in the survey to specifically include such information, the reported rates of violence jumped to 43.7 per 1,000 women. This change most likely reflects the change in the survey and not a sudden increase in the rate of violence against women. The NFVS found a 6.6 percent drop in the rate of intimate violence against women from the 1975 survey to the 1985 survey, although the drop was not statistically significant.

In addition, the 1975 survey was conducted by face-to-face interviews and the 1985 survey was conducted by telephone: this difference may account for some of the drop in reported rates. Although the United States has significantly higher rates of most violent crimes than most other developed countries, rates of violence against women may be more similar. The recent Canadian Violence Against Women Survey found that 29 percent of ever-married women had experienced physical or sexual violence at the hands of an intimate partner; in comparison, Straus and Gelles (1986) estimated that violence occurred in 28 percent of marriages in the United States. The Canadian survey also found that nearly 50 percent of all Canadian women had experienced at least one incident of physical or sexual assault since the age of 16. The Canadian survey is remarkable in that it interviewed a random sample of 12,300 women who were 18 years of age and older and investigated physical and sexual violence as well as emotional abuse.

ACCOUNTING FOR DIFFERENCES IN FINDINGS

As with all research, a variety of methodological factors can be linked to the differences in study findings. Sample composition and locale, data collection method, and question construction and context are among the most important methodological differences in U.S. studies. Study samples vary widely. Although some include large numbers of African Americans or Hispanics, most focus on European American (white) populations. With a few exceptions, most studies were conducted with urban residents. Given differences in the geographic location, age, and ethnic composition of the samples, one would not expect similar prevalence estimates. Data collection methods also vary across the studies. Paper-and-pencil self-report instruments, once thought to be preferable because they allow for anonymity, have the lowest participation rates and produce the lowest prevalence estimates of adult sexual assault. Telephone interviews have been shown to be a substantial improvement over paper-and-pencil surveys because some rapport between the interviewer and the woman can be established and because more detailed and specific information can be collected.

Face-to-face interviews, the most costly data collection method, are generally preferred for the investigation of sensitive topics, such as violence in intimate relationships, because they allow for the greatest interviewer-respondent rapport. Sexual assault prevalence rates obtained in studies that gathered data through in person interviews are generally higher than those obtained in telephone interviews; those rates, in turn, are generally higher than the rates obtained in paper-and-pencil surveys.

Definitions of violence against women vary from study to study. Some studies of sexual assault were limited to rape; others included physical contact in addition to rape; and still others used a very broad definition that included noncontact abuse. Given the discrepancy in definitions used to assess the phenomenon, differences in prevalence rates are to be expected. Multiple, behaviourally specific questions are associated with greater disclosure by study participants. Studies of sexual assault that use a single screening question (e.g., "Have you ever been raped or sexually assaulted?") no matter how broad it is obtain lower prevalence rates than studies that use several questions that are behaviourally specific (e.g., "Did he insert his penis into your vagina?"). Asking directly about sexual violence does not appear to offend study participants. In one community-based survey, a number of respondents talked about their assaults for the first time when responding to a direct question by the interviewer. Also, consistent with decades of social science research that documents similar patterns with regard to sensitive topics, respondents in surveys were more likely to refuse to answer questions about income than they were to refuse to answer questions about sexual assault. Prevalence estimates are also related to the context in which questions about sexual or intimate partner violence are asked. For example, the NCVS recently was amended to ask directly about sexual assault.

Although such a change is an improvement over previous NCVS practice (to clearly define events such as robbery and burglary but not to name or directly ask about sexual assault), asking about sexual or intimate partner violence in the context of a survey about crime requires the respondent to define her experience as a criminal act. Research consistently shows, however, that women often do not define experiences that meet the legal definition of a rape as a rape, so they may be unlikely to respond affirmatively to questions about sexual assault that are asked in the context of a survey about criminal acts. The context of the data collection is important in another way: women are known to be less likely to reveal incidents involving their male intimates, a common assailant according to survey research. There are a number of reasons for this phenomenon.

Women may believe assaults by an intimate are family matters that should not be disclosed; they may fear losing their children should the violence become known; they may have concerns about involving the criminal justice system if the violence becomes known; and their assailants may be nearby at the time of the interview. Like investigations into other sensitive topics, most investigations have tried to reduce the differences between interviewers and study participants. One study that included both male and female interviewers and male and female respondents found that the sex of the interviewer had little effect on prevalence estimates. Responses may vary on more subtle matters, however, and the issue of interviewer-respondent similarity on socio-demographic characteristics, such as gender and race, has not been deeply investigated.

USING THE AVAILABLE DATA

Policy decisions—such as how many resources to allocate to service delivery—require solid data about the incidence and prevalence of violence against women. Rather than viewing the discrepancies in prevalence estimates as a problem, the range of findings may be very useful to decision makers. For example, differing estimates on the prevalence of sexual assault research results that are related to methodological differences can be used for different purposes. Research investigations ask directly about sexual assault (and which obtain relatively low prevalence rates) ascertains the number of women who are willing to label themselves as survivors or victims of sexual assault and, therefore, who might seek sexual assault services. At the same time, it is important to estimate the number of women whose experiences are legally defined as sexual assault although they themselves might not define them that way: research indicates that those women use health services more frequently than women who have not been sexually assaulted, even when their health status and health insurance coverage are nearly identical. Thus, the "true" prevalence of violence against women may be less important for policy and other decision makers than understanding the methodological differences that resulted in various estimates.

Recognizing the commonalities in study findings of various investigations is critical to both policy and research. Research consistently documents those men known to women are those most likely to assault them (whether physically or sexually) and that young women are at high risk. These consistent findings suggest that scarce resources designated for men's violence against women should be allocated not to "stranger danger," but to the problem of violence by intimates and acquaintances. The research indicates the relative importance of preventing violence against young women.

Although some policy decisions can be based on existing research, improving estimates of the rates of violence against women is important for a number of reasons. Without solid baseline rates for the general population and for various groups within the population, it is difficult to assess the effectiveness of interventions, particularly preventive interventions and interventions aimed at community-wide change. Good incidence and prevalence data—though they may measure different phenomena—are also important for the allocation of service resources. A number of substantial gaps exist in the knowledge base. First, there is relatively little information about violence against a growing segment of the nation's population—women of color. Second, research on violence against women has advanced knowledge along categorical lines (i.e., sexual assault, physical assault) rather than on what are believed to be patterns of victimisation that include multiple forms of violence.

Third, studies have focused primarily on the victims, not the offenders, so there is little information on rates of perpetration. Estimates can be made of the number of women likely to experience sexual assault or intimate violence at sometime in their lives, but there is a lack of data with which to estimate the lifetime prevalence of violence perpetration. The scope of perpetration has implications for designing preventive interventions. The studies conducted to date present a complex picture of ethnic differences in violence against women. National survey studies suggest that African Americans are more likely than white Americans to report physical violence in an intimate relationship. However, how much of the variance may be explained by socio-economic factors and how much by cultural factors remains unclear and requires further study. Studies that included Hispanics showed contradictory conclusions. Hispanics were reported to be at higher, similar, or lower risk than non-Hispanic whites for physical violence in marriage. It is possible that this range of findings is due to sample differences, study contexts, and different data collection methods. It is also important to consider intra-group differences: for example, one study of four Hispanic groups—Puerto Rican, Mexican, Mexican-American, and Cuban—found prevalence rates for wife assault varied among them.

In-person interviews with representative samples of women reveal little difference in sexual assault prevalence between African American and white women. By contrast, unlike the findings for physical violence, studies have found Hispanic women (mostly of Mexican descent) to be at significantly lower risk of sexual assault than their non-Hispanic white counterparts. However, a substantial and consistent proportion of sexual assaults, regardless of respondent ethnicity, are perpetrated by the woman's male intimate. There are no survey studies, to the panel's knowledge, of Asian American women's experiences of intimate violence. Such research is important because, according to Ho (1990:129): "traditional Asian values of close family ties, harmony, and order may not discourage physical and verbal abuse in the privacy of one's home; these values may only support the minimization and hiding of such problems."

Moreover, we have few data on different Asian and Pacific Islander populations, despite prevailing differences among these subgroups in terms of culture, value systems, immigration history, and other factors. There is also limited information on the prevalence of violence against women in American Indian and Alaska Native communities. There may be significant intertribal differences with the tremendous diversity in tribal cultures and over 250 recognized tribes, 209 Alaska Native villages, and 65 communities not recognized by the federal government. There are reports that domestic violence was rare, at least in some tribes, prior to contact with Europeans. It is possible that traditional family structures and social and religious functions may have served as protective factors. Recent immigrants often are not represented in survey samples because of language and cultural barriers, immigrants' fears of officials and deportation, and fear that applications for relatives to immigrate to the United States might be affected. One study that examined immigrant status (i.e., whether the respondent was born in the United States) in association to physical or sexual assault by intimates offered surveys in either Spanish or English and found that persons born in Mexico evidenced a much lower risk of both physical and sexual violence in their intimate relationships than their U.S.-born Hispanic counterparts. These differences in risk patterns were not identified in two other studies of Latinos; in no small part because relatively recent immigrants were not likely to have been sampled since neither of these latter two studies interviewed anyone in Spanish. Diversity in the primary variable of interest, culture, is attenuated when monolingual non-English speaking populations are excluded.

There is a further methodological problem. Most studies have used measures and instruments developed on Anglos and simply applied them to members of other ethnic groups, for whom the instruments' validity is unknown. There may be differences in the intent of a question and a respondent's interpretation related to patterns of expression and idioms that may vary across cultures. This may explain, in part, the lack of consistency of results across studies. Clearly, unique cultural manifestations of violence against women cannot be identified if such experiences are not measured. The failure to include women of color in the development of instruments designed to assess violence against women has left the field with a major gap in the data.

In addition to data gaps about the prevalence of violence among minority women, there is also little conceptual understanding of how structural factors relating to race or ethnicity and socioeconomic status interact with gender to create the specific context in which violence is experienced. These conceptual gaps can sometimes lead to oversights and omissions that can lead to policies that unintentionally exacerbate some women's vulnerability to violence. For example, immigration policies that required immigrant women to remain married to a resident spouse for 2 years before they could receive permanent residence status forced some women to remain in violent situations. Although there is anecdotal evidence that language barriers, immigrant status, geographical or social isolation and cultural insularity can influence the experience of violence and the accessibility of interventions, these dynamics have not been systematically researched. Additionally, there is little systematic information about the intersection of different forms of violence. One could speculate that a woman who is beaten by her husband on a regular basis is likely to be sexually victimized and psychologically maltreated as well, but survey research seldom investigates the co-occurrence of various forms of violence against women.

Most surveys have focused on single aspects of women's experiences of violence, such as rape or physical violence. For example, studies of intimate partner violence that neglect to ask about sexual violence may miss information on and understanding of marital rape. Case studies of battered women indicate that the most severely battered women also experience severe sexual violence. Another source of data may be studies of women's health and behaviour that include unanalyzed information pertinent to violence against women.

Identification and secondary analysis of these types of data sets could yield much information and at a relatively low cost. The inclusion of research questions pertaining to violence against women in other studies, such as those pertaining to women's health, alcohol and drug use, prenatal care, or unplanned pregnancy, could further help illuminate the context in which women experience violence and its impact on their lives. For example, existing health surveys could be amended to include questions about violence in women's lives. Research suggests that pregnant women who are battered are more likely to delay obtaining prenatal care and to have low-birth-weight babies than pregnant women who are not battered. Cigarette smoking, alcohol and other drug intake, mental health status, and other relatively sensitive topics have been investigated in numerous studies of pregnancy. Including questions about being hit, kicked, or otherwise injured by one's male intimate may yield key information for understanding of pregnancy complications and outcomes, as well as of violence itself. Physical and sexual violence may account for some of the unexplained factors in women's health status that have been noted. Violence against women has been recognized as an important field of scientific inquiry, and the research to date has illuminated many aspects of women's experiences with violence. However, that research has often been narrowly focused, and comparisons across studies have been hampered by methodological differences.

Research definitions of violence against women have been inconsistent, not only making study findings difficult to compare, but also contributing to controversy over the scope of the problem. More consistent definitions and improved measures covering all aspects of violence against women would facilitate needed research on violence against women and improve knowledge as a basis for both research and policy.

Researchers, policy makers, and service providers from a wide spectrum of disciplines and fields—including public health, criminal justice, medicine, sociology, social work, psychology, and law—work on violence against women, and they need to ensure that others can understand and use their findings. The definitions need to take into account the full range of abuse experienced by women—sexual, physical, and psychological—and acknowledge the commonalities among, as well as unique aspects of, those forms of violence. Definitions that take into account the multidimensional aspects of violence against women will allow for the assessment of multiple types of violence against women in the same sample. Definitions should also specify severity, duration, and frequency of violent acts. There has been much controversy in the field over instruments used to measure violence against women, and the paucity of validated instruments is a serious barrier to improved research on violence against women. The context in which questions are asked and the wording used may influence the willingness of respondents to report violence. The context and wording of questions may also have different meanings for different subpopulations. In fields in which few measurement instruments are available, determining construct validity (the extent to which the association between a measure and other variables is consistent with theoretical or empirical knowledge) and concurrent validity (the extent to which a measure is related to other presumably valid measures) may be difficult.

Repeated use and refinement of the test instrument, with careful attention to such aspects of measurement as format, administration conditions, and language level, may be necessary. Instrument developers may receive guidance on validity determination from the *Standards for Educational and Psychological Testing*. After work on instrumentation, including investigations of effective questioning strategies in relevant subpopulations, funding is needed for survey studies of varying sizes and scope (including different age groups and ethnic or racial groups) to rigorously document the extent of violence against women. Although some national surveys have estimated the frequency of violence against women, few national lifetime prevalence data exist, especially for racial and ethnic subgroups and other subpopulations. Because most surveys include persons who have experienced violence and sought services, those who have experienced violence but not sought services, and those who have not experienced violence, they can investigate the range of experiences and exposures. Documentation in official records (e.g., law enforcement records, medical charts) also needs to be improved so that more research can be conducted using available records.

An improvement in official records would reduce, to some degree, the need for and expense associated with investigating certain research questions in one-time studies. A consideration of the context in which women experience violence is vital to understanding the nature of the problem, as well as to the consequences to the woman, and effectiveness of interventions.

There is little understanding of how such factors as race, ethnicity, socioeconomic status, culture, and sexual orientation intersect with gender to shape the particular context in which violence occurs. Because women's experiences differ on these dimensions, those differences must be understood and incorporated into the body of knowledge about violence against women in order to design intervention strategies. Other factors that warrant consideration include disability, religion, homelessness, and institutionalization. Investigators should be encouraged to undertake studies that examine risk factors for victimisation as well as groups at risk of victimisation. In other words, in addition to identifying target groups for prevention and intervention, research needs to identify elements that might be amenable to change.

8

Violent Victimisation and Offending

The purpose of this chapter is to:

- Summarize current knowledge on individual-, situational-, and community-level sources of criminal violence;
- Identify key problems of causal interpretation in existing research; and
- Suggest new directions for future research and policy. Although violence has not been an understudied phenomenon in American criminology, a synthesis of the causes and consequences of criminal violence across multiple levels of analysis has not been undertaken. Indeed, most of the more than 2,000 studies of violence published since 1945 have been descriptive and focused either on individual-level correlates of violent offending or, to a much lesser extent, on community-level correlates of violence rates. As a consequence, extant reviews tend to emphasize individual-level factors (especially age, race, and sex) or particular classifications such as family violence and criminal career violence.

By contrast, our goal in this review is to show how a multilevel perspective on both victimisation and offending may substantially increase the understanding and control of violence. Because there appears to be little consensus in the social science literature on how multilevel factors should be defined, we describe in more detail our conceptualization of these terms. Our use of the terms "individual," "situational," and "community" corresponds closely to Short's (1985) definition of the "individual," "micro-," and "macro-" levels of analysis. The individual level of explanation typically inquires as to characteristics of individuals that explain behaviour. In our discussion of individual-level risk factors for violence, we specifically focus on the ascribed and achieved characteristics of individuals that are statistically associated with violent victimisation and offending.

For example, we examine how the risks of violent victimisation and offending are distributed across characteristics such as age, sex, race, marital status, lifestyle, and socioeconomic status. Our intention, though, is not only to provide a descriptive summary of statistical findings, but to suggest how, and in what ways, individual characteristics are causally related to the risk of violent victimisation and offending. By situational-level risk factors, we are referring to those factors, broadly defined, that influence the initiation or outcome of a violent event. This conceptualization corresponds to Short's (1990:11) definition of the micro level, where attention is focused on the unfolding of events and the interaction of parties involved in events. Situational-level analyses usually treat the violent incident, or event, as the unit of analysis. Included in our review is a discussion of such factors as the presence and type of weapon, the presence of drugs or alcohol, the role of bystanders or third parties during violent events, and victim resistance and retaliation.

However, we expand the traditional conceptualization of situational-level analyses to include a discussion of the victim-offender overlap and how victim-offender relationships are related to violence. These factors are included because we believe that the simultaneous consideration of victims, offenders, and their past and present interactions provides a more complete context for studying the initiation and outcomes of violent events. The macro social or community level of explanation asks what it is about community structures and cultures that produces differential rates of crime. For example, what characteristics of communities are associated with high rates of violence? Are communities safe or unsafe because of the persons who reside in them or because of community properties themselves? Can changes in community structure affect violent crime rates? As implied by these questions, the goal of macro level research is not to explain individual involvement in criminal behaviour but to isolate characteristics of communities, cities, or societies that lead to high rates of criminality.

Examples of macro level risk factors include residential mobility, population density, heterogeneity, and income inequality. These and other factors are assessed for both intra urban (e.g., local community, neighborhood) and interurban (e.g., city, metropolitan area) units of analysis, although for substantive reasons discussed below we place more weight on between-community variations in rates of criminal violence. Conclusions about the correlates of violence are naturally linked to the universe of studies under consideration. Because our review is highly focused we applied systematic criteria for inclusion of research. Although exceptions arise, the studies analyzed in this chapter were selected based on the following criteria:

1. Studies in which serious interpersonal violence (e.g., assault, homicide, robbery, and rape) is measured directly are our primary focus. Issues surrounding the measurement of violence are discussed as needed; however, we should note that our intention herein is to avoid studies that present overall measures (e.g., total scales, index crimes) in which violence is confounded with property or other crime types (e.g., drug use, status offenses). Also, many delinquency studies focus on such events as schoolyard theft ("robbery") and minor fighting. Except where important for historical or theoretical reasons, these studies are generally not considered.

2. Analyses of objective social characteristics of individuals, situations, and community context are emphasized, as opposed to those studies focusing on internal psychological states, perceptions, or biological/constitutional conditions.

Because individual-level social characteristics have received disproportionate attention in the past, we tend to highlight the theoretical and policy implications of community-level factors. As we make clear, however, the study of community-level processes is not possible without a thorough understanding of individual-and situational-level correlates.

3. We emphasize studies that present empirical data, especially those that have representative (e.g., national-level) or large enough samples to draw reasonable conclusions.

   However, this does *not* rule out the selective use of important ethnographic work that bears directly on issues of concern.

4. We focus on American studies or those written in the English language, particularly those published in refereed journals. Moreover, we emphasize urban-based research from the past 20 years that has formed the bulk of multivariate studies of violence.

5. In general, we attempt to assess the substantive and (where appropriate) causal importance of key factors. Consequently, we focus on the magnitude of effects as opposed to mere statistical significance.

Although not strict criteria for inclusion, we also make a special effort to highlight (a) micro-macro linkages (i.e., the simultaneous consideration of both individual-and community-level risk factors in violence) and (b) the connection between violent victimisation and violent offending. We believe that much previous research on violence is problematic because of the causal confounding and alternative causal interpretations that can arise in designs relying on a single level of analysis. Furthermore, we contend that the victim-offender overlap can provide fundamental insights into the etiology of violence; hence we pay close attention to studies that allow assessment of the causal role that offending may play in increasing victimisation risk, and vice versa. Too often in the past these issues have been treated separately as if they were unrelated.

In contrast, by highlighting micro-(individual/situational) and macro-(community) linkages in the study of violence, in addition to victim-offender relationships, we believe that our understanding of the social structural and contextual sources of violence is improved. To our knowledge the literature on violence has not been critically assessed from this perspective before, especially in a framework that points to future research designs needed to address remaining etiological questions. Before turning to a road map outlining our review, two issues deserve further clarification. Given the vast literature and multiple measures of both violence and community factors, we do not present in tabular form the magnitudes of effect for all studies and factors-preliminary efforts found this to be unworkable. As noted above, the Bridges and Weis (1989) review located more than 2,000 studies of violence-a universe larger than that relevant to other comprehensive reviews.

Perhaps more of a problem, we discovered an almost unlimited supply of incomparable measures and incomparable techniques, especially in community-level studies. For example, a concept as seemingly straightfor-ward as "poverty" has been measured in at least 20 different ways, ranging from dichotomous groupings of communities through census-based percentage measures to factor-analytic scores. Complicating matters further, researchers have employed many different analytical techniques and styles of data presentation. This issue is discussed more below, but we emphasize at the outset that the nature of past research makes it difficult to present summary figures representing magnitudes of effect that are comparable across studies.

Second, there is a plethora of theories of violence that have been advanced in the criminological literature. Some of these, such as the subculture of violence theory, are well known and have been explicated quite well in other sources. A seemingly reasonable strategy, then, especially in a review devoted to empirical risk factors in violence, is simply to ignore theory and concentrate on the findings. However, findings alone do not speak for themselves and are generally devoid of meaning when stripped of substantive content. More to the point, empirical research designs are valid only to the extent that the substantive model under consideration is valid and properly specified. Our compromise is therefore to couch, no matter how briefly, the correlates of violence in substantive perspective.

We refer readers to appropriate sources on theoretical issues for more detail, particularly individual-level theories that are more widely known. Thus, theories per se are not reviewed, but key substantive themes are emphasized in an effort to shed light on the importance of empirical findings, especially multivariate, community-level, or contextual studies. This review is divided into seven major sections. First, the literature on factors underlying an individual's risk of violent victimisation is assessed. This section includes a review not only of demographic correlates (e.g., age, race, and sex) emphasized in previous research, but of lifestyle and routine activity factors as well.

In a similar fashion, the second section reviews the individual-level correlates of violent offending. In the third section, an overview is presented of situational-level risk factors in violence, along with analyses that consider victim-offender relationships and the concept of a victim-offender overlap. The fourth and fifth sections assess community-level determinants of violent crime and metropolitan (i.e., city-level) sources of violence, respectively. In the sixth section, some key problems and pitfalls in attributing causal interpretations to findings from past research are examined. Finally, the last section identifies promising directions for future research designs and public policy initiatives.

Our focus in this section is on factors related to the risk of violent victimisation among individuals. Here, we address the following questions: What are the overall risks of violent victimisation to individuals? How are these risks distributed across individual characteristics such as age, sex, race, marital status, and socioeconomic status? Are these differences stable over recent time periods? How are individual-level differences in risk explained by theories of victimisation? Finally, how might some of the limitations of extant victimisation research is minimized? We begin with a brief overview of the general aspects of violent victimisation.

Victimisation research over the past 20 years has produced several consistent findings. One of the primary findings is that the annual risk of becoming a victim of a crime of personal violence (i.e., homicide, rape, robbery, or assault) is relatively low. For example, the combined risk of suffering a violent victimisation by rape, robbery, or assault in 1987 was estimated at approximately 1 in 33. The risk of suffering a victimisation from a personal crime of violence is considerably less than that of suffering a theft victimisation-in 1987, the rate of reported theft victimisation (approximately 1 in 14) was more than twice the rate of reported violent victimisation. Although this risk may seem low on an annual basis, the lifetime risk of violence for any particular crime is much higher. For example, the annual risk of becoming a victim of homicide is about 1 in 10,000, but the lifetime risk of being murdered is approximately 1 in 369 for white females, 1 in 131 for white males, 1 in 104 for black females, and as high as 1 in 21 for black males.

As suggested by the differences in lifetime homicide risks, the second major finding in individual-level analyses is that the distribution of violent victimisation is not random. Rather, the risk of experiencing personal violence varies considerably across demographic and social groups. The pattern of systematic differences found across different demographic and socioeconomic subgroups has been fairly consistent across analyses utilizing either the Uniform Crime Report (UCR) data or the National Crime Survey (NCS) data in the United States. Patterns of association similar to those found in the United States have also been found in analyses using data from other countries such as England, the Netherlands, and Australia. To describe these patterns of violent victimisation, we present, as briefly as possible, bivariate and then multivariate findings of research examining individual-level risk factors associated with victimisation by homicide, assault, robbery, and rape. Particular attention is paid to the magnitude and consistency of findings in multivariate research, as well as their theoretical importance. Limitations of these analyses and their consequences for our understanding of violent victimisation are discussed.

BIVARIATE FINDINGS

It should be mentioned at the outset that the vast majority of knowledge about the risk of violent victimisation has been obtained through analyses of National Crime Survey data. The NCS is an ongoing survey conducted by the Bureau of Justice Statistics, designed to measure the extent of personal and household victimisation in the United States. Interviews are conducted at six-month intervals with all persons 12 years of age or older living in a household. By using NCS data, it is possible to estimate the extent of victimisations that are not reported in official police data (due to non reporting of incidents, arrest bias, etc.) and to calculate prevalence measures of violent victimisation for specific individual subgroups. Therefore, the NCS constitutes the best available data source on the risk of victimisation for persons living in the United States.

Age is one of the most important predictors of an individual's risk of violent victimisation. The NCS data for 1987 indicate that the risk of personal violent victimisation is highest for persons less than 25 years of age. After age 25, the risk of such victimisation gradually declines such that by age 65, the risk of suffering a violent victimisation is approximately one-tenth that of persons under 25 years of age. This bivariate age-victimisation relationship-a relatively high level of victimisation in youth and young adulthood followed by a gradual decline in risk-is observed for the crimes of homicide, rape, and assault (and, therefore, violent victimisation in general). Differences in the risk of robbery victimisation across age groups are not as great as those found for other violent crimes.

In addition to contributing to the overall risk of violent victimisation, age appears to be related to the nature of crime-specific victimisations. In an analysis of NCS victimisation narratives for juvenile victims (age 12-17) of personal crime, Garofalo et al. (1987) found that assaults reported by juveniles were overwhelmingly minor in nature-that is, they were often the result of an inability to resolve common disputes and rarely led to serious injury on the part of the victim. For robbery as well, the relative nature of the event was reported to be less serious among juvenile victims than among adults. Although a large proportion of all victimisation reported in the NCS is relatively minor in nature, juvenile victimisation appears to be least serious overall in terms of both injury levels and monetary loss. Therefore, although juveniles appear to be at high risk for violent personal victimisation, the victimisations they do suffer are more likely to have minor consequences compared to those of adults.

For all crimes of personal violence—with the obvious exception of rape—males are at greater risk for victimisation than females. The annual rate of homicide victimisations for males is nearly three times greater than the annual rate for females. The lifetime risk of becoming a victim of homicide is estimated to be between three and four times greater for males (1 in 84) than females (1 in 282). For the crimes of robbery and assault, males are approximately 1.5-2 times more likely to become victims. On the other hand, women are overwhelmingly the victims of rape. NCS data estimate the risk of attempted or completed rape for females to be approximately 1 in 770 annually. Furthermore, these relationships between sex and the risk of violent victimisation have remained fairly constant over the last decade. Smith (1987), for example, reports that the proportion of female victims of robberies and assaults has remained stable, whereas the proportion of female homicide victims has increased slightly over the past 10 years.

As was true for the relationship between age and overall risk of violence, the nature of victimisation for males and females differs. First, for assault and robbery victimisations, men are more likely than women to report injury. Second, according to victim reports, offenders attacking males are more likely to be armed: between 1973 and 1982, approximately 41 percent of male and 29 percent of female victims of violent crime were attacked by offenders with weapons. Rape is an obvious exception to this pattern. Excluding homicide, rape is the crime with the highest level of injury and is perpetuated largely against females.

Both NCS and UCR data confirm that blacks are disproportionately the victims of homicide, rape, and robbery. Blacks are approximately five times more likely than whites to become victims of homicide and approximately three to four times more likely to report victimisation by rape and robbery. Higher rates of black victimisation by homicide (compared to whites) have been found throughout the last century, and recent trends indicate a continuation of this differential. As noted earlier, the lifetime risk of homicide victimisation is approximately three times greater for black women than for white women, and approximately four times greater for black men than for white men. Assault victimisation rates for blacks and whites do not differ significantly in magnitude, although the majority of assault victimisations reported by blacks are incidents of aggravated assault, whereas among whites, simple assaults comprise the majority.

The lack of race differences in assaults overall may be the result of differences in reporting. For example, it has been suggested that blacks underreport less serious forms of assault and/or that whites over report minor assaults. Two-and three-way associations for age, sex, and race suggest that the relationships among these factors are generally speaking, additive. Thus, for certain subgroups the relative risk of violent victimisation is quite high. In particular, young, black males are approximately 22 times more likely than older, white females to become the victims of violent crime. Within these three-way associations, age continues to have the largest independent effect followed by sex and race.

Although somewhat less studied than age, race, and sex, marital status has also been found to be substantially related to the risk of violent victimisation. Overall, NCS estimates suggest that unmarried persons are nearly four times more likely to become the victims of robbery, rape, or assault than are those currently married. The exception to this pattern is for widowed persons who have the lowest risk of violent victimisation. Never-married persons have the highest risk of victimisation, followed closely by divorced and separated persons. At the extreme ends of the scale, those never married are approximately 11 times more likely than widowed persons, and more than 3 times more likely than currently married persons, to become the victims of assault. On the other hand, the differences by marital status for robbery and rape are not as pronounced. Finally, when sex and marital status are considered simultaneously, marital status is more strongly related to victimisation risk among females than among males.

SOCIO-ECONOMIC STATUS

Not surprisingly, family income is inversely related to the risk of personal victimisation. However, the overall magnitude of the effect of family income is not as large as the magnitudes for the individual-level characteristics previously discussed (namely, age, race, sex, and marital status). For violence in general, the risk of victimisation is approximately twice as great for persons whose family income is reported to be less than $7,500 compared to those whose family income is higher than $50,000. Specific crimes of violence also have varying relationships to family income. For example, there is little relationship between rape and family income, although women whose families earn less than $7,500 are again most likely to become victims. The risk of rape among women in the remaining income categories is approximately equal. Income is somewhat more strongly related to the risk of assault, with those at the lowest end of the income distribution reporting twice the risk of victimisation as those at the highest end. Of all violent crimes, income is most strongly related to the risk of robbery-poorer persons report a robbery rate about three times higher than persons at the upper ends of the income distribution.

The relationship between education and violent victimisation is less consistent than the relationship between family income and personal victimisation. In fact, persons with the least amount of education report the lowest level of violent victimisation. Excluding this category of education, and with slight fluctuations, the general relationship between education and victimisation is negative but small in magnitude. It has been suggested that the ability to accurately recall victimisations may be affected by one's level of education. For example, highly educated respondents in the NCS appear to be more "productive" when recalling victimisation events. The relationship between socioeconomic status (either income or education) and rape victimisation is also small in magnitude and is more uniformly distributed across women in different income and education groups.

Finally, of the common indicators of an individual's socioeconomic status, unemployment is most strongly related to the risk of violent victimisation. Those who are unemployed are at the greatest risk of robbery, assault, and rape, followed by persons in school, the employed, those unable to work, those keeping house, and the retired. Overall, the unemployed are more than twice as likely as the employed to suffer a violent victimisation. It is thus clear that the risk of suffering a violent victimisation is differentially distributed across social and demographic groups.

Extant data suggest that age has the largest bivariate relationship with the risk of homicide, assault, robbery, and rape. Sex and race are also related to violent victimisation, as is marital status, although these effects are slightly smaller in magnitude. Two-way relationships among most forms of violent victimisation and each of the indicators of socioeconomic status are generally negative in direction, but even smaller in magnitude. Although each of the individual-level characteristics discussed above appears related to victimisation, it is possible that these associations are spurious. To assess this possibility, we direct our attention to the research literature that has considered some or all of these individual-level factors simultaneously.

Despite the rather large body of research on the

individual-level risk of victimisation, there have been relatively few multivariate analyses that directly examine the risk of violent victimisation in the United States. This is due in part to the relative rarity of violent crime: because of its infrequency, it is difficult to test reliably for the independent effects of many of the above-mentioned correlates. Nevertheless, some major studies have examined the interrelationships among demographic and socioeconomic (as well as other) characteristics and violent victimisation in the United States.

More specifically, Hindelang et al. (1978) analyzed the 1972 NCS (eight-city survey) data in order to examine the independent effects of social and demographic factors on whether or not a person reported a personal victimisation (defined as assault, robbery, rape, and personal larceny with contact). Cohen et al. (1981a) examined robbery victimisation using 1973 to 1977 NCS data combined, and Cohen et al. (1981b) analyzed similar factors for their effects on the risk of assault victimisation using 1974 and 1977 NCS data combined.

Miethe et al. (1987) also examined a set of demographic and socioeconomic factors for their effects on violent victimisation using the 1975 NCS (13-city survey) data. Although the dependent variables and statistical techniques differed across studies, the general patterns and relative magnitudes of effects found in each of the analyses are compatible. Hindelang et al. (1978) for example, found that the most important predictors of personal victimisation were age, marital status, sex, and employment status: young, single, unemployed males had the highest risk of personal victimisation. Cohen et al. (1981a) found that age, employment status, race, and income had significant and independent effects on robbery victimisation. Namely, younger persons, the unemployed, blacks, and poorer persons had the highest risk of being robbed. Cohen et al. (1981b) also found that age, marital status, and employment status had the greatest independent effects on the probability of assault.

Finally, Miethe et al.'s (1987) findings agree: age, sex, and marital status are the predominant demographic risk factors predicting violent victimisation. Miethe et al. (1987) also found a relatively small but significant negative effect for income. Only in the case of robbery victimisation was race found to be a significant predictor (Cohen et al., 1981a). The lack of an independent race effect on assault is not surprising when one considers the negligible bivariate effect found in the NCS data. Direct comparisons of the magnitude of effects found in prior analyses of violent victimisation are not possible given the variety of statistical controls and analytical techniques.

However, in the analyses noted above, partial effects were most often no more than twice the risk of the reference group-a magnitude that is determined in part by the measurement level of the independent factors. Miethe et al. (1987), for example, found that males were approximately twice as likely as females to suffer a violent victimisation, independent of race, income, marital status, and age. However, certain combinations of these risk factors produce much higher risks of victimisation for some subgroups. In particular, Cohen et al. (1981a) estimated that young, poor, unemployed black males living alone had a risk of robbery victimisation nearly 10 times greater than the national average.

THEORETICAL INTERPRETATIONS

These individual-level correlates of victimisation have formed the basis of "lifestyle" or "routine activity" theories of victimisation risk. The essential proposition of "lifestyle-routine activity" theories is that the convergence in time and space of suitable targets and the absence of capable guardians may lead to increases in crime, independent of the structural and cultural conditions that may motivate individuals to engage in crime (e.g., poverty, unemployment, sub-cultural values). Derived from this general proposition, the "principle of homogamy" in lifestyle theory states that persons are more likely to be victimized when they disproportionately associate with, or come in contact with, members of demographic groups that contain a disproportionate share of offenders. Young single males, for example, are more likely to pursue social activities outside the household than are older, married, or female persons, and hence are more likely to place themselves in situations where victimisation exposure is increased. Moreover, younger persons may suffer a higher risk of violent victimisation than older persons because the former are more likely to associate with other youth who are themselves disproportionately involved in violence.

The limitations of lifestyle-routine activity theory and research have been discussed at length elsewhere. The most common criticism of empirical research has been the inadequate measurement of explanatory variables; demographic and social characteristics of individuals are used primarily as proxies or indirect indicators for lifestyle activities that persons engage in routinely. Social and demographic characteristics are argued to have effects on the risk of victimisation because they determine, to a large extent, "systematic differences in role-structured behaviour" via differences in expectations, constraints, opportunities, and preferences for activities. The principal critique of much of the multivariate literature is thus that direct measures of lifestyle activities are not included in the models containing social and demographic characteristics. Consequently, the effects of routine activities or specific behaviours have not been distinctly separated from the ascribed and achieved characteristics of victims. Exactly what types of behaviours put individuals at higher risk for violence has not yet received thorough attention.

Exceptions to the lack of direct indicators of lifestyle include measures of activities such as employment status that specifically ascertain what people do during a relatively large portion of their day. The extent of nighttime activities away from the home is also considered to be a direct measure of lifestyle in that activities away from home and activities typically occurring at night are assumed to be more likely to involve either decreased guardianship or increased contact with offenders. These factors-nighttime and daytime activities away from the home-were considered by Miethe et al. (1987) in their analysis of violent victimisation. They found that although extent of nighttime activity significantly and positively influenced risk of violent victimisation, the effect was smaller in magnitude than most of the other demographic variables considered. Furthermore, the inclusion of these activity measures did not significantly attenuate the magnitude of the effects of sex, income, marital status, and age. Major daytime activity as measured was found to have no significant independent effect on risk of violent victimisation.

In light of these findings, Miethe et al. conclude that there is "little support for the mediational role of routine activity/ lifestyle variables on the demographic correlates of violent victimisation.". By contrast, there were much larger effects of lifestyle on theft victimisation. These findings are intriguing but not definitive. First, nighttime activity was measured as a dichotomy and consequently may underestimate victimisation risk for persons who engage in night activities most often. Second, as measured, this variable was not able to capture the nature of away-from-home activities, nor whether particular activities were engaged in alone or with strangers, friends, or family. Third, the measurement of the major activity variable was constructed on the basis of predictability of behaviours. In other words, persons in school were included in the same category as the employed because they presumably depart and return to their homes at predictable times during the day-an element of routine activities assumed to be of interest to motivated offenders.

However, as analyzed, the comparison group for major activity included homemakers, retirees, those unable to work, and the unemployed. Thus, included in one category was those with high risks (the unemployed) and low risks (homemakers and retirees). Measurement problems, then, may have been responsible for the lack of effect of major daytime activity on the risk of violent victimisation. More direct tests of lifestyle-routine activity hypotheses have been conducted with data from countries other than the United States. Similar examinations have not been conducted for the general U.S.

population, primarily because the major source of victimisation data-the NCS-does not include measures of routine activities detailed enough for adequate assessment of lifestyle-routine activity hypotheses. Indeed, the lack of direct measures coupled with the rarity of personal violence has made lifestyle-routine activity hypotheses of violence extremely difficult to test with U.S. data. On the other hand, direct measures of routine activities derived from foreign data sets-especially the number of nights per week out alone, type of activity typically engaged in at night, mode of transportation used, extent of drinking, and self-reported offending behaviours-have been significantly linked to the risk of personal victimisation. Corrado et al. (1980), for instance, found a similar demographic pattern in Canadian data compared to that in the United States. However, the inclusion of a crude measure of out-of-home activities (divided at the median) had a significant effect on the risk of violent victimisation (robbery, assault, and sexual assault): persons who spent more time away from home were approximately three times more likely to be victimized than persons who centered their time at home.

The inclusion of this variable did not attenuate the effects of sex and age but did decrease the magnitude of the effect of marital status. Smith (1982) similarly finds that those out-of-home activities that increase contact with strangers are most victimogenic. Similarly, Hough and Mayhew (1983), van Dijk and Steinmetz (1983), and Gottfredson (1984) found that frequency and type of nighttime activities are related to the risk of violence. In particular, Gottfredson (1984) reports that the use of public transportation and nighttime activities such as drinking or going out to pubs increase personal victimisation in Great Britain whereas activities such as attending church are associated with lower risk.

Also, using data from Great Britain, Hough and Mayhew (1983) found that the frequency of nighttime activity combined with the extent of drinking was important for determining the level of risk among persons under 30 years of age. Finally, Kennedy and Forde (1990), using Canadian data, examined the relative effects of a variety of routine activities on assault and robbery victimisation. They report that certain types of activities-especially how often one goes to bars or takes walks at night-are directly related to the risks of violent victimisation.

Furthermore, these effects persisted despite statistical controls for traditional demographic factors (age, sex, and family income) and neighborhood characteristics (e.g., percent single person households and percent low income families). In sum, recent analyses strongly suggest that details concerning the type and extent of daytime and nighttime activities are necessary for adequately assessing lifestyle-routine activity models of violent victimisation. Previous analyses using the NCS data have been limited because of the unavailability of measures such as the type of nighttime activities engaged in, the use of public transportation, drinking, and other self-reported deviance such as offending.

It is thus possible that the patterns regarding direct effects of lifestyle are unique to countries such as Great Britain, where cultural and structural conditions (e.g., racial composition) are quite different. Consequently, we can only speak generally about individual-level lifestyle factors associated with the risk of violent victimisation for the U.S. population as a whole, and we are unable to specify precisely why it is that traditional social and demographic factors (including age, sex, race, and employment status) are related to differences in the risk of violent victimisation. Clearly, future research on violence needs to focus more specifically on the development of individual-level measures necessary to test lifestyle-routine activity hypotheses using U.S. data.

RISK FACTORS IN VIOLENT OFFENDING

Having reviewed the individual-level factors underlying the risk of violent victimisation, we now turn our attention to the issue of violent *offending*. This section is similar in scope to the previous section in that we review basic individual-level correlates. For example, we focus on questions such as: How are the individual-level factors of age, sex, race, socioeconomic status, and family structure related to the likelihood of committing violent crimes? Are these patterns consistent across sources of data? Have they remained stable over time? Also, what are the current limitations of individual-level analyses of violent offending? Prior research on individual-level correlates of offending has discussed in great detail the methodological issues that may limit the generalizability of findings; therefore, we will mention only a few of these limitations here. One of the primary concerns is the source of data on offending-whether or not the findings are based on official, self-report, or victimisation data.

Findings based on official data (e.g., UCR arrest data or imprisonment data) are limited to the extent that apprehended offenders differ in some way from non apprehended offenders, whereas findings based on self-report surveys may be limited either by the respondents' intentional or unintentional errors in reporting or by sampling restrictions (e.g., an almost exclusive focus on juveniles or males).

A third source of data-the NCS-also provides information on the *perceived* age, race, and sex of offenders; however, it should be reiterated that victims have been found to underreport certain types of incidents, especially those involving victimisations by family members and acquaintances. These potential sources of error should be kept in mind as we review the correlates of violent offending. Age is one of the major individual-level correlates of violent offending. In general, arrests for violent crime peak around age 18 and decline gradually thereafter. More than two-thirds of those arrested for violent crimes are age 30 or younger. The relationship between age and violent crime is less peaked than that for age and property crime in that a larger proportion of violent crimes are committed by persons over age 20. In other words, the age-specific rate of violent offending declines more gradually and after a later peak, than the age-specific rate of property offending. Victim reports of offender characteristics in NCS data support the age patterns found in UCR data: victims estimate that the majority of (lone) violent offenders are less than 30 years of age. Steffensmeier et al. (1989) also report that there are differences in age distributions within types of violent crime. Analyzing 1980 UCR data, they report that the mean age of offenders arrested for robbery (17 years) is lower than the mean age of homicide (19 years) or assault (21 years) arrestees. Personal offenses against family members peak even later, at about 24 years old. Furthermore, the age distribution for robbery is much more peaked than the normal distribution whereas age distributions for other violent offenses are flatter than normal. These analyses suggest that robbery offending declines more rapidly with age than does assault or homicide offending, especially when these crimes are committed against family members. The NCS victim reports support these findings; the estimated age distribution for lone robbery offenders is more peaked than the estimated age distributions for assault and rape offending.

Even though sex is one of the strongest demographic correlates of violent offending, analyses of violence have concentrated almost exclusively on male offending. Consequently, detailed accounts of male-female differences in violent offending are rare. When sex differences are examined, males are far more likely than females to be arrested for all crimes of violence including homicide, rape, robbery, and assault. Females constitute, on average, only 11 percent of arrestees for all of these crimes (U.S. Department of Justice, 1988a); however, the proportion of female offenders arrested for the crime of rape (1%) is estimated to be far lower. The NCS data closely parallel findings from UCR arrest data in that approximately 14 percent of (lone) violent offenders were reported by their victims to be female.

Hill and Harris (1981) compared sex-specific arrest rates for violent crimes using 1953 and 1977 UCR arrest data. They found that in 1953, males were approximately five times more likely than females to be arrested for murder. The ratios for manslaughter (12 to 1), robbery (23 to 1), and aggravated assault (5 to 1) indicate that females were much less involved in violent offending than were males in the early 1950s (1981:661). Robbery offending in particular, along with rape offending, appears to be the most disproportionately male crime. By 1977 these sex ratios had changed to 6 to 1 for murder, 9 to 1 for manslaughter, 13 to 1 for robbery, and 4 to 1 for aggravated assault. Therefore, although sex-specific *rates* for all crimes increased over this period, the 1977 *ratios* suggest that the proportion of violent crimes committed by females increased more quickly over these two decades for the crimes of manslaughter, robbery, and aggravated assault. Only for the crime of murder has there been a greater acceleration in the male crime rate than in the female crime rate. Smith and Visher (1980) conducted a meta-analysis of studies investigating the sex-crime relationship to examine the extent to which statistical associations varied according to study characteristics. They found that, overall, the relationship between sex and crime is greater when violent and officially recorded crimes are examined (versus property offenses and self-reports) and is greater among whites than nonwhites. They also found that the magnitude of the sex-crime association has decreased slightly over time, supporting the findings reported by Hill and Harris (1981). Simon and Baxter (1989) reach a similar conclusion in their analysis of cross-cultural data on female homicide offending rates: women continue to play a minor role in violent offending around the world.

Race is another individual-level factor found to be substantially related to violent offending. Although whites are arrested for the majority of all violent crimes (approximately 52%), blacks are significantly overrepresented in arrest data: blacks comprise 47 percent of violent crime arrestees yet constitute 12 percent of the U.S. population (U.S. Department of Justice, 1988a). For persons under 18 years of age, the ratio of black to white arrest rates for violent offenses is approximately 9 to 1. The NCS victim reports support the finding of disproportionate black involvement in violent crime, but these data suggest that the race and violent crime association may not be quite as strong. Victims report that in long-offender violent crime incidents, blacks constituted about 25 percent of the offenders. This percentage varies by crime type; black representation was higher in rape and robbery incidents, whereas white representation was higher in assaults.

Hindelang (1978) has investigated the extent to which black over-representation in official data is due to differential involvement in violent crime or to differential selection into the criminal justice system via arrests by police. In comparing the distribution of arrestees by race from the 1974 UCR to the distribution of perceived race of offenders derived from the 1974 NCS, he found some evidence for the differential selection hypothesis with respect to assault and rape.

Overall, though, NCS victim reports suggest that most of the race difference found in arrest rates for violence is due to greater black involvement in personal crimes, especially robbery. For example, in 1974 both the NCS and the UCR estimate the proportion of black offenders committing robbery to be 62 percent. We compared similar data for personal violent crimes using 1987 NCS and 1987 UCR data and found much the same pattern as reported earlier by Hindelang (1978). However, we found a somewhat larger discrepancy between the two estimates of racial involvement. For instance, the NCS estimate of the extent of black involvement in robbery in 1987 is 51 percent, whereas the UCR data show that 63 percent of robbery arrestees were black. These differences between UCR and NCS data do not necessarily indicate a change in the underlying relationship between race and violence, particularly if race is related to group versus lone offending and this changed over time. In the 1987 data there was also a higher proportion of reported "other" racial group involvement in violent crime than in 1974.

Each of the above ascribed characteristics of individuals combines to produce substantial variation in age-race-sex-specific offending rates. In particular, Hindelang (1981) has examined rape, robbery, and assault offending rates (estimated from 1973 through 1977 NCS data) for demographic subgroups. The subgroup with the highest rate of offending for each of these crimes was 18- to 20-year-old black males. Black males of all ages had rates of offending that were higher than those estimated for white males. Overall, offending rates were approximately three, five, and fourteen times greater among black males compared to white males for the crimes of assault, rape, and robbery, respectively. Female rates of violent offending were substantially lower than male rates with one exception-white males ages 12 to 17 had offending rates for robbery and assault that were roughly comparable to those of black females of the same age. Between ages 18 and 20, white males' violent offending rates increase (as do rates for black males), but black and white female rates decline.

Apparently, females are most likely to engage in violent offending before age 17, whereas male involvement peaks somewhat later (between 18 and 20 years of age). Race differences among females for assault offending are roughly the same magnitude as those among males, whereas female race differences for robbery are less pronounced than male race differences in part because of lower level of involvement in robbery offending. Laub and McDermott (1985) report that between 1973 and 1981 there was a decline in race differences among female juvenile offenders for assault crimes and that this decline could be attributed to a decrease in black female offending. The limitations of these findings are discussed at length by Hindelang (1981), including the concern that race-age-sex estimates are based solely on NCS victim reports of lone offender crimes and that the NCS data produce incidence rates instead of prevalence rates. This problem of incidence rates versus prevalence rates is important to the extent that each age-race-sex subgroup contains different proportions of repeat offenders. The UCR data share a similar limitation in that arrest incidents (and not offenders) are used as the unit of analysis. The potential inaccuracy of victims' reports of an offender's age, race, and perhaps sex in the NCS data is also a concern but is not considered a serious limitation.

Hindelang (1981), for example, compared NCS rape victims' reports of their offender's age and race to police reports of the offender's demographic characteristics and found substantial agreement. Victims' reports of race agreed with police reports in more than 96 percent of the cases.

Similarly, the accuracy of age estimates was very good (89% or higher) and was highest for offenders less than 20 (96%) and more than 45 years of age (96%). Of course, these findings are not definitive because arrests are often made on the basis of victims' descriptions of offenders. Bridges and Weis (1989) conducted a meta-analysis of correlations reported in studies examining sex, race, and violent crime. They found that variation in the magnitudes of these relationships across studies was related to differences in the level of the data used (e.g., individuals, households, cities, etc.) and whether the analysis was based on offenders as opposed to victims.

In the case of sex, male-female differences were greater in violent offending than in violent victimisation. For race effects, analyses of offender data produced greater race-violence coefficients than did analyses of victimisation. The presence of statistical controls diminished the effect of race on violence but had no effect on the overall magnitude of the sex-violence relationship. Consequently, their results suggest that the relationship between sex and violent offending is strong and stable, whereas the association between race and violent crime is particularly sensitive to the level of analysis and the presence or absence of statistical controls.

SOCIO-ECONOMIC AND FAMILY FACTORS

The association between social class and violent offending continues to be one of the most contested relationships in the literature. Hindelang et al. (1979) and others have noted the methodological problems in this area: "Unlike sex and race, social class data are not available for either UCR arrestees or for offenders in victimisation surveys. Thus, if understanding the relationship of social class to serious offending is our aim, data limitations are much more severe for social class than for sex or race". The reliance, then, on self-report data has led to questions concerning the validity of such data for examining violent crime. Still, Hindelang et al. (1979) have argued that the self-report method is capable of dealing with serious offending behaviour and, further, that no evidence of differential self-report validity has been found by social class. Bridges and Weis (1989), in their meta-analysis, also examined variation in the social class-violent crime association. They report, as did Hindelang et al. (1979), that much of the discrepancy in findings across studies of violent offending is due to the level of analysis and to the presence or absence of statistical controls. As was true for race, they found that the magnitude of association between social class and violent offending decreased when individual-level data were used and when statistical controls for correlates of violence were included. The type of data used (i.e., official versus self-report) also had a marginal effect on the relationship; findings that used official data show a stronger negative effect than findings based on other sources. With the exception of Thornberry and Farnworth (1982) and the vast research in the area of family violence, most of the recent literature directly examining social class and violence has been based on samples of adolescents. For example, Elliott and Ageton (1980) used self-report data from a nationally representative sample of 1,716 adolescents in the National Youth Survey and found that social class (based on a comparison of middle-, working-, and lower-class youth) was negatively related to the mean frequency of predatory crimes against persons (a scale including robbery and aggravated, simple, or sexual assault).

This relationship was due in part to the differences across social classes in high-frequency offending. The authors also found an interaction between race and class, which suggests that lower-class black youth were particularly likely to report higher levels of involvement in these personal violence offenses. Elliott and Huizinga (1983) report more extensive data from the National Youth Survey on the relationship between social class and offense-specific prevalence and incidence scales of violence for both males and females. In analyzing several waves of this longitudinal data base, their results suggest that class differences are more apparent when incidence measures as opposed to prevalence measures are used. They also find class differences in the frequency of minor and felony assault by males such that lower-class youth are more likely to commit offenses than middle-class youth.

Few differences were found between middle-and working-class or working-and lower-class males. Among females there were comparable class differences in levels of felony assault but no differences in minor assault levels. A more extensive analysis of female offending behaviour using the National Youth Survey found class effects for aggravated assault offending in the first two waves of data and for involvement in gang fighting in four out of five waves of data. In these instances, lower-class females, like males, were more likely to report involvement in assaults against persons. The above research emphasizes the importance of the measurement of violent offending; findings using incidence measures may differ from findings using prevalence measures. Additionally, the measurement of "social class" is a concern.

Although there appears to be differential involvement in serious violent offending by social class, these findings depend to some extent on the conceptualization and operationalisation of the social class measure. Brownfield (1986) finds that the strength of the class-violence relationship among individuals varies depending on whether a neo-Marxist conception of class categories is used, versus a more gradational measure of socioeconomic status that combines occupation and education measures. A small relationship was found in two studies of youth using the gradational measure, but none was found using the alternative measure.

Additional limitations of the class-violence literature are discussed by Thornberry and Farnworth (1982), who argue that although the overall relationship between class and juvenile violence is weak, the relationship among adults may be stronger. In fact, they found in a reanalysis of Wolfgang's (1958) Philadelphia cohort data that for white adults the father's occupational status was negatively related to violent behaviour, whereas for black adults the respondent's own education level was negatively related to arrests for violence. The causal implications of these findings are not yet clear-it is possible that there is a reciprocal relationship between the social class of an adult and levels of criminality. Among juveniles this is less problematic, but it is an issue that has not yet been adequately resolved.

FAMILY STRUCTURE AND PROCESS

There are at least three ways in which family factors have been examined in the literature on violent offending. The first pertains to the marital status of offenders. Studies of prison inmates have found that most offenders are not married (78 percent) and that white inmates are disproportionately divorced or separated. Black inmates, on the other hand, are just as likely not to be married as blacks in the general population. These findings, of course, are quite limited. We do not know whether an offender's marital status is a consequence of his or her offending behaviour, and data representing the prison population may not be representative of the overall population of violent offenders. Consequently, the meaning of these findings is unclear.

Second, and more importantly, family structure and intervening "family processes" have been correlated with aggression and other serious criminal behaviours among children and adolescents. The relationship between juvenile delinquency and these family factors has been reviewed extensively elsewhere, but we find that studies focusing exclusively on family factors and violent behaviour are rare. This is, perhaps, to be expected given that we are focusing our discussion on those serious violent behaviours not typically engaged in by youth. Nonetheless, extant research suggests that children living in "broken" homes are slightly more likely to engage in aggressive behaviours than children living in two-parent homes. However, the magnitude of this relationship is weak, and these results are not unanimous across adolescent subgroups or types of aggressive behaviours.

Rankin (1983) also reports a small effect of family structure on fighting (children in single-parent homes are more likely to report fighting), but no differences in other assaultive behaviours. Research on family functioning or intervening family processes typically examines factors such as parental neglect, punishment styles, punitive ness, marital conflict, parental attitudes toward deviance, and parental criminality for their effects on children's offending behaviours. Parental neglect in the form of either lack of supervision or lack of other involvement has been found to be positively related to aggressive behaviours in children. Punishment styles of parents are also related to aggressiveness and serious criminality: yelling, threatening, and hitting children is associated with increased aggressive behaviours among children. Factors such as marital discord and conflict have similarly shown positive, but small, associations with aggression and serious criminality. Finally, parental criminality also tends to show a positive correlation with aggression among children as does parental aggressiveness and paternal alcoholism.

Loeber and Stouthamer-Loeber (1986) summarize in tabular form the overall relationships between these family factors and juvenile delinquency. In general, family functioning or process variables such as those discussed above were more consistently associated with delinquency than were family structure variables. Recent multivariate analyses focusing exclusively on violent behaviour (assault, robbery) also suggest that the quality of family life may be more important than family structure. For example, Van Voorhis et al. (1988) found that family structure had no independent effect on violent behaviour (fighting and assault combined), whereas overall home quality was negatively and significantly related to violence. Although there are many methodological limitations in the family-aggressive behaviour literature, these findings suggest that family functioning may be a more important factor than family structure and that more explicit attention should be paid to the effects of family functioning on juvenile aggression and its relationship to later violent offending as an adult.

A third, related, way in which family factors have been studied with respect to violence has been in the "cycle of violence" or "violence breeds violence" literature. These recent and extensive reviews suggest that the research on intergenerational transmission of violence is inconclusive and plagued with methodological problems. Although there is agreement concerning the correlation between suffering abuse as a child and perpetrating abuse as adults, the magnitude of the relationship is quite small and many violent offenders report no history of child abuse. It is also the case that most abused children do not go on to commit abusive or violent acts as adults. Consequently, recent analyses have sought to discover the factors that break the "cycle of violence."

Kruttschnitt et al. (1987) report that children who suffer from emotional neglect (in addition to physical abuse) and who have no emotional support system inside or outside the home are more likely to be abusive as adults. Widom (1989a) found that age at the time of abuse, sex, temperament, and intelligence were protective factors from future involvement in violence. However, Widom argues for caution when interpreting these results: to say that certain factors appear to protect children from perpetuating future violence does not imply that the effects of child abuse are eliminated. The effects may be manifested in other ways, including depression, anxiety, or even suicide, and these links have not been adequately assessed. A variety of other factors have been studied in conjunction with violent behaviour among juveniles including analyses of school achievement and attachment, associations with delinquent peers, and prior involvement in crime. Perhaps surprisingly, analyses of school and peer factors and their relationship to violence have not been as extensive as investigations of relationships discussed earlier (e.g., age, sex, social class). Nevertheless, small and relatively consistent effects have been reported.

Friedman and Rosenbaum (1988) found that time spent doing homework was inversely related to juvenile assault and robbery offending, and that time spent with delinquent peers was positively related to juvenile violence (this is also consistent with Elliott et al.'s, 1985, analysis of "index" offending). Liska and Reed (1985) considered the reciprocal effects that parental attachment, school attachment, and violence might have on each other. They found that for white males, parental attachment decreased violent behaviour and that violent delinquency led to future decreases in both school and parental attachment.

They argue that for white males at least, "parents, not the school, are the major institutional sources of delinquency control" (1985:558) and that their findings imply that factors associated with school attachment and achievement may be *consequences* of violence and not causal factors. Finally, it should be noted that by distinguishing prevalence of offending from incidence (or frequency) of offending, "criminal career" research suggests that certain individuals are disproportionately involved in violent offending. However, research by Blumstein et al. (1988) and Farrington et al. (1988) suggests that offenders do not typically "specialize" in violent crimes such as homicide, assault, and robbery, and that "escalation" in terms of the seriousness of offending over periods of time is not common. A possible exception to the lack of specialization holds for persons who have prior involvement in robbery. Overall, "the more impulsive, violent crimes of homicide, rape, and weapons violations were among the least specialized". Consequently, although violent offenders often have prior records of extensive involvement in crime, the prediction of violence from these records is very difficult. Of all the individual-level correlates discussed above, ascribed demographic characteristics appear to have the strongest associations with violent offending. Sex and age are clearly and consistently associated with all forms of violent behaviour, whereas race and social class have smaller and less consistent relationships to violent offending.

Family structure and functioning are associated with juvenile violence and aggression, but multivariate analyses suggest that family functioning or process variables such as parental neglect and punishment styles (i.e., quality of family life) are more important than family structure characteristics (i.e., one versus two parents). Physical abuse as a child also appears to be related to future violent behaviour, but the reasons for this association are not yet clearly understood. Other correlates of violence such as school attachment and achievement are even smaller in magnitude, and causal analyses suggest that school factors may not be as important as family factors or other social and demographic characteristics. Finally, although violent offenders typically have prior criminal records, the prediction of future violence from these records has been extremely difficult.

As noted throughout the above discussion, much of the extant literature in each of the areas relating social factors to violent offending suffers from methodological or causal interpretation limitations.

These limitations include sampling (e.g., a focus on males or juveniles only, unrepresentative samples), the domain of the dependent variable (studies of specific violent crimes are surprisingly rare), analytical techniques (multivariate statistical controls are also rare), issues of causal direction (temporal ordering and reciprocal effects are typically ignored), the general failure to distinguish participation in violent offending from frequency of violent offending, and the paucity of studies examining the intervening mechanisms and social processes that might explain the effects of demographic factors such as age, race, and sex. An equally important limitation of prior individual-level analyses of both violent offending and victimisation is that they generally have not considered the possible effects that situational-or community-level factors might have on an individual's experiences with violence.

It is possible that individual-level correlates of victimisation and offending are the same because of the structural or situational contexts in which particular demographic subgroups typically find themselves. Situational-level variables or community-level factors may thus be responsible for a small or large portion of the individual-level risk for violent victimisation and offending.

Additionally, individual-level research has for the most part treated victims of violence and violent offenders as though they were mutually exclusive groups. The remainder of the chapter therefore considers the additional and perhaps crucial role of victim-offender relationships and the structural context-both situational and community-in which violence occurs. Our contention is that a consideration of these other levels of analysis may help to better explicate the sources of both violent victimisation and offending.

9

Domestic Violence against Children

IN AFGHANISTAN AND SRI LANKA

To date, research on the psychosocial consequences of mass trauma resulting from war and organized violence on children has primarily focused on the individual as the unit of treatment and analysis with particular focus on mental disorders caused by traumatic stress. This body of research has stimulated the development of promising individual-level treatment approaches for addressing psychological trauma. In contrast, there is virtually no literature addressing the effects of mass trauma on the family and community systems. Research conducted in Sri Lanka and Afghanistan, two long-standing war-torn societies, found that in addition to multiple exposures to war or disaster-related traumatic events children also indicated high levels of exposure to family violence.

These findings point to the need for conjoint family and community-based programmes of prevention and intervention that are specifically tailored for the context of the affected society. In particular, programmes should take issues such as poverty, child labor, and parental alcohol use into account in assessing and treating children in the aftermath of mass trauma.

There are currently over 40 wars and armed conflicts occurring throughout the world, including the highly publicized wars in Iraq and Afghanistan. These wars are characterized by high levels of violence against the civilian population that impact society at multiple levels, including the individual, family, and community. Children are a particularly vulnerable group who often suffer from devastating long-term consequences of experienced or witnessed acts of violence. Child survivors of war must cope with repeated traumatic life events, such as the loss of loved ones, displacement, lack of food, and interruption of school and other aversive experiences, all of which can hamper the healthy development of a child and his or her ability to function adequately even after the violence has ceased.

Research studies on the psychological consequences of war on children have primarily focused on the individual and have shown increased rates of mental disorders in traumatized children, particularly posttraumatic stress disorder (PTSD). PTSD is a chronic disorder that can develop following traumatic events. Symptoms of PTSD may include intrusive thoughts, flashbacks, or nightmares; avoidance behaviours; and increased levels of arousal. PTSD is thought to have particularly harmful effects on children's social, affective, and cognitive development. Many studies in various war zones of varying cultures have reported high rates of PTSD in children. For example, Saigh (1991) found that 20% of Lebanese children who had been exposed to bombings and terror attacks met the DSM-IV criteria for PTSD. In another study, Thabet and Vostanis (1999, 2000) showed that 41% of Palestinian children from Gaza reported moderate to severe PTSD symptoms.

Results from studies conducted by our research team and colleagues at the University of Konstanz and vivo Foundation have demonstrated similar findings of high PTSD prevalence rates in child survivors of war and organized violence. In 2005, Ruf and colleagues interviewed 102 refugee children living in Germany, who were seeking asylum from countries affected by war and other forms of organized violence. The authors found that 19.6% of children met the criteria for PTSD. Schaal and Elbert (2006) found a prevalence rate of 44% in surviving orphans 10 years after the Rwandan genocide. Most recently, an epidemiological survey of Tamil school-children exposed to war in the northeastern provinces of Sri Lanka revealed that 1925% of the sample was suffering from PTSD. Epidemiological studies in war-affected populations have found that cumulative exposure to trauma is one of the major risk factors for PTSD in children and adults. For example, the prevalence of PTSD in Sri Lankan children affected by both the civil war and a natural disaster was as high as 40% after the tsunami. Thus, a high level of mental disorders, especially PTSD, has been identified in war-torn populations as a result of extensive violence.

TREATMENT OF WAR-TRAUMATIZED CHILDREN

Given the pervasiveness of war and conflict-related trauma, especially in resource-poor countries, interventions tailored to a large group of survivors are especially important. However, treatment outcome studies in this field are still scarce. Many interventions were derived from methods developed for adults, such as cognitive behavioural therapy (CBT). The recent guidelines of the British National Institute for Clinical Excellence (NICE) recommend psychotherapeutic treatments like CBT that involve talking about the traumatic experience in detail (i.e., exposure methods) in favor of anxiety management approaches or medications. Most controlled clinical trials employing CBT for traumatized children have focused on victims of sexual abuse living in industrialized countries.

One exception is a study by Goenjian and colleagues (1997) in which a school-based grief-and-trauma-focused CBT intervention effectively decreased symptoms of depression in teens following the earthquake in Armenia. Other interventions currently used with children include psychopharmacological treatments, play therapy, psychological debriefing, and testimony therapy. Many of these approaches have not been tested in randomized clinical trials nor have they been used with post-conflict populations of children and adolescents living in non-industrialised countries. Our team developed Narrative Exposure Therapy (NET) as a standardized short-term approach based on the principles of cognitive behavioural exposure therapy by adapting the classical form of exposure therapy to meet the needs of traumatized survivors of war and torture. In exposure therapy, the patient is requested to repeatedly talk about the worst traumatic event in detail while re-experiencing all emotions that are associated with this event. In the process, the majority of patients undergo a habituation of the emotional response to the traumatic memory, which consequently leads to a remission of PTSD symptoms. As most of the victims of organized violence have experienced many traumatic events, it is often impossible to identify the worst event before treatment. To overcome this difficulty, we based our approach on Testimony Therapy (TT), a method of therapy created by Lira and Weinstein to treat traumatized survivors of the Pinochet regime in Chile. Instead of donning a single event as a target in therapy, the patient constructs a narration about his whole life from birth up to the present situation while focusing on the detailed report of the traumatic experiences.

The focus of the NET procedure is twofold. As with exposure therapy, one goal is to reduce the symptoms of PTSD by confronting the patient with the memories of the traumatic event. However, recent theories of PTSD and emotional processing suggest that the habituation of the emotional responses is only one mechanism to improve-ment of symptoms. Other theories suggest that the distortion of the explicit autobiographic memory about traumatic events leads to a fragmented narrative of the traumatic memories, which results in the maintenance of PTSD symptoms. Thus, the reconstruction of autobiogra-phic memory and a consistent narrative should be used in conjunction with exposure therapy. NET puts a focus on both methods, the habituation of emotional responding to reminders of the traumatic event and the construction of a detailed narrative of the event and its consequences.

NET has been tested in a variety of countries and settings with refugee adults and children who suffer from PTSD. For example, results from one randomized controlled trial with Sudanese refugees comparing NET with supportive counseling (SC) and psycho education (PE) showed significant treatment effects for NET 1 year post-treatment, with 29% of refugees meeting DSM-IV criteria for PTSD compared to 79% for the SC group and 80% for the PE group. The efficacy of KIDNET, a version of NET adapted for use with children, has also been tested in a pilot study with Somali refugee children diagnosed with PTSD. Results of the study demonstrated a significant reduction in symptoms immediately following the completion of the KIDNET treatment.

The treatment effects were even more pronounced at the 9-month follow-up, indicating that KIDNET is a promising intervention to treat children with war-related trauma. Very recently, several randomized controlled treatment trials with KIDNET have been completed in post-conflict settings such as Rwanda and Sri Lanka as well as with traumatized child war survivors in Germany. Results consistently showed the successful application of KIDNET with traumatized children and adolescents leading to considerable symptom reduction, to the extent that the majority no longer met the diagnostic criteria for PTSD after treatment.

THE CONTEXT OF WAR IN AFGHANISTAN

A quarter century of conflict in Afghanistan has led to a countless number of civilian casualties and displacement amongst Afghan nationals. Despite the first democratic elections in 2005, security has not yet returned to the country. Hundreds of Afghans have died in disputes over recent years, and violence and threats by the Taliban and other militant groups continue to destabilize peace and safety of the population. Civilians are still suffering from disabling physical and psychological consequences of the violence that has characterized the country over the last two decades. Even though younger children in Afghanistan were not directly exposed to war related events, such as bombings, physical attacks, or killings of others, they still suffer from indirect consequences of the war. Several families are impoverished and lack the basic necessities such as food and shelter. Many are reliant on the earning capacity of their children for survival. A survey published in 2002 found child labor to be a common problem in the Afghan urban community. In Kabul alone, 36,000 children were reported to be working as carpet weavers. Previous studies evaluating the mental health status of Afghans exposed to violent conflicts reported a high incidence of traumatic experiences in adults. Psychopathology was also reported to be high with both men and women exhibiting symptoms of depression, PTSD, and other anxiety disorders. A qualitative study in the Herat province reported a general increase in psychosomatic problems, anxiety, depression, and family violence, indicating the harmful effects that parental traumatisation can subsequently have on children.

WAR AND NATURAL DISASTER IN SRI LANKA

In Sri Lanka's northeastern provinces, traumatic experiences were already common prior to the tsunami in December 2004. For two decades, thousands of people have been killed and many more were displaced as a result of conflict and violence in the country. The Liberation Tigers of Tamil Elam (LTTE) has been fighting for political autonomy, which resulted in ongoing conflict in the northern and eastern areas of the country. Civilians have become casualties of war; landmines and unexploded ordnance pose a constant threat; hospitals and schools have been destroyed; and the economy has been shattered. In spite of a cease-fire that was called in December 2001, violent incidences between the LTTE and the government have dramatically intensified, costing the lives of nearly 3,000 people in the last year alone.

INCREASE OF DOMESTIC VIOLENCE IN SRI LANKA AND AFGHANISTAN

Recently, we have carried out two surveys of school-attending children in Sri Lanka and Afghanistan. Data were collected in the Dashti Barchi area of Kabul, Afghanistan, and the Vadamarachi school district (Point Pedro area) at the northern tip of Sri Lanka. Dashti Barchi is an urban district in the Afghani capital Kabul which, in the past, has been particularly affected by war and violence because of the Taliban regime. Point Pedro and the surrounding northeastern part of Sri Lanka have been exposed to two decades of civil war and, more recently, to the tsunami. In Kabul, 287 children from age 7 to 14 from two schools participated in the screening. In Sri Lanka, 286 children from age 9 to 15 from 15 different schools in the Vadamarachi educational zone took part in the survey.

Socio-economically, the two samples were comparable. Both reported a relatively poor living standard, particularly with respect to the number of family possessions (beds, mats, kitchen utensils, etc.). As expected, there were similarities as well as remarkable differences with regard to the impact of war experiences on children in these two societies. In Afghanistan, the number of war-related event types was only moderately high, with 39% of the children reporting at least one type of war-related traumatic event during their lives. Given the young age of the sample interviewed, a higher exposure to war events was not expected as the majority of the armed conflict occurred before their births. In contrast, the Tamil northeastern province in Sri Lanka is politically unstable and insecure, resulting in frequent incidences of violence affecting the civil population, including children.

This was mirrored in the children's reports of their war-related experiences. Almost half of the interviewed sample (48.6%) had experienced at least one event related to war in the past year. The great majority of children (82.4%) reported at least one war-related event during their lifetimes, and 47.6% of the interviewed group had experienced three or more war-related event types. In addition to war experiences, children in both samples frequently reported a high degree of domestic violence. The term domestic violence is being used here to encompass the range of violence that might take place within and across different family subsystems (e.g., inter-partner, parent-child, and sibling-sibling). Afghani children had experienced or witnessed an average of 4.3 different types of violent incidences at home with the majority of children (54.1%) reporting three or more event types. In Sri Lanka, rates were higher with children having experienced or witnessed an average of 5.2 types of events related to family violence.

Even more impressive is the finding that more than half of the sample interviewed in Sri Lanka reported more than five different types of aggression occurring at home. In the majority of the cases studied here, domestic violence was found to be ongoing. Results also indicated that violence at home was not only inflicted on children but on a wider range of family members. Both children in Kabul and children in Point Pedro reported several family members committing physical violence. Wife beating turned out to be a major issue in both samples, reported by 31.5% of Afghan children and 41.2% of children in Sri Lanka. Children in the Tamil sample reported sexual abuse of children and witnessing sexual acts against other family members only rarely.

To do a comparative analysis of these data to rates of domestic violence reported in previous studies with populations from industrialized countries is difficult for two reasons. First, the definition of what constitutes an act of domestic violence is still controversial second, there is a paucity of representative data on child maltreatment prevalence rates. In fact, prevalence data are most often based on official records of legal and social service agencies, on parents' reports through community surveys, or on retrospective population surveys. All three of these methods are assumed to underestimate the actual occurrence of domestic violence. In fact, there are no population-based studies reporting data, which were directly obtained from a representative sample of children. With these cautions in mind, however, available data suggest that children's exposure to domestic violence is a prevalent problem in industrialized countries as well. A survey in the United States based on official records from child protective services and other agencies in the year 2004 reported about 1% of children to be victims of child abuse or neglect. Community surveys such as the study carried out by Strauss, Hamby, Finkelhor, Moore, and Runyan (1997) suggest much higher rates of child abuse and maltreatment. The authors reported prevalence rates for physical abuse of 5% in American children.

Even though the present data are not directly comparable

to surveys on child exposure to domestic violence, tentative conclusions about the severity of family violence can be drawn from indicators such as the frequency of injuries and the need for medical treatment because of the physical abuse at home, as described by the children in our samples. In Kabul, 10% of children reported to have suffered at least one injury resulting from maltreatment at home. In the Sri Lankan sample, this figure reaches 18%, indicating an alarming level of violence experienced by children in their families. Even using a strict criterion of definition of child abuse results in rates higher than in the United States. Other findings from these two studies pointed at major differences between these war torn societies. Whereas no child in Sri Lanka reported child labor (defined as work contributing to the family's income generation), child labor was found to be very common in the Kabul sample, with 39% (49% of the boys vs. 29% of the girls) of schoolchildren reporting daily work. On average, children forced to contribute to the family's income generation worked 6.7 hr/day (SD = 3.01) with a range of 1-13 hr/day.

The majority of children who reported working held jobs as carpet weavers. Seven boys also reported working in small retail stores. Another major difference between the countries refers to drug consumption. In the Afghani sample, drug use (e.g., the use of hashish, alcohol, opium) did not turn out to be a noteworthy issue in children or in parents. In contrast, drug use by fathers appeared to be much more prevalent in Sri Lanka, with 50.5% of the children reporting that their fathers used alcohol and 73.6% reporting use of other types of drugs, including betel nut (34.1%), tobacco (27.9%), and tobacco plus betel nut (37.5%). In the majority of cases, drug use was reported to be an occasional occurrence (once a month); however, 33.5% of children said their fathers use alcohol and/or other drugs more than 3-4 times a week.

TRAUMA AND DOMESTIC VIOLENCE

The commonalities and differences between Afghanistan and Sri Lanka as two examples of war-torn societies are relevant for understanding the impact of mass trauma on children and their families. In countries, the types and degree of domestic violence as an additional source of trauma for children is startling. In regression analyses, a history of war trauma for the child and family size were significant predictors of domestic violence in both samples. In addition, child labor and poverty predicted domestic violence in Afghanistan, and fathers' drug abuse predicted child maltreatment in Sri Lanka. Results from these studies confirm previous findings related to risk factors associated with family violence. In particular, poverty has repeatedly been linked to an increased risk for child abuse even though the interpretation of this finding is still controversial. However, most studies concur that poverty reflects limited family economic resources and support that expose children to additional risk factors, which often leads to an increased potential for domestic violence. Family size has also been reported to be a predictor of domestic child abuse. For instance, Stair (1988) found that larger families present with more violence toward children compared to families with fewer members, hypothesizing that elevated stress and higher economic strain may be related to the increased level of violence.

With regard to parental alcohol use as a predictor of domestic violence, the Sri Lankan sample supported our initial assumption that increased levels of parental use of substances such as alcohol are associated with higher levels of child abuse. In fact, fathers' use of alcohol proved to be a significant predictor of the number of domestic violence experiences of Tamil children. This finding is in line with previous research showing that children of substance-abusing parents are more likely to be exposed to family violence. Beyond these relationships that have also been found in countries experiencing times of peace, one striking finding points toward a difference between countries in war and peace. In both Afghanistan and Sri Lanka, we found a correlation between exposure to war and domestic violence. One explanation might be that the parents of the war-affected children in Sri Lanka and Kabul have experienced more war events themselves. Therefore, the outcome may be in line with previous studies that argue for a link between the traumatizing effects of warfare on men's propensity for domestic abuse. Even with respect to milder and non traumatic stressors in the lives of families, research has shown that stressful life events affect parental violence inflicted on children. Several investigations have found that abusive families report more life stressors than do non-abusive families. Taking into account the potential relationship between war trauma and substance abuse, the alcohol intake in fathers, as reported by the children here, could be related to the individual problems associated with war trauma as suggested by the "self-medication" hypothesis. However, the hypothesized links between war exposure, increased intake of substances, and increased levels of abusive behaviour toward children must be investigated further. These studies would ideally include interviews with both parents and their children.

Summarizing findings from both samples, it can be asserted that children in postwar societies are affected not only by aversive events occurring within the framework of organized violence, but also by family-related stressors, such as domestic violence and parental substance use, and by community-level stressors such as child labor and poverty. There is no one single factor at play. Conversely, it appears as if the interplay of these multilevel stressors leaves families particularly vulnerable to engaging in child abuse.

CONSEQUENCES OF DOMESTIC VIOLENCE FOR CHILDREN

Domestic violence in children-defined by neglect, physical abuse, sexual abuse, and emotional maltreatment experienced or witnessed at home-has been shown to result in detrimental long-term effects on various areas of child development. In particular, PTSD and PTSD symptoms have been linked with sexual and physical abuse experienced during childhood. Maltreatment in childhood is considered to be both a cause and a risk factor for PTSD, with sexual abuse representing a particularly salient risk factor for acute and chronic PTSD, as well as other negative developmental consequences.

Aggression, anxiety, depression, suicidal behaviour, and increased hyperactivity and attention deficit are part of the wide-ranging psychological consequences associated with child abuse. In addition, exposure to domestic violence seems to be associated with long-lasting cognitive impairments. Perez and Widom (1994) showed that child abuse and neglect represent significant risk factors for poor long-term intellectual and academic outcomes. Further evidence proves that child abuse and chronic maltreatment during childhood have significant aversive effects on the child's biological stress systems and on brain development. De Bellis et al. (2001) have extensively summarized the variety of findings in this area and suggest the term "environmentally induced complex developmental disorder" for the psychobiological sequel of child maltreatment.

In addition to childhood trauma experiences resulting from war and/or natural disasters, the alarming number of children exposed to domestic violence found in war countries-taken together with the knowledge about the harmful and lasting consequences of child maltreatment on various levels of children's development-points toward an urgent need for targeted programmes of prevention and intervention that extend beyond individual treatment. Treatment approaches in post-conflict settings should be carefully tailored to fit the specific context and requirements of the given population and address not only the war trauma but also problems present at the family and community level which may arise as an indirect consequence after violent conflict. With respect to individual trauma-focused treatment, the application of psychotherapeutic approaches such as KIDNET with traumatized children and adolescents in post-conflict settings have shown promising first results.

However, future studies must be conducted to better understand particular family dynamics that increase the potential for domestic violence within single families. Findings from our studies point toward potential mechanisms that might take place if the whole family is affected by war-related violence. Traumatization and symptoms of PTSD in adults are typically linked to affect dysregulation and irritability, which might result in aggressive behaviour toward their children. In the most severe cases, particularly if PTSD is a factor, we purport that parents have to be treated with trauma-focused therapy first. Only then can additional family or parenting programmes be effective in changing parenting practices and family dynamics within families characterized by a long history of domestic violence and child maltreatment.

However, studies that include experimental research designs that include multi-component interventions targeting children as well as parents and the family system (as well as the larger community) are sorely needed in order to provide a deeper understanding of the relational impact and dynamics between trauma, domestic violence, and child/family functioning.

Studies that have investigated intervention programmes for child abuse argue for the beneficial effect of parenting and family interventions on parental discipline methods as well as emotional regulation and management of stress affecting the family. Those approaches, including modeling and practice to improve parenting skills, might also be adapted for the specific needs of families in postwar communities experiencing a range of trauma-related symptoms and maladaptive individual and family system functioning, including domestic violence.

In particular, our findings in Sri Lanka highlight another critical problem that must be addressed: alcohol abuse by fathers, which again might be related to traumatic experiences of war violence. Here, addiction therapy needs to be examined in combination with trauma therapy in order to address the core problem (trauma) as well as its consequences (self-medication through alcohol). Marital/couple therapy and parenting programmes for abusive fathers should be finally added to address problems affecting the family system.

Additionally, the fact that poverty and child labor are often found to predict domestic violence points to larger developmental issues present at the community level that cannot be solved with psychosocial individual-level interventions alone. Poverty is a complex and crucial issue, given its intersecting connection to the problems of child labor and child maltreatment.

Alternative forms of earning income must be developed for adults to prevent children from having to participate in the family's wage earning to such a degree that it compromises their healthy emotional and physical development and typically prevents children's ability to seek basic education. Likewise, macro-level policy changes and advocacy for proper monitoring of international child labor regulations are essential components to the sustainable protection of children's rights. Interventions which promote children's rights and psycho-emotional wellbeing must carefully analyze these corroborating factors that often lead to the violation of their human rights.

Although addressing the multiple complexities and endless variables that impact children and families after exposure to mass trauma is daunting, we believe that it is vital that clinical scholars hold these contextual realities and become immersed in understanding the intersection between micro- and macro-level factors as they develop programmes of prevention and intervention for affected communities. We are currently collaborating with a team of family therapists with the vision of developing studies that implement and test narrative exposure therapy in conjunction with parenting and family programmes of intervention. We hope to develop a better understanding of how and in what sequence interventions might be implemented with traumatized populations in different parts of the world to demonstrate effectiveness as well as sustainable improvements in mental health for both children and families.

ADDRESSING BARRIERS TO DEVELOPMENT AND LEARNING

Every day, too many youngsters encounter external and internal barriers that interfere with healthy development and positive learning. This unfortunate reality ultimately makes it difficult for them to become productive members of society. Among those living in poverty, major inequities of opportunity interfere with school readiness, and this contributes to the large proportion of learning and behaviour problems in urban and rural schools, especially those serving economically impoverished families. For all youngsters, a host of interfering factors arises from physical, mental health, and psychosocial concerns such as neighborhood and domestic violence, physical and sexual abuse, exposure to disease, relationship difficulties, school adjustment and attendance problems, encounters with the juvenile justice system, substance abuse, youth pregnancy, dropping out of school, homelessness, and so forth.

This chapter underscores the nature and scope of barriers to young people's development and learning, stresses the importance of collaboration for efforts to address such barriers, and offers a few implications for future policy and practice. With respect to collaboration, the emphasis is on highlighting the value of adopting a unifying concept around which prospective partners can rally and illustrates how one state, New Mexico, is doing this. From the perspective of schooling, barriers to development and learning encompass any factor that interferes with satisfactory performance at school, including factors that make it difficult for teachers to teach effectively. The problems are exacerbated as youngsters face the frustrations of confronting barriers to development and learning and the debilitating effects of performing poorly at school.

The number of youngsters affected is large and growing. How many are affected? Estimates vary. With specific respect to mental health concerns, between 12 percent and 22 percent of all children are described as suffering from a diagnosable mental, emotional, or behavioural disorder, with relatively few receiving mental health services. Of the approximately 20 percent of children with mental health problems, however, 50 to 80 percent do not receive mental health care; 70 to 80 percent of children from disadvantaged families do not receive critical mental health services. If one adds the many others experiencing significant psychosocial problems, the numbers grow dramatically. Harold Hodgkinson, director of the Center for Demographic Policy, estimates that 40 percent of young people are "in very bad educational shape" and "at risk of failing to fulfill their physical and mental promise". The problems these students bring to the school setting often stem from restricted opportunities associated with poverty, difficult and diverse family circumstances, lack of English language skills, violent neighborhoods, and inadequate health care.

The reality for many large urban and poor rural schools is that over 50% of their students manifest learning, behaviour, and emotional problems. One view of this issue is provided by a 1997 survey of 28,000 New Mexico public school students, grades 7 through 12, by the state's Office of Epidemiology in the Department of Health. The survey focused on substance use, self esteem, depressive symptoms, and school behaviour. The number of students abusing substances other than alcohol showed an increase from a previous study done in 1993. Of particular note: Marijuana use increased to approximately 25 percent of boys and 22 percent of girls, and other drugs of abuse, particularly inhalants and crack cocaine, continued to increase. Those who reported any substance use were much more likely to have had problem behaviours at school, such as having stolen things, ditched school, put down others, or hit others on purpose.

Students who reported higher rates of depressive symptoms, such as feeling sad, discouraged or hopeless, also reported more problem behaviours at school. Those reporting high rates of substance use, too, had higher scores on a measure of depressive symptoms (e.g., they too indicated feeling sad, discouraged, and hopeless), raising the suspicion that the students reporting more substance use also were the students reporting depressive symptoms. It was not clear whether the depression these students identified was a result of their substance use or their substance use secondary to self medication for depression. National data indicate that 20 to 40 percent of adolescents with substance abuse problems also may have co-morbid depressive disorders. Similar problems were seen in a "snapshot" study of incarcerated youth done by the New Mexico Children, Youth, and Families Department (1996). Among a sample of approximately 550 incarcerated youth in New Mexico detention facilities in 1995, high proportions reported histories of school failure (67 percent), substance abuse (63 percent), mental health problems (52 percent), special education involvement (36 percent), and abuse and neglect (34 percent).

Among students served by the six school-based health center sites operated through the University of New Mexico in 1997-98, an average of 37 percent of students had a mental health diagnosis or problem. These numbers are particularly large at the middle schools, where more than half of the students seen had primary mental health or substance abuse issues. The most frequent diagnoses were depression and dysthymic disorders, general counseling needs, family disruptions, and academic problems leading to potential adjustment disorders. Many face high rates of poverty, lack of support at home, and multiple stresses that make it hard for them to be successful in a school environment. For many, the problems were so severe as to raise concerns about posttraumatic stress disorder.

Clearly, young people are facing many barriers to their successful development and learning. It is critical to deal with these barriers in ways that enable more youth to achieve successfully in school and become productive members of society. As is widely acknowledged, however, the tendency has been to address these matters in a marginalized and highly fragmented manner in policy and practice. Many of these youth, in fact, often do not end up with the educational supports to which they may be entitled, such as Section 504 of the Rehabilitation Act or the Individual with Disabilities in Education Act (IDEA). Frequently, at least in New Mexico, many of these students are suspended or expelled, or drop out, leaving them on the streets, where they end up in trouble and in the juvenile justice system. In the 1999 Kids Count poll, New Mexico led the nation with the most students in the nation out of school and not working. Many students throughout New Mexico are suspended or expelled from school or drop out without first receiving an adequate assessment of their individual barriers to successful learning. Clearly, New Mexico's data show that a major part of their school behavioural problems are tied to a failure to identify children early who may have mental health or substance abuse issues. Providing such an assessment identifies children at risk for problem behaviours or violence, as well as children with potential disabilities. Unfortunately, the majority of the current school and community processes that are supposed to lead to early identification and intervention for children and teens in New Mexico lack a strong mental health component. Early Periodic Screening, Diagnosis, and Treatment screens, a part of the federal Medicaid programme, do not include a mental health component and often are administered by providers with no mental health training.

Under Medicaid Managed Care, fewer students are being identified, as community services for children have not been expanded, and inpatient and residential services are decreasing. New Mexico's State Children's Health Insurance Plan (SCHIP) provided for funds for school mental health assessment, but this plan was rejected by the Health Care Finance Administration (HCFA) and is in legal limbo. As a result of this lack of mental health assessments from medical providers, as well as the responsibilities schools face with the Individuals with Disabilities in Education Act (IDEA) and Section 504 to identify children with disabilities, schools must bear the burden for most of these assessments. Unfortunately, schools do not currently have the systems or resources in place to provide these critical assessments.

This may be related to the fact that New Mexico was the last state in the United States to accept funding from IDEA. Even those early educational processes that do include mental health assessments and supports (Child Find and Head Start) often fail to help preschoolers make the transition into the general school system, and individual progress is lost. Furthermore, parents frequently are left out of the assessment and evaluation process and are not aware of their rights to have their child assessed. The New Mexico State Department of Education General Screening Process most often consists of simple vision and hearing tests and does not address children's mental health needs. Student Support Processes, which also are mandated by the State Department of Education, are functioning below par in some schools and are nonexistent in others. The quality of school-based assessments is too dependent upon an individual school's commitment and the expertise and availability of trained personnel.

Many special education or 504 evaluations that do take place have minimal mental health and substance abuse components, and often psychological staffing on children provide only cursory mental health evaluations. As stated, most of the students who are involved in school violence show early warning signs of mental health or substance abuse issues prior to these incidents. The ratio of school counselors, social workers, and other school personnel to students, however, is so poor that schools are not able to take on the sole responsibility of evaluating the vast numbers of these children.

Even when children's behavioural issues become serious enough that administrators consider suspension or expulsion, children and teens rarely have a mental health or substance abuse evaluation. The lack of assessment at this critical juncture leaves many students on the street without school or treatment. This results in high costs both in terms of increased violence in our communities and general fund expenditures for juvenile justice intervention. The need for improving collaboration among schools, families, and communities in meeting these overwhelming demands cannot be overstated. In recent years, an increasing number of collaborative arrangements within, between, and among agencies, schools, families, and communities have emerged to address the needs of young people and their families, and a growing body of literature helps to clarify the policy and conceptual bases and available data related to these endeavors. The nature and scope of collaborative activity varies from community to community and site to site and may be initiated by one or more agencies, schools, family-oriented organisations, or a wide variety of community entities. Terms used to designate their activity include school linked services, integrated services, school-community partnerships, family resource centers, one-stop shopping, wraparound services, seamless service delivery, systems of care, comprehensive school health programmes, co-location of services, and community schools. The arrangements encompass concerns for promoting well-being, preventing problems, and addressing existing problems through early intervention and remediation/ treatment of chronic and severe problems. Prevention programmes and interventions may be offered to everyone, to those in specified cohorts, or to those identified as at-risk. For the most part, however, high poverty communities don't come close to having enough resources to meet their needs, which makes collaborative use of existing resources an essential strategy in maximizing use of what is available.

Analyses of trends indicate that a basic intent of policies for collaboration is to move from fragmentation to cohesive intervention and from a narrow focus on specific problems and specialist-oriented services to strategies that encompass comprehensive approaches. Partnerships offer hope for reducing fragmentation and minimizing wasteful use of limited resources and also seem fundamental for enhancing efficacy by weaving limited resources together into increasingly comprehensive, multifaceted, and integrated approaches. Moving toward comprehensive approaches requires more than a desire to collaborate. It involves overcoming marginalization and fragmentation by elevating the priority level assigned to the policies that address the problems that young people experience and creating stronger linkages between policy and practice. For this to happen, the many forces currently advocating for specialized concerns have to develop partnerships around a concept that unifies responses to a wide range of psychosocial and health factors that are interfering with young people's learning and performance. Adoption of such an inclusive unifying concept is pivotal in convincing policy makers to move to a position that recognizes the essential nature of comprehensive, multifaceted, and integrated approaches. The concept of addressing barners to development and learning represents such a unifying concept.

New Mexico's children currently face some of the highest rates of poverty, substance abuse, suicide, and school dropout of any children in the United States. New Mexico has the largest number of children in poverty, the third highest teen pregnancy rate, the fourth highest dropout rate, and the fifth highest teen suicide rate in the United States. No wonder New Mexico is consistently rated one of the two or three worst states in which to raise a child. Unfortunately, as indicated in The Status of Children's Mental Health in New Mexico, the majority of those with problems are not receiving appropriate support or intervention. In part, this lamentable state of affairs is a result of the limited availability of school- and community-based programmes and services, and in part from the difficulty public systems have in working together to address these matters. New Mexico has been taking active steps to alleviate many of these difficulties.

One trend across the country for improving the situation involves expanding school-based and linked programmes and services by enhancing the policy focus at the state level. In New Mexico, the strategy for accomplishing this builds on current windows of opportunity that have opened because of policy initiatives encouraging collaborative infrastructures to enhance how schools address physical and mental health. As a result, school health has become a high priority within New Mexico. In establishing relevant collaborative arrangements throughout the state, the concept of addressing barriers to development and learning has had a unifying and energizing influence.

In recent years, various opportunities have emerged for funding and working with schools to address a variety of barriers to development, learning, and teaching. State agencies in New Mexico have been aggressive in taking advantage of the open windows.

Of particular note is the way the state has used federal initiatives designed to encourage states to build a collaborative infrastructure to enhance (a) coordinated school health, and (b) mental health in schools. As new initiatives were introduced, establishing collaborative to enhance the focus on school health clearly would require strategies that accounted for the reality that schools are not in the health business. Their primary mission is to educate. Therefore, any effort to establish high-priority collaborations with education agencies and schools must operate within a framework that reflects their mission. In this respect, schools were found to value the idea of working with others to address the barriers that get in the way of their students benefiting from instruction. Therefore, many of the efforts to expand physical and mental health in schools were pursued by framing them as facets of a comprehensive component for addressing barriers to learning. From this perspective, it was much easier to connect school health initiatives with federal educational initiatives such as the Safe and Drug Free Schools programme and with special education. It also was easier to encourage building collaborative that combined the efforts of agencies, schools, families, and communities and to incorporate a strong school health emphasis in the plan for the state's Children's Health Insurance Programme (SCHIP).

The work of New Mexico's Office of School Health illustrates the progress being made. The Office, with its 18 staff members, is in the Health Systems Bureau of the Public Health Division of the New Mexico Department of Health. Its role is to promote school health programmes and services for all children, whether in school, home-schooled, suspended, or expelled. Programmes and services promoted by the Office of School Health range throughout the whole continuum of care, from prevention to early intervention to treatment services. Programmes supported by the Office include prevention efforts such as the A+ Awards programme, which supports schools in developing successful school/ community partnerships in one of the eight school health component areas promoted by the Center for Disease Control's model of coordinated school health.

Other programme include development and expansion of School Based Health Centers (SBHCs) throughout the state, with a particular focus on the mental health and substance abuse services that these centers provide. Furthermore, the Office of School Health has grown dramatically in the last few years, with expansion of the New Mexico School Mental Health Initiative. Funded by a federal Maternal and Child Health grant, this collaboration of state agencies, schools, families, and community partners has made great strides in expanding both programmes and support for addressing the mental health needs of students so they may be successful in school.

As one of the key agencies working to develop an effective infrastructure for a health focus in schools, the School Mental Health Initiative has played a catalytic role in enhancing connections among divisions within the Health Department (e.g., collaborations among the Office of School Health, the Behavioural Health Division, and the Division of Health Improvement, which monitors the effectiveness of interventions). It also has had to deal with the challenge of how to enhance collaboration among the various state agencies responsible for health, education, juvenile justice, child protective services, and the Human Services Department. (This last agency has been actively involved in school health issues because it administers both Medicaid-managed care and the Medicaid in the Schools Programme, and because under welfare reform, it requires children to stay in school for a family to receive financial benefits.) The task of establishing interagency partnerships and other collaborative working relationships has been facilitated by emphasizing the reality that addressing barriers to development and learning is an overlapping concern for all public agencies that deal with youth and their families.

Adopting the unifying concept of "addressing barriers to learning," the staff of the School Mental Health Initiative reached out to organisational representatives and other key stakeholders to create the Interdepartmental School Behavioural Health Partnership. This state level, interdepartmental collaborative has coordinated and expanded critical school mental health programmes for New Mexico's children. Members include representatives from the Divisions of Public Health, Behavioural Health, and Health Improvement in the Health Department; Data and Analysis and Special Education Divisions in the Department of Education; staff from the Children, Youth and Families Department; and the Medical Assistance Division of the Human Services Department. Together, these agencies have combined to provide more than $ I million in staff and programme support for school mental health programmes in a true state-level partnership.

Initially, the staff of the School Mental Health Initiative consisted of the child psychiatrist director (funded through three different state agencies and the federal grant), a master's-level social worker as programme director, and an administrative assistant. To be responsive to the needs of schools for training in school mental health directed to teachers, it became important to obtain state support to add a position for a teacher with strong background in working with the social/ behavioural needs of students in a classroom. For this reason, the Behavioural Educational Consultant position was created, and a former special education teacher with a strong background in teacher training was hired. Later, as the four existing staff worked to meet the demand for their technical assistance, support, and training services, the four School Mental Health Advocate positions were created.

Each regional School Mental Health Advocate, a master's-level trained therapist with school mental health experience, was assigned to one of the four state Public Health district offices to work closely with local schools, parents, health professionals, and mental health providers. These critical community partners have provided essential technical assistance, training, and support to schools, families, and communities to expand regional and local capacity to provide collaborative prevention, early intervention and treatment support for students. These School Mental Health Advocates worked with more than 37 communities statewide and provided more than 120 trainings to more than 4,000 people in school mental health during 1999. They also have played a critical role in bringing community partners together to address the barriers to learning unique to each school and community. The first step in implementing the initiative at the community level was to establish statewide workgroups. An Advocacy Workgroup was created to promote legislation and expand policy support for school mental health. A Training Workgroup focused on expanding the capacity of school teachers and other school health professionals to recognize children at risk for problems so they can be properly directed to help and also to enhance University linkages for pre-service and in-service training of school and community providers. The initial emphasis of the Families, Schools, and Communities Linkages Workgroup was on ways to improve understanding and use of Section 504 of the 1973 Rehabilitation Act, which provides general education classroom modifications for children with behavioural and physical disabilities. These workgroups played a critical role in expanding initial linkages between state government and community partners in determining local priorities and providing direction for future initiatives.

An additional step has involved interagency and community partnerships to develop four demonstration sites across the state for use as models of school/community school mental health collaboration. Funded by the Interdepartmental School Behavioural Health Partnership, these pilot programmes were designed to expand mental health and psychosocial interventions to the schools by expanding linkages to the community and provide additional resource support for these school/community partnerships. Projects at these sites include the restructuring of student support teams in schools, the development of parent and peer mentorship models in middle schools, and improving access to case management and other mental health services on school grounds. Other non funded sites throughout the state receive regular technical assistance and training for developing school/community mental health collaboration to expand their capacities to provide school-linked services and programmes. In fact, 10 sites that were not initially funded received mini-grants for education and training opportunities that led to many of them obtaining other funds for their collaborative.

School-Based Health Centers (SBHCs) are important components of school health interventions in New Mexico. The Office of School Health, with additional financial support from the Interdepartmental School Behavioural Health Partnership, currently provides funding for 17 school-based health centers statewide, which serve more than 40 schools. In New Mexico, at least one-third of children who come to school-based health centers have a primary mental health or substance abuse issue, which becomes apparent after several visits. While most states with school-based health centers have a large number of mental health providers, New Mexico initially had mental health providers in only one-third of its school-based health centers.

One of the goals over the past several years has been to expand the capability of these sites to provide mental health and substance abuse support by linking them more effectively with community children's mental health and substance abuse providers. In 1999, the Office of School Health restructured its request-for-proposals process to reflect this by expanding the level of funding available to school-based health centers that provide coordinated primary care, mental health, and substance abuse services on site. Also in 1999, funding was created for stand-alone school-based mental health centers. In addition, the Office of School Health is in the process of developing state standards for provision of mental health and substance abuse services, including the provision of psychotropic medication in school-based health centers.

New Mexico moved to Medicaid-managed care in the middle of 1997. Since that time, community-based services have not yet been expanded to a great degree under Medicaid-managed care and New Mexico's public mental health systems continue to have difficulty identifying and bringing children into treatment services.

As New Mexico moved to Medicaid managed care, the School Mental Health Initiative worked to develop relationships with community Medicaid providers to link them with schools through the behavioural health systems of Medicaid-managed care. A pilot project in school-based Medicaid managed care behavioural health services in the Albuquerque Public Schools now provides for full-time clinical social work services for Medicaid-eligible children in all 12 schools in one high school cluster. Through this pilot, social workers from community provider agencies work in conjunction with school health professionals employed by the school district and are able to see students regardless of their assigned Medicaid provider.

As a result of statewide efforts to expand this model, the Medical Assistance Division of the Human Services Department, in a joint effort with the Health Department and the Medicaid-managed care providers, is awaiting final approval for a grant from the Center for Health Care Strategies to expand the relationship between Medicaid-managed care and school-based health centers. In addition, the School Mental Health Initiative is collaborating with other state and school partners on a Medicaid in the Schools Guidebook. This document will give schools additional technical information on how to utilize their Medicaid in the Schools dollars more effectively to support school mental health and other programmes.

As stated, the School Mental Health Initiative has worked to expand the statewide effort to provide school behavioural health assessments for students. The Initiative took the lead in developing the School Behavioural Health Assessment component of the state SCRIP plan. This meant convening a group of more than 30 representatives of state and local agencies, parent organisations, school health providers, and others to come to consensus about how to develop a system of school-based behavioural health assessment. As stated earlier, New Mexico's entire Phase II SCRIP plan was rejected by HCFA and is still under negotiation. If it is finally approved, the plan will provide for more than $9 million per year for school behavioural health assessment and school health interventions. The SCRIP Assessment component, which would take place in childcare, daycare, or schools whenever possible, focuses on identifying early risk factors in children and serves as a gateway to other SCHIP services and to Medicaid-managed care services, school interventions, and community resources and services.

As a result of the hold-up on the SCHIP plan, other efforts have been made to bring mental health assessments to schools. A legislative memorial was approved in 1999, and followed by legislation in the 2000 legislative session that, if approved, would target mental health assessments for students in K-grade 3. The goal would be early identification of high-risk youth, supportive intervention for the child and family, and a plan to get the child back on track and successful in the classroom. This legislation is accompanied by funds for teacher training in school mental health and funds for assessments tools, as well as service dollars.

An additional component of collaboration includes statewide and local community training with a specific focus on strategies for enhancing the capacity of schools to identify students with mental health issues early and linking to appropriate intervention. This effort includes a partnership with the Department of Education's Special Education Division as well as New Mexico State University and is designed to expand awareness and training for teachers on how to identify children's mental health issues in the classroom and link them to intervention. This train-the-trainers model, known as Supporting Teachers Supporting Students, is based on a model developed by the Training Workgroup of the School Mental Health Initiative. In this model, teachers, administrators, and school health professionals from local school districts are trained in adult education techniques and then an array of school mental health topics. The trainees then practice their own presentation skills with others being trained before going back to their home districts and providing two workshops for colleagues in their home schools.

In the first training pilot in the spring, of 1999, 30 teachers from five New Mexico school districts attended the training and then provided workshops for 600 colleagues at their home schools. This group's presentations were well rated, with requests for more training in specific school mental health areas. Currently, 55 school personnel from nine school districts are participating in this training process. It is hoped that additional funds will be obtained to expand this training in the coming year and give it a truly regional focus. This effort represents true collaboration among state, university, and school agencies. In addition, the School Mental Health Initiative collaborates with the Office of School Health in the yearly Head to Toe: A Conference on School Health. This conference is now in its fourth year with attendance of more than 400 and brings together school personnel, parents, students, and providers from throughout New Mexico to collaborate on school health issues. Also, in collaboration with the Department of Education's Special Education Division, Section 504 training has been implemented for teachers and administrators throughout the state. Other workshops have focused on topics ranging from adolescent substance abuse to grant-writing (so school/community collaborative partners can learn how to pursue additional funds for needed interventions).

Collaboration with parents and parent advocates has been one of the critical priorities of the School Mental Health Initiative. With parent organisations, the initial thrust has been one of joint advocacy for increased support to address children's mental health concerns such as expanded awareness of mental health symptoms and improving access to services. The School Mental Health Initiative is currently colaborating with Parents for Behaviourally Different Children, New Mexico's parent advocacy organisation for children with neurobiological disorders, to develop a Guide for Parents on School Mental Health Issues, which includes diagnostic and resource information, as well as updates on parent rights under Section 504 and IDEA. The School Mental Health Initiative provides for reimbursement for parent transportation and time to attend meetings and asks for parents to co-present to legislative committees. Acknowledgement of parents as the true experts in understanding the needs of their children and the community has been one of the cornerstones of the School Mental Health

Initiative's collaborative model.

With youth organisations, one emphasis has been on ensuring students a greater voice in policy and legislation, particularly regarding efforts to provide alternatives to suspension and expulsion. An additional youth-related effort is development of the Peer Navigator's Programme, a peer mentorship model and training guide, created by School Mental Health Initiative staff with community and youth involvement. This prevention programme and workbook for school personnel provide a leadership model for high-risk youth to develop self esteem and find success in school through positive peer role-modeling. Now implemented in seven school districts within New Mexico, schools are finding strategies to reach out to some of their at-risk students to keep them involved in their schools in productive ways.

With institutions of higher education, the focus has been on expanding pre-service and in-service training for school personnel and for community mental health providers who work within schools. The Initiative is working with a statewide school health collaborative on higher education to bring models of school mental health to teachers, administrators, school nurses, and counselor training. Some of the School Mental Health Initiative social work staff provides linkages for state social work training programmes to develop internships for their social work students at local schools. Furthermore, the School Mental Health Initiative staff is linking with the state Legislative Education Study Committee and the State Board of Education to develop a plan for prioritizing school mental health issues in classroom education and state curricula.

With the state Pupil's Services Alliance, the emphasis has been on linking with school nurses, school social workers, school psychologists, school counselors, and child psychiatrists to bring a collaborative effort to expand attention to the mental health needs of our students. These efforts include multidisciplinary training on school mental health issues, as well as advocacy to expand the ratios of school health professionals and community providers on site in schools.

The School Mental Health Initiative also has undertaken major efforts to expand statewide awareness of the mental health needs of children. In the summer of 1999, the School Mental Health Initiative, along with the Interdepartmental School Behavioural Health Partnership, brought together parents, religious leaders, school personnel, legislators, providers and youth from throughout the state to discuss the need to expand support for children's mental health. With consultation from a national media firm with expertise in children's mental health campaigns, the New Mexico Children's Mental Health Awareness Project was born.

The target audience of this effort is parents and families, school personnel, and policy makers. The two priorities of the project are (a) to promote issues of awareness of children's mental health problems in the state, and (b) to improve access to programmes and services.

The first activity of the group is to bring the art exhibit Childhood Revealed to New Mexico in the spring of 2001. This exhibit was coordinated by staff from the New York University Child Study Center and highlights artwork of children with mental illness from across the United States.

Plans are under way to bring this exhibit to three sites in New Mexico. The Awareness Project intends to build a series of lectures, media events, and materials around this exhibit, which will highlight these critical issues. Schools and universities from around the state are joining the project to develop curricula and classroom projects to help New Mexico youth derive the maximum understanding from this exhibit. This exhibit certainly will galvanize community collaborative from around the state to discuss the impact of childhood mental illness while also addressing the stigma issues that complicate communication around this issue.

Indications of the initial impact of the various collaborative efforts with respect to enhancing statewide attention to youth problems is reflected in establishment of the first state Summit on Children's Mental Health (done in conjunction with the Governor's Mental Health Planning Council) and passage by the legislature of a special Memorial in support of expanded school mental health. In the fall of 1998, the School Mental Health Initiative took the lead in developing the first New Mexico Summit on Children's Mental Health. Attended by more than 200 people its first year, this summit brought together statewide advocates for youth, parents, and providers, to share information about children's mental' health in New Mexico.

The Mental Health in the Schools Memorial formally called for maximizing intra- and interagency collaboration and training to enhance school mental health programmes. State agencies involved were the Departments of Health; Public Education; Children, Youth, and Families; Human Services; Corrections; the Administrative Office of the Courts; the Children's Subcommittee of the Governor's Mental Health Planning Council; the Developmental Disabilities Planning Council; and the IDEA Council. In addition, the text called for inclusion of consumers, advocates, and providers working in the mental health field and schools. The Memorial recommendations were made following four regional meetings on school mental health around the state. More than 240 New Mexicans spent one-half day discussing these issues in small groups and making recommendations. Some of the final recommendations, such as the SCHIP plan and other legislation, became policy, but are still awaiting final state approval. With awareness of the expanding numbers to be served and the growing emphasis on wraparound services, New Mexico's legislature and state government is increasingly coming to understand that effective collaboration is essential to addressing barriers to development and learning. In keeping with this understanding, the state is making school and community-level collaboration a priority and is building an infrastructure that can effectively turn policy into practice.

New Mexico's efforts to enhance collaboration for addressing barriers to development and learning represent moves in the right direction. Nevertheless, the problems of fragmentation and marginalization related to efforts for addressing barriers to learning are generally well entrenched and difficult to change. These problems frequently stem from categorical policy making and funding, along with the specialized, self protective focus and relative autonomy of units within agencies and among agencies. It is well documented that, although agencies often are dealing with "the same client", they tend to do so with little in the way of a "big picture" framework, little or no coordination, and sparse attention to moving toward integrated efforts.

Ultimately, addressing barriers to learning and enhancing healthy development must be viewed from a social policy perspective. It is becoming increasingly clear that a major policy shift is needed to move (a) from fragmented to cohesive interventions, and (b) from narrowly focused, problem specific, and specialist-oriented services to comprehensive programmatic approaches. This shift encompasses an expanded focus on addressing barriers and enhancing the cohesiveness of existing policy. It also should include efforts to fill critical gaps in current initiatives designed to reform and restructure education and link to those efforts to restructure community health and human services. From a societal perspective, the goal is to foster development of a comprehensive, multifaceted, and integrated continuum of community and school programmes for local catchments areas. The framework for the continuum emerges from analyses of social, economic, political, end cultural factors associated with the problems of youth and from reviews of promising practices. It is built on holistic and developmental perspectives that are translated into an extensive continuum of programmes focused on fostering the well-being of individuals, families, and the contexts in which they live, work, and play.

This continuum ranges from primary prevention and early-age intervention, through approaches for treating problems soon after onset, to treatment for severe and chronic problems. Included are programmes designed to promote and maintain safety at home and at school, programmes to promote and maintain physical and mental health, preschool programmes, early school-adjustment programmes, programmes to improve and augment ongoing social and academic supports, programmes to intervene prior to referral for intensive treatments, and programmes providing intensive treatments. Implied is the importance of using the least restrictive and non-intrusive forms of intervention required to address these problems in a culturally appropriate manner. This scope of activity underscores the need to develop formal mechanisms for essential and long lasting inter programme connections (collaboration in the form of information sharing, cooperation, coordination, integration) on a daily basis and over time.

One tool to foster greater cohesion in educational and health policy and practice is Adelman and Taylor's concept of an enabling component as a policy-oriented notion around which to unify efforts to address barriers to learning. The concept is intended to underscore two major concerns.

1. Current reforms are based on an inadequate two component model for restructuring school and community resources, with the result that efforts to address barriers to development and learning are marginalized.
2. It is essential to move to a three-component model if student achievement is to increase significantly. (As delineated in the publications cited above, a three-component model calls for elevating efforts to address barriers to the level of one of three fundamental and essential facets of education reform and school and community agency restructuring. All three components are seen as essential, complementary, and overlapping.)

By calling for reforms that fully integrate a focus on addressing barriers to learning, the concept of an enabling component responds to a wide range of factors interfering with development and learning. By providing a framework for restructuring school-owned enabling activity and blending school and community resources, the concept provides a helpful unifying focus upon which to formulate new policy and foster collaboration. A policy shift and programmatic focus are necessary but insufficient. For significant systemic change to occur, policy and programme commitments must be demonstrated through allocation and redeployment of resources (e.g., finances, personnel, time, space, equipment) that can adequately operationalize policy and promising practices. In particular, there must be sufficient resources to develop an effective structural foundation for systemic changes.

Existing infrastructure mechanisms must be modified in ways that guarantee that new policy directions are translated into appropriate daily practices. Well designed infrastructure mechanisms ensure local ownership, a critical mass of committed stakeholders, effective capacity building (including staff development), processes that can overcome barriers to stakeholders working together effectively, and strategies that can mobilize and maintain proactive effort so changes are implemented and renewed over time. Institutionalizing comprehensive approaches requires redesigning mechanisms for governance, capacity building, planning-implementation, coordination, daily leadership, communication, information management, and the like. In reforming mechanisms, new collaborative arrangements must be established and authority (power) must be redistributed. All this obviously requires adequate support (time, space, materials, and equipment) - not just initially but over time - to those who operate the mechanisms. And appropriate incentives and safeguards must be provided for those undertaking the risks involved in making major changes.

As Melaville and Blank (1998) note:

One of the most important, cross-cutting social policy perspectives to emerge in recent years is an awareness that no single institution can create all the conditions that young people need to flourish.

Here it is evident that agencies, schools, families, and communities must work closely with each other to meet their mutual goals. For example, schools find that they can provide more support for students, families, and staff when they are an integral and positive part of the community. Reciprocally, agencies can make services more accessible to youth and families by linking with schools, and they can connect better with and have an impact on hard-to-reach clients. The interest in working together is bolstered by concern about widespread fragmentation of interventions. The hope is that by integrating available resources, as New Mexico is attempting, a significant impact can be made on at-risk factors. In particular, appropriate and effective collaboration and teaming are seen as key facets in addressing barriers to development, learning, and family self sufficiency. Though informal linkages are relatively simple to make, establishing major long-term connections is complicated. These require vision, cohesive policy, and basic system reform. The difficulties are seen readily in any attempts to evolve comprehensive approaches. Enhancing the effectiveness of intervention in addressing barriers to development and learning requires collaboration among agencies, schools, families, and communities that is cohesive; provides the resources necessary for transforming the nature and scope of intervention efforts so comprehensive, multifaceted, and integrated approaches can be developed; creates necessary infrastructure and provides for effective capacity-building to ensure appropriate implementation of these comprehensive approaches provides the resources necessary for implementing widespread scale-up.

Inadequate policy support related to any of these matters decreases the likelihood of enhancing intervention effectiveness on a large scale. Thus, the task ahead is one of ensuring that policy makers appreciate this fact and act appropriately.

10

Prevention Primer for Domestic Violence

In the past several decades, shelters and advocacy programmes have proliferated throughout the United States to provide vital services to victims of domestic violence (DV) and their children. On a daily basis, DV advocates face the harsh reality that the number of women who experience DV far exceeds the availability of services that women from diverse backgrounds face many barriers to accessing services, and that abuse has many long-term consequences. Consequently, advocates have expanded the scope of their work beyond direct victim services to include prevention. Advocates have been engaged in prevention through a wide range of activities including school-based curricula, community education, mass media campaigns, legal reform, and policy development.

Meanwhile, public health professionals have become increasingly aware that DV is a leading determinant of health and has a direct impact on most areas of service delivery ranging from reproductive health to injury prevention. As a result, DV has been identified as a public health priority. The high prevalence of DV, the enormous cost to society, and the high rate of recidivism among perpetrators makes a strong case to focus on prevention. The public health approach emphasizes primary prevention and working with community partners to develop a coordinated response to violence. The purpose of this chapter is to provide an introduction to basic prevention concepts from a public health perspective.

Following a brief outline of the public health approach to prevention, two classification systems for prevention are discussed along with examples of DV prevention strategies.

These classification systems provide a framework to conceptualize how prevention can be designed to occur at different points in time (before, during, and even after an adverse event) to address different aspects of a problem and how strategies can be directed to different populations according to their levels of risk. A planning tool that can be used to develop more comprehensive prevention initiatives is introduced along with specific examples for preventing DV. The importance of understanding prevention terminology relative to grants and funding opportunities is emphasized throughout this chapter, which concludes with an overview of a national partnership between public health and domestic violence coalitions that is supported through public health funding.

FINDING COMMON GROUND

It is important to acknowledge that prevention terminology and tools developed by public health practitioners will not be a perfect fit for DV. Public health has its roots in science and medicine and consequently places considerable emphasis on empirical evidence and structure. As part of the larger social justice issue of violence against women, DV brings together many disciplines and perspectives. Public health and DV practitioners have different philosophies and missions, and often use different terminology that can be confusing or even conflicting. Nevertheless, both of these fields have strong underpinnings in social equity. DV advocates are dedicated to ending social injustices against women. Public health is committed to reducing health disparities. Health disparities are factors that are associated with reduced access to health care and compromised health.

DV, a well-documented barrier to health care, is associated with a myriad of health problems and health risk behaviours. DV is a health disparity issue for adult victims and their children.

The health disparities and social justice aspects of DV are inextricably interwoven, and this interface provides common ground for public health and DV practitioners to learn from one another and work together. The magnitude of DV as a social equity and public health problem, the limited resources available to fund research, intervention, and prevention, and the potential for maximizing the effectiveness of prevention through collaborative leadership and teamwork provide the groundwork for promoting DV-public health partnerships.

PUBLIC HEALTH APPROACH TO PREVENTION

Public health uses a systematic approach to prevention that has four basic steps. The first two steps of the public health approach to prevention are data-driven and research focused. In Step 1, surveys, surveillance systems, and other data collection methods are used to gather information that is used to describe the magnitude of the problem.

In Step 2, more advanced research is conducted to identify the causes of a problem, factors that are associated with an increased risk of the problem occurring (risk factors), and protective factors that may prevent the problem from occurring. The information that is gathered during Steps 1 and 2 is applied during Step 3 to translate science into data-driven prevention strategies that are evaluated. Step 4 focuses on disseminating what has been learned and helping communities to adapt and implement proven prevention strategies.

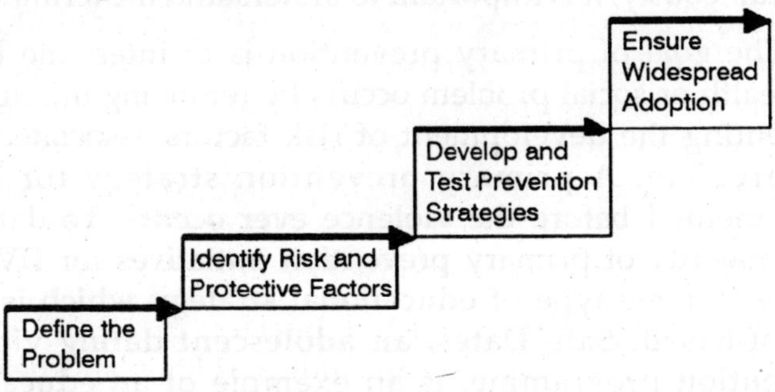

Figure: Public Health Approach to Prevention (Lutzker, 2006)

CLASSIFYING PREVENTION STRATEGIES

Two different systems for classifying prevention strategies are described below. The original classification system, referred to as the "levels of prevention," categorizes a prevention strategy based on what point in time the intervention is implemented relative to when the problem occurs. This classification system has three levels of prevention: *primary, secondary, and tertiary*. The second classification system categorizes prevention strategies according to the population that is being designated for the intervention. For the purpose of this discussion, this classification system is referred to as the "targeted population" approach. The three categories of prevention using this system are: *universal, selective, and indicated*. Grants and funding sources may explicitly state what types of prevention activities are eligible for funding.

For example, the following statement appeared in a recent violence prevention grant announcement from the Centers for Disease Control and Prevention: "only proposals that evaluate a strategy, programme, or policy that is focused on primary, not secondary prevention of perpetration of violence, and focuses on a target population that has not already engaged in the perpetration of violence will be considered responsive...". Because both of these classification systems are used in publications and grant proposals, sometimes simultaneously, it is important to understand the terminology.

The goal of primary prevention is to intervene before the health or social problem occurs by removing the cause or preventing the development of risk factors associated with the problem. A primary prevention strategy for DV is implemented before the violence ever occurs. To date, the vast majority of primary prevention initiatives for DV have involved some type of educational strategy which is often school-based. Safe Dates, an adolescent dating violence prevention programme, is an example of an educational strategy that has been evaluated. Eighth and ninth graders who participated in Safe Dates reported less sexual and physical dating violence perpetration and victimisation and the reduction in violence persisted four years after students had completed the programme compared to students who did not receive the intervention. The school-based, primary prevention strategies include a theater production performed by peers, a 10-session curriculum, and a poster contest.

The conceptual framework for Safe Dates is that changing norms associated with partner violence, decreasing gender stereotyping, and improving conflict management skills will prevent the perpetration of dating violence. It is important to note that primary prevention does not have to be limited to risk factors or problems that increase the risk of victimisation or perpetration. Primary prevention strategies can focus on protective factors. In one study, parental monitoring reduced the likelihood of dating violence among African American girls and boys. In another study by Howard and colleagues (2005), having a stronger sense of self was protective against dating violence for Latina girls while spending weekly time with a mentor was protective for Latino boys. Culturally relevant, gender-specific prevention strategies for dating violence can promote development of the appropriate protective factors.

The goal of secondary prevention is to identify a risk factor or problem and take the necessary actions to eliminate the risk factors and the potential problem. While strategies at this point may sound more like intervention than prevention, the objective is to create opportunities to identify the problem before it becomes evident and to intervene as soon as possible to *prevent* the problem from occurring or progressing. Screening programmes in the health care setting are an example of secondary prevention. By screening patients for DV, health care providers can offer support and referrals to patients who disclose abuse to reduce the likelihood of future victimisation and prevent long-term health consequences. To date, there is very limited evidence to support the effectiveness of screening as a preventive measure. Two studies have shown that screening for DV and offering a wallet-sized referral card to patients who disclosed abuse was associated with reduced physical violence over time when compared to the level of violence disclosed at the time of screening.

Home visitation services that are targeted to women with identified risk factors for DV is another example of secondary prevention. For example, the Nurse-Family Partnership home visitation programme offers services to low-income pregnant women who are then screened for a wide range of risk factors, including DV. Women who disclose abuse receive additional support and referrals. Without this screening, home visitors may not become aware of the DV until much later when there is overt evidence of physical harm or the client chooses to self-disclose due to escalating violence. In one evaluation of the Nurse-Family Partnership, women who received home visits reported less DV two years after home visitation services had ended compared to women who did not receive home visits. Other examples of secondary prevention strategies for DV include self-defense training and community watch programmes.

Tertiary prevention occurs after the adverse event or illness has occurred and interventions are designed to minimize the impact and restore health, wellness, and/or safety as soon as possible. It is sometimes argued that tertiary prevention should not be called prevention because the violence has already happened. However, a rapid, coordinated response and follow-up can reduce the impact of victimisation, and prevent predictable, long-term consequences and revictimisation.

Tertiary prevention for DV encompasses all of the services directed to survivors and perpetrators once the violence has occurred, and it is important for first responders and caregivers to understand that they can have a role in prevention when prompt, appropriate services and follow-up are provided. These services may address immediate needs such as medical care for physical injuries, restraining orders, safety planning, and shelter services, long-term needs such as trauma counseling, support groups, employment assistance, transitional housing, children's services, parenting after domestic violence initiatives, and strategies to enhance the quality, coordination, and access to victims' and batterers' interv ention programmes. Legal advocacy programmes to help victims navigate the legal system are an example of tertiary prevention. An evaluation of a legal advocacy programme in Washington, DC found that women who worked with legal advocates reported significantly less abuse six weeks after contact with the advocate. Tertiary prevention strategies are not limited to first responders and service providers.

For example, the Mentors in Violence Prevention (MVP), a college-based empowerment programme to prevent gender violence that focuses on primary prevention, also has a tertiary level "bystander" component to empower friends and students to be proactive when they witness or become aware of abusive behaviours among their peers. The MVP initiative is an example of multi-level prevention as described in the next section.

MULTI-LEVEL PREVENTION

Prevention initiatives can address more than one level of prevention by integrating strategies that intervene for DV at different stages or points in time such as before the violence has occurred (primary prevention), during (secondary prevention), or after the violence has occurred (tertiary prevention). For example, Expect Respect, a school-based programme developed by Safe Place: Domestic Violence and Sexual Assault Survival Center to promote safe and healthy relationships for youth, combines strategies to prevent relationship violence from ever occurring while also providing support to youth who have or are currently experiencing abuse.

Expect Respect's primary prevention strategies include classroom presentations to educate youth in grades 6-12 about dating violence, sexual assault, sexual harassment, and healthy relationships. It also has a summer teen leadership programme that provides intensive training on social justice and violence prevention to teen leaders through a paid internship. Counseling and support groups are offered to students who are currently in abusive relationships and students who have already experienced sexual, dating, or domestic violence (secondary and tertiary prevention).

APPROACH TO CLASSIFYING PREVENTION

While the classification system for the three levels of prevention *(primary, secondary, and tertiary)* seems fairly clear-cut, there can be considerable disagreement when actually classifying prevention strategies. As science has advanced our understanding about risk and protective factors and the complex relationship between these factors and health, a new classification system was developed. Referred to as the "targeted population" approach, this classification system categorizes prevention strategies by the group or population to whom the intervention is directed and for whom it is most likely to be beneficial. There are three categories for classifying prevention strategies using the "targeted population" approach: *universal, selected,* and *indicated.*

Knowledge about risk factors is needed to use this classification system. While a discussion of risk factors for DV is beyond the scope of this chapter, a review of the literature on risk factors for physical partner abuse perpetration and victimisation by Stith and colleagues (2004) provides a comprehensive overview on this topic. This different approach to classification (*universal, selected, and indicated*) and how these terms related to the three levels of prevention (*primary, secondary, and tertiary*) are described below.

Universal preventive measures are targeted to the general public, or all members of a specific group such as young boys or all adolescents, to reduce the likelihood of a problem ever occurring (IOM, 1994). The population is identified on the basis that the prevention strategy will benefit everyone in that group versus on the basis of a risk factor or problem. An example of a universal preventive strategy for DV is the Family Violence Prevention Fund's "Coaching Boys Into Men" initiative. This public education campaign is directed to all men based on the belief that encouraging men to teach boys about healthy relationships and respecting women will benefit all boys. This campaign employs a wide array of strategies including public service announcements (PSAs), posters, awareness materials, leadership development, an interactive website, and event sponsorship with national sports and media figures who speak out on violence against women. Over a four-year period during which the PSAs were aired, the percentage of men who had actually taken action and spoken to boys about violence against women increased from 29% to 41%.

Selective preventive measures are directed to individuals or groups that have an above average risk of developing a problem. The Youth Relationship Project is an example of a selective preventive measure. These project recruits youth, ages 14-16, with a history of maltreatment to participate in classroom sessions designed to reduce gender-based violence. This intervention offers education on healthy relationships, conflict resolution and communication skills, and social action activities. Youth who received the intervention reported a significant reduction in perpetrating physical and emotional abuse against a dating partner over time. Indicated prevention strategies are directed to high-risk individuals or groups that have minimal but detectable signs of the problem.

For example, indicated preventive measures could be directed to women who disclose early signs of emotional abuse in a relationship, immigrant women who are not allowed to apply for citizenship and teens whose dating partners are tracking them by cell phone. Any identifiable risk factor or condition that makes it highly likely that these individuals are experiencing or perpetrating DV would constitute a population that is eligible for an indicated prevention measure. In a school-based survey of Latino youth, teens who reported recent fearful dating experiences reported less knowledge about abuse and less endorsement of nonviolent attitudes. Teens who disclosed fearful dating experiences could be identified as the population for an indicated prevention measure and be offered a culturally relevant intervention to enhance their knowledge about abuse and healthy relationships, improve their communication skills, and change their attitudes towards violence.

MAKING THE CONNECTION

As previously mentioned, terminology from both the "levels of prevention" and the "targeted population" classifica-tion systems can be used to describe the same prevention strategy so it is useful to understand how the two systems are related to one another. While caution must be advised in making such broad generalizations, universal preventive measures are usually primary prevention strategies. For example, the Coaching Boys into Men initiative is a primary prevention strategy that is also a universal preventive measure since it is directed to all young boys. Selective prevention measures typically focus on secondary prevention strategies while indicated prevention measures usually involve tertiary prevention strategies directed to high-risk groups. The classification systems described above illustrates how there are different approaches to prevention. The following section describes a tool that helps practitioners to recognize that there are many pathways to prevention. This tool facilitates planning and coordination of multi-level strategies that comprehensively address the problem to maximize our prevention potential.

THE SPECTRUM OF PREVENTION

Public health promotes multifaceted prevention strategies that address individual risk factors within the larger context of the socio-cultural environment. The Spectrum of Prevention provides a framework for developing comprehensive prevention initiatives. The spectrum has six action levels. The levels are not hierarchal or mutually exclusive – that is to say that one level is not considered more effective than another and the levels are designed to overlap because they are inter-related. The relationship between the levels is synergistic and the potential for prevention is maximized by strengthening the linkages between the levels with multiple, complimentary strategies. When used as a planning tool, the spectrum promotes a systems approach that helps practitioners move beyond educational strategies to develop broader initiatives that address institutional practices (level 5) and policy development and legal reform (level 6). Reducing childhood exposure to violence against women in the media as a prevention strategy for DV is shown below as an example of how the spectrum can be used. The Spectrum of Prevention does not directly address all of the issues or possible levels that may need to be considered in DV prevention initiatives but practitioners can adapt or modify the tool as needed to be more responsive. For example, issues on cultural sensitivity may need to be a separate action step to ensure that this issue is systematically addressed in a comprehensive DV prevention initiative. When designing prevention strategies or evaluating what is missing in their prevention agenda, advocates can use this tool to explore opportunities at each action level and add other levels as needed to develop a culturally relevant, comprehensive approach.

As previously noted public health prioritizes primary prevention and working collaboratively with community partners. The U. S. Centers for Disease Control and Prevention (CDC) have partnered with domestic violence coalitions in fourteen states on a prevention initiative called DELTA (Domestic Violence Prevention Enhancements and Leadership Through Alliances). DELTA focuses on three key areas of violence prevention: leadership, capacity building, and partnership. Funded coalitions have created interdisciplinary work groups that are engaged in a wide range of activities which includes conducting needs assessments that will provide national baseline data on DV prevention activities, collecting and disseminating information on new prevention models, and providing education, technical assistance, and funding to evaluate DV prevention through local initiatives called coordinated community responses (CCRs). The DELTA initiative, which focuses on primary prevention, uses a social ecological model that identifies four levels of factors that can contribute to DV: individual, relationship, community, and society. By identifying risk and protective factors associated with these four levels, communities can then identify new pathways and comprehensive strategies that address prevention at all four levels. Lessons learned during this initiative will provide insight on collaborative opportunities and the challenges of integrating the diverse philosophies and practices of DV advocates and public health practitioners.

The expertise of DV advocates and service providers is essential to develop safe and effective prevention strategies. The field of public health provides a systematic approach that prioritizes primary prevention, provides terminology to categorize strategies and tools to develop comprehensive initiatives, and promotes community-based partnerships. DELTA is an important step forward for comprehensive, primary prevention initiatives developed through the collective efforts of domestic violence and public health practitioners and other community partners. There are many challenges and opportunities for collaborative approaches to DV prevention. The public health model, which has traditionally focused on diseases, must be adapted to accommodate complex social issues such as DV. There are important lessons that have been learned from the public health approach that are transferable.

The advantage of designing comprehensive prevention initiatives that address many different aspects of a problem is applicable to DV. To date, primary prevention for DV has focused almost exclusively on educational strategies, which limits our prevention potential. Another lesson learned in the field of public health is the importance of integrating evaluation into prevention to obtain the necessary data to determine and compare the effectiveness of different strategies.

As government agencies and foundations place more and more emphasis on evidence-based practices, collecting and using evaluation data has become essential to compete for funding. Unfortunately, only a few preventive strategies for DV have been rigorously evaluated. These challenges should be viewed as opportunities for DV and public health practitioners to work together to adapt public health resources to address DV, to enhance the scope and evaluate the effectiveness prevention initiatives, and to advocate for more prevention funding.

NATURE AND EFFECTS OF SEXUAL VIOLENCE

There are various forms of sexual violence. Rape, the most often cited form of sexual violence, is defined in many societies as sexual intercourse with another person without his/ her consent. Rape is committed when the victim's resistance is overwhelmed by force or fear or other coercive means. However, the term sexual and gender-based violence encompasses a wide variety of abuses that includes sexual threats, exploitation, humiliation, assaults, molestation, domestic violence, incest, involuntary prostitution (sexual bartering), torture, insertion of objects into genital openings and attempted rape. Female genital mutilation and other harmful traditional practices (including early marriage, which substantially increases maternal morbidity and mortality) are forms of sexual and gender-based violence against women which cannot be overlooked nor justified on the grounds of tradition, culture or social conformity.

Since perpetrators of sexual and gender-based violence are often motivated by a desire for power and domination, rape is common in situations of armed conflict and internal strife. An act of forced sexual behaviour can threaten the victim's life. Like other forms of torture, it is often meant to hurt, control and humiliate, while violating a person's physical and mental integrity. Perpetrators may include fellow refugees, members of other clans, villages, religious or ethnic groups, military personnel, relief workers and members of the host population, or family members (for example, when a parent is sexually abusing a child). The enormous pressures of refugee life, such as to live in closed camps, can often lead to domestic violence. In many cases of sexual violence, the victim knows the perpetrator.

Because incidents of sexual and gender-based violence are under-reported, the true scale of the problem is unknown. The World Bank estimates that less than 10 per cent of sexual violence cases in non-refugee situations are reported.

Two principal types of under-reporting are found in

refugee situations:

- Under-reporting by the victims, which can lead to distorted figures that suggest there is no problem; and
- Absence of figures relating to sexual violence within official statistics.

It is essential to know that the problem of sexual violence is serious. Reporting and interviewing techniques should be adapted to encourage both victims and relief workers to report and document incidents. Reporting and follow-up must be sensitive, discreet and confidential so no further suffering is caused and lives are not further endangered. In reporting, it is recommended that definitions (such as confirmed rape cases or sexual violence, in general) are provided and a rate calculated (for example, the number of reported cases per 10,000 people over a given period of time). This rate would allow for monitoring of trends and comparisons with other areas.

Sexual and gender-based violence has acute physical, psychological and social consequences. Survivors often experience psychological trauma: depression, terror, guilt, shame, loss of self-esteem. They may be rejected by spouses and families, ostracised, subjected to further exploitation or to punishment. They may also suffer from unwanted pregnancy, unsafe abortion, sexually transmitted diseases (including HIV), sexual dysfunction, and trauma to the reproductive tract, and chronic infections leading to pelvic inflammatory disease and infertility.

CAUSES AND CIRCUMSTANCES OF SEXUAL VIOLENCE

Sexual and gender-based violence can occur during all phases of a refugee situation: prior to flight, during flight, while in the country of asylum, during repatriation and reintegration. Prevention and response measures must be adapted to suit the different circumstances of each phase. In conflict situations, sexual violence may be politically motivated — when, for example, mass rape is used to dominate or sexual torture is used as a method of interrogation. It may result from long-standing tensions and feuds and the collapse of traditional societal support. In situations in which the refugees are considered to be materially privileged compared to the local population, neighbouring groups may attack the refugees.

The psychological strains of refugee life may aggravate aggressive behaviour towards women. Male disrespect towards women may be reinforced in refugee situations where unaccompanied women and girls may be regarded by camp guards and male refugees as common sexual property. If men are responsible for distributing goods and necessities, women may be subject to sexual exploitation. Those women without proper personal documentation for collecting food rations or shelter material are especially vulnerable.

Women may have to travel to remote distribution points for food, water and fuel; their living quarters may be far from latrines and washing facilities; their sleeping quarters may be unlocked and unprotected. Lack of police protection and lawlessness also contribute to an increase in sexual violence. Police officers, military personnel, relief workers, camp administrators or other government officers may themselves be involved in acts of abuse or exploitation. If there are no independent organisations, such as UNHCR or NGOs, to ensure personal security within a camp, the number of attacks often increases.

VIOLENCE IN REFUGEE SITUATIONS

A multi-sectoral team approach is required to prevent and respond appropriately to sexual and gender-based violence. A committee or task force should be formed to design, implement and evaluate sexual violence programming at the field level. Refugee representatives, UNHCR, UN partners, NGOs and government authorities should be members of this task force. Each member of the task force, representing relevant sectors/ partners (such as protection, health, education, community services, security/ police, site planning, etc.), should identify his/ her role and responsibilities in preventing and responding to sexual and gender-based violence.

The most effective measures require that the refugee community participates in promoting a safe environment for all. Women leaders need to be involved; and women's refugee committees and groups should be established to represent women's interests and to help identify and protect that most vulnerable to sexual violence. Traditional birth attendants (TBAs) can be a valuable source of information and a channel for disseminating protection messages. It is important to have at least one trained female protection officer at the site. Host countries and international relief organisations have a responsibility to provide the refugee community with funding, technical assistance and the safety measures necessary to allow the refugees to design and implement responses to the problem. Experience has shown that community-based groups, commonly called anti-rape or crisis intervention teams should be established. These groups can help raise awareness of the problem, identify preventive measures and be at the forefront of providing assistance to survivors.

INFORMATION, EDUCATION AND COMMUNICATION

Public information campaigns on the subject of sexual violence should be launched (while respecting cultural sensitivities). Topics could include preventive measures, seeking assistance, laws prohibiting sexual violence, and sanctions and penalties for perpetrators. Pamphlets, posters, newsletters, radio and other mass media programmes, videos and community entertainment can all be used to transmit information about preventing sexual violence. The refugee community and health workers must understand the importance of the problem and have the confidence to report all cases of sexual violence as soon as possible.

DESIGN, LOCATION AND PRACTICAL ARRANGEMENTS

Refugee camps can be designed to enhance physical security. Alternatives to closed camps should always be sought. When designing and organising camp facilities, help protect refugees by:

- Locating latrines, water points and fuel collection areas in accessible places;
- Making special arrangements for housing unaccompanied women, girls and lone heads of households;
- Locking washing facilities;
- Providing adequate lighting on paths used at night;
- Providing security patrols; and by
- Avoiding shared communal living space with unrelated families.

Essential items, such as food, non-food and shelter materials, should be distributed directly to women. That way, women will not have to exchange sexual favours for these items. Women should be involved in, if not administer, the food distribution system. Women and men should not be detained together unless they are family members. Appropriate organisations must be allowed access to detainees to monitor their safety and living conditions.

SOCIAL AND PSYCHOLOGICAL FACTORS

Life in refugee camps can lead to a breakdown of traditional social structures, frustration, boredom, alcohol and drug abuse, and feelings of powerlessness that may contribute to aggression and sexual violence. Therefore, educational, recreational and income-generating activities must be promoted.

The response to each incident of sexual violence must include protection, medical care and psychosocial treatment. Immediately following an incident of sexual violence, the physical safety of the survivor must be ensured. All actions must be guided by the best interests of the survivor and her wishes must be respected at all times. Wherever possible, the identity of the survivor should be kept secret and all information kept locked and secure from outsiders.

Health workers should give the survivor as much privacy as she needs and reassure her about her safety. She may want a family member or friend to accompany her throughout the procedures. She should not be pressured to talk or be left alone for long periods. If the incident occurred recently, medical care may be required. The survivor should then be escorted to the appropriate medical facilities. It also may be necessary to contact the police, if the survivor so decides. The likely course of events and all the procedures that may follow should be carefully explained to her to ensure informed consent and preparedness.

The key elements of a medical response to sexual violence are described below. Health care professionals must be specially trained to undertake post-sexual violence medical care. Psychosocial support should begin from the very first encounter with the survivor. A protocol should be adopted to guide the medical and psychosocial care provided to survivors. A doctor (or qualified health worker) of the same sex should conduct the initial examination and follow-up. The survivor should be prepared for the physical examination and perhaps accompanied (if she so wishes) by a staff member who is familiar with the proceedings, or by a family member or friend. Strict confidentiality is essential. Staff dealing with the survivor must be sensitive, discreet and compassionate.

The survivor should not shower or bathe, urinate or defecate, or change clothes before the medical examination, as evidence may be destroyed. A detailed history of the attack should be documented, including the nature of the penetration, if any, whether ejaculation occurred, recent menstrual and contraceptive history, and the mental state of the survivor.

Procedures for medical examination after rape should be established and follow national laws, where they exist. The results of the physical examination, the condition of clothing, any foreign material adhering to the body, any evidence of trauma, however minor, scratches, bite marks, tender spots, etc., and results of a pelvic examination should be documented. Health workers should collect materials that might serve as evidence, such as hair, fingernail scrapings, sperm, saliva and blood samples.

The following tests may be indicated to establish pre-existing conditions: syphilis blood test, pregnancy test and HIV test. Treatment for common sexually transmitted diseases (STDs), such as syphilis, gonorrhoea and chlamydia, may be indicated. A tetanus vaccination should be considered.

Emergency contraceptive pills (ECPs) can prevent unwanted pregnancies if used within 72 hours of the rape. As described by WHO "emergency contraceptive pills (ECPs) work by interrupting a woman's reproductive cycle – by delaying or inhibiting ovulation, blocking fertilisation or preventing implantation of the ovum. ECPs do not interrupt pregnancy and thus are not considered a method of abortion." WHO acknowledges that this description does not command consensus and that some believe that ECPs are abortifacients. Women and health workers holding such belief may be precluded from using this treatment and women who request this service need to be offered counselling so as to reach an informed decision.

ECPs should not be seen as a substitute for regular use of contraceptive methods. Women should be counselled concerning their future contraceptive needs and choices. Copper-bearing IUDs can be used as a method of emergency contraception. They may be appropriate for some women who wish to retain the IUD for long-term contraception and who meet the strict screening requirements for regular IUD use. When inserted within five days, an IUD is an effective method of emergency contraception. However, IUD insertion requires a much higher degree of training and clinical supervision than ECPs. Clients must be screened to eliminate those who are pregnant, have reproductive tract infections, or are at risk of STDs, including HIV/ AIDS. As for ECPs, some women and health workers may be precluded from using this treatment and women who request this service need to be offered counselling so as to reach an informed decision.

PROVIDE FOLLOW-UP MEDICAL CARE

A woman should be counselled to return for follow-up examinations one to two weeks after receiving initial medical care. Health care providers should monitor her follow-up care. Further tests and treatment, such as testing for or treatment of STDs or referral to other RH services, may be indicated during follow-up. Further visits may also be required for pregnancy and HIV testing.

PSYCHOSOCIAL CARE

Survivors of sexual violence commonly feel fear, guilt, shame and anger. They may adopt strong defense mechanisms that include forgetting, denial and deep repression of the events. Reactions vary from minor depression, grief, anxiety, phobia, and somatic problems to serious and chronic mental conditions. Extreme reactions to sexual violence may result in suicide or, in the case of pregnancy, physical abandonment or elimination of the child. Children and youth are especially vulnerable to trauma. Health care providers, relief workers and protection officers should devote special attention to their psychosocial needs.

Survivors should be treated with empathy, care and support. In the long term, and in most cultural settings, the support of family and friends is likely to be the most important factor in overcoming the trauma of sexual violence. Community-based activities are most effective in helping to relieve trauma. Such activities may include:

- Identifying and training traditional, community-based support workers,
- Developing women's support groups or support groups specifically designed for survivors of sexual violence and their families, and
- Creating special drop-in centres for survivors where they can receive confidential and compassionate care.

These activities must be culturally appropriate and must be developed in close cooperation with community members. They will need on-going financial and logistical support and, where appropriate, training and supervision. Quality counselling by trained workers, such as counsellors, nurses, social workers, psychologists or psychiatrists – preferably from the same background as the survivor – should also be provided as soon after the attack as possible. Reassurance, kindness and total confidentiality are vital elements of counselling. Counsellors should also offer support if the survivor experiences any post-traumatic disturbances, if she has difficulty dealing with family and community reactions, and as she goes through any legal procedures.

The objectives of counselling are to help survivors:

- Understand what they have experienced,
- Overcome guilt,
- Express their anger,
- Realise they are not responsible for the attack,
- Know that they are not alone, and
- Access support networks and services.

SEXUAL VIOLENCE IN DOMESTIC SITUATIONS

Caution should be exercised before intervening in domestic situations because the survivor and/ or other relatives could be subjected to further harm. If the survivor has to return to the abuser, retaliation may follow, especially if the abuser learns that the matter has been reported. Each situation needs to be individually assessed in close cooperation with colleagues to determine the most appropriate response. Health care providers may choose to refer the matter to a disciplinary committee, inform the authorities, or provide discreet advice to the survivor about her options.

These children may be mistreated or even abandoned by their mothers and families. They must be closely monitored and support should be offered to the mother. It is important to ensure that the family and the community do not stigmatize either the child or the mother. Foster placement and, later, adoption should be considered if the child is rejected, neglected or otherwise mistreated.

Legal Aspects

The government on whose territory the sexual attack occurred is responsible for taking remedial measures, including conducting a thorough investigation into the crime, identifying and prosecuting those responsible and protecting survivors from reprisal. In all cases, the wishes of the survivor should be respected when pursuing the legal aspects of the case. Confidentiality must be ensured. All agencies should advocate the enactment and/ or enforcement of national laws against sexual violence in accordance with international legal obligations. These should include prosecution of offenders and the implementation of legal measures to protect the survivor. The local UNHCR Protection Officer must be familiar with the national criminal and civil law on the subject of rape and sexual violence before an incident occurs so he/ she will know what procedural steps should be taken and what advice should be given to survivors.

Monitoring

Monitoring cases of sexual violence should be a routine task of health care providers, protection officers and others, as appropriate. In addition, there should be regular assessments of the providers' ability to offer comprehensive medical and psychosocial care for rape survivors. Ideally, care should be given as soon after a rape as possible.

Sexual Violence Indicators

Indicators to be collected from the health-facility level

- Incidence of sexual violence (reported cases/ 10,000 population)
- Coverage of services for survivors
- Timely care for survivors

Indicators that might be measured annually:

- Prosecution of sexual violence offenders
- Coverage of health-worker training that serves survivors of sexual violence

Key Interventions — Preventing Sexual Violence:

- Ensure proper documentation for women

- Increase availability of female protection officers and interpreters and ensure that all officers have knowledge of UNHCR Protection Guidelines and UN Security Guidelines for Women
- Facilitate the use of existing women's groups or promote the formation of women's groups to discuss and respond to issues of sexual violence
- Improve camp design for increased security for women
- Include women in camp decision-making processes, especially in the areas of health, sanitation, reproductive health, food distribution, camp design/ location
- Distribute essential items such as food, water and fuel directly to women
- Train people at all levels (NGO, government, refugee, etc.), to prevent, identify and respond to acts of sexual violence.

Key Interventions – Responding to Sexual Violence:

- Develop/ adapt protocols and guidelines that would limit further traumas to survivors of sexual violence
- Engage socially and culturally appropriate support personnel as a first contact with people who have been subjected to sexual violence
- Provide prompt and culturally appropriate psychosocial support for survivors and their families
- Provide medical follow-up immediately after an attack that also addresses STDs, HIV infection and unwanted pregnancy
- Establish closer links among protection officers, women's groups, TBAs and community leaders to discuss issues related to the attacks
- Document cases while respecting survivors' wishes and confidentiality.

EFFECT OF DOMESTIC VIOLENCE ON PREGNANCY AND LABOUR

Because the issue of violence against women is such an important social problem with serious health consequences for abused women and their children, health professionals providing care to pregnant women need to consider how the experience of abuse in current or past intimate relationships could affect their patients during pregnancy, labour, and delivery. This chapter reviews current evidence from the medical, nursing, and midwifery literature, with a particular focus on clinical issues, and identifies some important, but as yet unresolved issues. For a more comprehensive analysis of these issues, readers are referred to other materials, some of which are listed in the bibliography. For the purposes of this chapter, we use the terms violence and abuse interchangeably, to mean the use of physical force and verbal threats to intimidate another person with whom one has an intimate or other close family relationship. The abuse can manifest as physical, psychological, or sexual abuse. Why violence against women is an important health issue.

In a 1993 Statistics Canada survey of 12, 300 adult women, 29% of the women who had ever been married or involved in common-law relationships reported that they had been assaulted by their partners and 51% reported at least one incident of physical or sexual violence since the age of 16. Younger women (18 to 24 years), women whose household incomes were less than $15 000, and women whose marriages (or common-law partnerships) had lasted less than 2 years reported higher rates of abuse; neither educational level nor geographic location was associated with variation in the rate of abuse. When asked about the occurrence of violence in association with their pregnancies, 21% of women abused by a partner reported being assaulted during pregnancy. The incidence of physical abuse in pregnancy has been examined in two Canadian studies. When women receiving prenatal care from family physicians and obstetricians working in either private, community-based, or university teaching clinics in Toronto were asked about their experience of physical abuse in pregnancy, 6.6% reported physical abuse during the current pregnancy and 11% reported being abused prior to the current pregnancy.

Similarly, a recent study of pregnant women attending a publicly funded, community-based health programme in

Saskatoon found that 5.7% reported physical abuse during pregnancy and 8.5% reported experiencing abuse in the year prior to their third-trimester interview. The risk of abuse for this group of women was greater if they were aboriginal, if their partners had a problem with alcohol, and if they had high levels of perceived stress in the preceding year. Numerous studies have shown that abuse accounts for a substantial proportion of the injuries that bring women to hospital emergency departments. Abused women are more likely to present with physical symptoms, such as headache, irritable bowel syndrome, and chronic pelvic pain, than non abused women.' The prevalence of psychological problems, such as depression, suicidal behaviour, and substance abuse, is higher in abused women as well.'

Looking at 1992 Canadian homicide statistics spousal homicides accounted for 17% of solved murders, with men killing their wives in 84% of these cases and women killing their husbands in 16% of cases; 42% of family-related homicides involved a history of domestic violence reported to police. During the period from 1974 to 1987, 31% of men who killed their wives went on to commit suicide immediately following the incident. Although a systematic review of the literature found no consistent relationship between violence during pregnancy and adverse pregnancy outcomes, some of the studies reviewed did find a difference between abused and non abused women's outcomes of pregnancy in mean birth weight and incidence of low birth weight. Both direct and indirect causal pathways have been postulated to explain such adverse outcomes.

Blunt trauma to a maternal abdomen has been shown to lead to placental abruption, preterm labour and delivery, fetomaternal hemorrhage, and fetal death. Assaults resulted in more pregnancy complications than motor vehicle accidents or falls, the two other major causes of trauma during pregnancy. Physical, sexual, or emotional abuse during pregnancy can lead indirectly to adverse pregnancy outcomes by affecting pregnant women's health behaviours. For example, abuse during pregnancy has been associated with delayed entry into prenatal care, increased behavioural risks such as the use of tobacco, alcohol, and illicit drugs, and poor maternal nutrition, all of which have been associated with increased risk of low birth weight and preterm delivery.

Labour and delivery can be particularly difficult for women with a history of sexual abuse, and physicians and other birth attendants unaware of the abuse could have difficulty understanding their seemingly unusual behaviour. As labour progresses, the increasing pain, the subsequent sense of loss of control, and the repeated pelvic and genital examinations by multiple caregivers can result in unexpectedly extreme responses from labouring women from too quiet and passive to screaming, crying, or uncontrollable terror. Other women respond by becoming overly controlling or demanding. Still others dissociate during labour or delivery. Some accoucheurs have even speculated that a history of abuse plays a role in inadequate fetal descent and prolonged second stage, based on their interactions with abused women during labour.

ROLE OF THE CAREGIVER

Because of the high prevalence of abuse in the general population, all pregnant women should be screened for past or current history of abuse. Rates of disclosure might be improved if women are asked about abuse at the same time that they are asked about other social risk factors. Some clinicians prefer to ask about abuse during history-taking, while others prefer to use standardized tools. The Woman Abuse Screening Tool is reliable and valid and has been shown to be effective in identifying abuse in adult women patients attending their regular family physicians for prenatal care or periodic health examinations or for assessment of particular health problems. It has been included in the Antenatal Psychosocial Health Assessment (ALPHA) form, an evidence-based screening tool that can be used as a checklist for psychosocial enquiry and will soon be incorporated into the Ontario Antenatal Record. Women should never be asked questions about abuse in the presence of their partners.

Caregivers might be particularly alerted to the possibility of abuse in the following clinical situations.

- Unwanted pregnancy
- Teenage pregnancy
- Delay in seeking prenatal care
- Inadequate attendance at prenatal education
- Recurring or unexplained psychosomatic illness
- Addiction to alcohol, tobacco, or psychotropic drugs, or use of illicit drugs
- Unexplained injuries, particularly to the breasts and abdomen
- History of psychiatric illness

Barriers to identification and disclosure- Women might be reluctant to disclose a history of abuse for a variety of personal and social reasons (e.g., shame, embarrassment, uncertainty about housing or financial options, etc) or because previous attempts at disclosure were met with disbelief or denial by other professionals or by family members or friends. Health care providers might be reluctant to ask about abuse because of a lack of understanding of the importance of abuse as a health issue or a lack of information about community resources. Caregivers' own experiences as victims, perpetrators, or child witnesses to abuse could also affect their readiness to ask about abuse.

When patients disclose a history of abuse, it is crucial that health care providers respond in a way that makes these patients feel believed and supported. It is not appropriate to question behaviour during the abusive episodes or to minimize the seriousness of the abuse. Patients should be provided with information about how to get help in dealing with their experiences. In situations where pregnant women have sustained direct trauma to the abdomen, continuous fetal heart rate monitoring and external tocodynamometry are recommended. Controversy exists over the duration of monitoring; recommended times range, from 30 minutes to 48 hours. Women who are Rh negative require Rh globulin.

Some abused women will need help in making changes in their lives as they sort out their experiences of abuse. In addition to providing clinical care, which might include helping them with their physical and psychological symptoms and providing support, health care providers might decide to refer such patients to other health care professionals or to community agencies for assistance in obtaining shelter, sorting out financial options, exploring legal options, and arranging further psychological counseling for themselves and their children. When abuse is disclosed, the importance of having a safety plan should be stressed by health care providers or other helpers from the community. Many community agencies can provide written materials to help women develop safety plans. If there are children in the family, health care providers should enquire about whether they have ever been abused or if there is risk of abuse and determine whether the physical and emotional environment is safe for the children. Any concerns about the safety of the children must be reported to the appropriate child protection agencies.

Family physicians typically provide medical care to members of pregnant women's families as well and might find themselves caring for partners or other family members who perpetrated the violence. In such situations, physicians must ensure that the needs of the abused women and the perpetrators are addressed independently, such that their rights to autonomy, confidentiality, honesty, and quality of care are maintained. Couple or marital therapy is contraindicated unless the woman's safety can be ensured and the man has taken responsibility for his abusive behaviour. If current abuse is disclosed, accoucheurs will need to determine whether the home environment is safe for a newborn (and for other children) and whether the woman and her partner are physically and emotionally able to care for a newborn appropriately.

CONFIDENTIALITY AND REPORTING ISSUES

Women will feel more comfortable disclosing if they know that the details of their disclosure will be kept confidential by caregivers. This is particularly important for family physicians that also provide care to other family members. Practitioners who are concerned that a history of abuse might affect their patients' tolerance of certain procedures (e.g., transvaginal ultrasound) should check with their patients about what information can be disclosed to these other caregivers (e.g., obstetrical consultants, delivery room nurses). Practitioners are not obliged to report past or current episodes of abuse, no matter how violent. Practitioners should, however, be aware of the recommendations of their provincial colleges with respect to the duty to warn in situations where they become aware of a serious risk of violence to a third person. If the possibility of child abuse arises, practitioners must inform local child protection agencies of their suspicions.

As in any clinical situation, disclosures of abuse and relevant positive and negative findings on physical examination should be well documented. Good records of repeated injuries or recurrent vague complaints might help physicians consider the possibility of abuse, even when women are reluctant to disclose. Moreover, thorough documentation might obviate the need for a court appearance should the case come to trial. Exactly what information should be recorded on the standardized antenatal record forms that are sent to the delivery room remains unclear. A history of violence before or during pregnancy can affect labour and delivery, but women might not want staff in the delivery room to know about their experience because they do not have long-term, trusting relationships with those caregivers. It is important that caregivers check with their patients about what information to share with other caregivers.

FUTURE DIRECTIONS

Because the frequency of an event is an important consideration in deciding whether to screen, it would be helpful for practitioners to have accurate, current estimates of the prevalence of violence in Canada, with attention to specific populations. We need to determine regional, social, and cultural differences that would assist policy planners and clinicians to provide better service to abused women and their families.

Practitioners would be helped by more research into the clinical clues that suggest violence is an issue in their patients' lives, including important risk factors. Given the increasing numbers of refugee and immigrant women coming to Canada, practitioners require more information about their needs. We need to know how to ask about abuse in a culturally sensitive fashion and how best to serve women with violence issues complicated by language barriers, immigration status problems, poverty, and isolation. Little attention has yet been addressed to meeting the needs of these particular women. More research is needed on the effect of violence on pregnancy outcomes. Attention is required to the particular physiologic mechanisms through which violence could affect pregnancy outcomes. In addition, little is known about the effect of aspects of our clinical care; for example, do violence-screening strategies help or hinder our patients? In a recent editorial, MacMillan emphasized the need to expand the extensive work on low birth weight to include an examination of its association with abuse during pregnancy. In addition, she stresses the need for a population-based study to determine the long-term clinical outcomes for women and their children.

Research needs to be done on the roles of various caregivers in identifying and managing domestic violence. Health care is changing rapidly, we are experiencing new kinds of caregivers (nurse-practitioners, midwives), changing types of practice, and increasing mobility of health care providers. With these changes come the challenges of communicating sensitive patient information, such as a history of violence and abuse, to colleagues and sharing care of patients in collaborative ways that best help women and their families.

Now that practitioners are becoming more aware of the importance and frequency of violence issues in the lives of pregnant patients, we need to examine how well we are helping these patients. We need to look at how extensively and how sensitively we screen. Are non-abused women intimidated or put off by our style of questioning? Do some screening efforts

harm abused women, and if so, which ones? Questions have been raised about the role of a practitioner's own gender in his or her ability to help abused women. If there are differences related to a physician's sex, what can practitioners do to minimize barriers to disclosure or assistance?

Another strongly held belief is that the duration of the doctor-patient relationship substantially affects disclosure or subsequent management of the problem. If a long-term relationship facilitates disclosure or helps the patient in any way, how can new caregivers short cut the development of a trusting or helpful relationship? Can other professionals or agencies use a family physician's previously established relationship to enhance their work with that family physician's patients? On the other hand, does a long-term relationship actually hinder screening, identification, and disclosure? Are practitioners and agencies new to patients better able to help with violence issues?

Further investigation is also needed into patients with multiple problems, e.g., patients with a history of abuse who abuse substances. Are we giving these women the comprehensive care they need? Can one practitioner respond to all their needs, and how do we share this type of care with colleagues whose expertise complements our own? More work needs to be done to determine whether certain interventions are better suited to specific patient populations (adolescents, new Canadians), and whether certain practitioners are better suited to specific roles (family physicians, delivery room nurses, community workers).

HEALTH SERVICES RESEARCH

Financing health care in Canada is undergoing great change. It is unclear how the current fiscal crisis affects practitioners' abilities and willingness to help abused women. Do time or funding constraints affect our identification, management, and referral of these women, and if so, how? If we take time to screen our pregnant patients for a history of violence, we need to be sure that referring agencies have the capacity to respond to the increased numbers of women seeking their help.

Research is needed into access to health care for women affected by violence. For example, do pregnant or postpartum women recently arrived in shelters have adequate access to medical, nursing, midwifery, or lactation consultant care? We need to know whether practitioners are defining their communities to the best advantage of women affected by violence. Which patients experience access problems due to geographical location, socioeconomic status, ethnicity, or other factors?

A great deal of community service and advocacy work is done after hours by health care practitioners, but this work is often poorly rewarded in any official way. Research into roles and service would enhance this recognition process. It could also invite new members and create new partnerships between community agencies and professionals or among different groups of professionals. Such research would promote public awareness of the extent of violence in our society and the roles and involvement of health care professionals in dealing with this issue. Finally, although we recognize that health care practitioners are exposed to violence in both their personal and professional lives, little work has been done to explore the extent to which they are affected by these experiences. We need to learn more about self care, coping strategies, peer support, and supervision of patients with difficult problems.

EDUCATION

Learners need to become familiar with the manifold presentations of violence and to become comfortable talking with patients about abuse. They need to be ready to refer to appropriate helping agencies. They need to see their preceptors and senior clinicians' role model these clinical skills. Education on violence for health care practitioners needs to be evidence based and properly evaluated. Effective methods for disseminating new findings to clinicians need to be implemented. We need to consider whether this education should be multidisciplinary or with groups of peers, and whether survivors of violence have a role in the education of professionals.

Special obstetrical education programmes, such as the Advanced Life Support in Obstetrics (ALSO) and Advances in Labor and Risk Management (ALARM) courses, need to incorporate violence issues directly into the curriculum. Domestic violence should not be marginalized by including it as a subsection of abdominal trauma. Although all practitioners should be aware of violence issues and be able to assist patients appropriately, some caregivers might be interested in developing advanced skills in this area.

Consideration should be given to creating educational opportunities for providing advanced training in psychosocial care of obstetrical patients. Strategies need to be developed, in conjunction with community agencies, to assist people affected by abuse and violence to use available community resources. Educational efforts must inform patients that violence in pregnancy is an important health issue and worthy of our attention. A variety of media, including pamphlets and posters in medical offices and hospital delivery rooms, should be used to inform the public of health care practitioners' awareness of violence as a health care issue and to encourage the public to discuss these issues with their family physicians and other health care professionals.

Public and professional educational endeavours need to be evaluated. We need to know which strategies have helped women and which have been ineffective or harmful. Involvement of survivors of violence, shelter workers, and other allied health professionals would greatly enhance such research. Not only can the experience of violence and abuse in past or current intimate relationships affect the physical health and psychological well-being of women and their children, these negative experiences can also play a role in pregnancy outcomes and in labour and delivery.

As health care professionals, we need to be aware of these issues and maintain a high index of suspicion for the possibility of abuse in our clinical work. Because of their long-term relationships with patients and because they focus on both physical and mental health issues with their patients, family physicians are in a unique position to identify patients with a history of abuse. As attention to these issues is relatively new, many questions remain unresolved. Collaborative projects with family physicians, obstetricians, midwives, patients, and others who work with abused women will help us all to better understand these women's experiences and to provide exemplary care.

The psychological and social sequels of HIV and AIDS infection is devastating to children, adolescents, women, and their families. HIV and AIDS is a chronic/terminal illness that forces individuals and their families to cope with an uncertain progression of disease, complicated medication regimes, and the grief related to the loss of health and possibly the loss of family members. Unlike other chronic/terminal illnesses HIV and AIDS infection is further complicated by the stigma related to the transmission of HIV infection (i.e., sexual activity and intravenous drug use). Due to disclosure fears and stigma associated with HIV and AIDS, many families isolate themselves from their extended family and communities to protect themselves and their children from maltreatment.

Thus, they are cut off from valuable supports. In conjunction with coping with the psychological and emotional ramifications of being infected with or affected by HIV and AIDS, these individuals are forced to deal with a multitude of stressors with little support. These factors place these individuals and their family members at risk for mental health disorders (e.g., depression, post-traumatic stress disorder, and anxiety), developmental deficits, and behavioural problems (e.g., drug or alcohol use, school failure, inability to maintain a job, and criminal behaviour). These issues complicate the HIV and AIDS infected children, adolescents, and women's ability to access medical care and comply with complicated medication regimens. The goal of this chapter is to provide an overview of the psychological and social issues, which impact families that are affected by HIV and AIDS.

EPIDEMIOLOGY

HIV and AIDS infection of adolescents and women is increasing, while the rate of vertical transmission of HIV to children has decreased with the use of medication during pregnancy. According to the United States Health and Resources Services Administration (HRSA) it is estimated that there are 40,000 new HIV infections annually, approximately 25% of these are believed to occur in individuals between the age of 13 and 21. HRSA also reported a higher percentage of females in the AIDS cases among adolescents and young adults: 55.5 percent from the age of 13 to 19 and 40.5 percent from the ages of 20 to 24. As of 1992, it has been estimated that 24,000 children have been orphaned by AIDS in the United States. According to the Bureau of HIV/AIDS of the Florida Department of Health, the numbers of HIV and AIDS case in Duval County through April 2000 were 688 and 3873, respectively. It is believed that the number of reported HIV cases is an underestimation of the number of actual cases, since reporting of positive HIV results began in 1997 in Florida. Duval County ranks number 5 in reported HIV and AIDS cases within the state.

FAMILY ISSUES

There are complex psychological and social issues that impact a family's ability to cope with HIV and AIDS infection. Individuals who participated in high-risk behaviour that lead to HIV infection may experience intense guilt, shame, and anger. These emotions may be intensified for women who transmit HIV infection to their children. Furthermore, the stigma related to HIV infection may lead to social isolation. Often, families do not disclose their HIV status to family members, including the infected child, and their community for fear that they and their children will be mistreated. This isolation prevents families from obtaining valuable social support during difficult times. It is important for members of the medical community to be aware of the fears that these families may have regarding disclosure, as women may not utilize services if they believe that their HIV status will be disclosed.

HIV and AIDS infection is viewed as a multi-generational illness. Individuals may be overwhelmed by the loss of a number of family members, as well as coping with their own diagnosis. Illness and grief interfere with a parent's ability to provide consistent care for children. Due to illness or death of the parents, primary care responsibilities often fall to extended family members.

In fact, grandmothers often become the primary caregiver for multiple children. Loss of parents and changes in caregivers interfere with mastery of developmental milestones and coping abilities of children and adolescents. Parent's failure to develop a permanency plan (create a will identifying a legal guardian for their children) further complicates this issue, particularly for children who are HIV infected. Development of a permanency plan and providing continuity of care are challenging tasks for parents with HIV and AIDS infection for numerous reasons. These reasons include denial of the severity of illness, fear of disclosure, health status of parent and HIV infected child, lack of reliable adult to provide care, psychological adjustment of parents, and domestic violence in the home.

Another complicating issue, is that HIV and AIDS disproportionately affects children, adolescents, and women of inner city, primarily minority communities. Individuals from inner city communities, such as Jacksonville, often struggle to cope with problems in their homes, schools, and neighborhoods that increase their chances of participating in high-risk behaviours. Examples of the problems that they face include single parent families, domestic violence, physical abuse and neglect, substance abuse, and mental health diagnosis.

To complicate matters many of these individuals suffer from cognitive and behavioural delays related to HIV and AIDS infection, poor education, and a history of physical trauma. These factors further place these individuals at risk for mental health illness (e.g., depression, post-traumatic stress disorder, conduct disorder, and anxiety), developmental deficits, and behavioural problems. Mental health treatment may be utilized to address the cyclic patterns of poverty, violence, abuse, and neglect. In addition, it is important to address both primary and secondary prevention issues with individuals in the community, particularly with adolescents, who are more likely to participate in behaviours that expose them to HIV or other sexually transmitted diseases.

ADHERENCE ISSUES

There are numerous issues that interfere with HIV and AIDS infected individual's ability to comply with complicated medication regimens.

Barriers to medication compliance include a lack of understanding of the long-term results of noncompliance, myths and misunderstandings about the effectiveness and necessity of medication, distrust of the medical community, conflicts with lifestyle choices, substance abuse, mental health illness, and side-effects of the medication. Adherence programmes developed to increase compliance in adolescents and adults have emphasized communication between patient and medical caregiver, development of a supportive medical setting, and determination of whether or not the HIV infected individual is ready to take medication. Psychological interventions also may include training children to swallow pills, identifying cognitive deficits, and difficulties in dealing with social issues that prevent compliance.

NEUROPSYCHOLOGICAL ISSUES

The progression of HIV infection to AIDS infection has been associated with central nervous system dysfunction. The signs and symptoms of HIV-related CNS infection include cognitive impairment (i.e., short term memory deficits and confusion), changes in personality (i.e., apathy and erratic behaviour), psychotic symptoms (i.e., hallucinations and suspiciousness), and motor symptoms (i.e., ataxia, and weakness). Careful assessment of symptoms is necessary to distinguish central nervous system dysfunction from the effects of mental health illness (i.e., depression and anxiety), as well as other factors that effect neuropsychological functioning.

These factors include, but are not limited to, prescribed and recreation drug use, stress of living with a chronic/ terminal illness, and nutritional deficiencies. It is important to note that a number of behavioural and psychosocial problems have been noted in HIV and AIDS infected children. These problems include hyperactivity, attentional deficits, social withdrawal, and depression.

In addition, cognitive deficits, learning disabilities, and developmental delays have been related to central nervous symptom dysfunction in children. Of course, it is possible that these disorders are related to environmental influences and due to HIV and AIDS infection. Careful assessment of a child's functioning will help to determine the cause of the deficit and appropriate treatment. HIV and AIDS infected individuals and their families are forced to cope with a multitude of stressors. Supportive psychotherapy may be utilized to improve quality of life, increase compliance with medical care and medication regimens, and address mental health disorders.

Historically, traditional psychotherapy and psycho educational interventions have not addressed the ethnically and culturally diverse issues often relate to HIV and AIDS infection. Therefore, professionals must offer flexible and effective interventions that encourage HIV and AIDS infected individuals to efficient coping and management skills. Psychologists and mental health counselors may help to foster a relationship between the medical care providers and the children, adolescents, and women who are

HIV and AIDS infected to ensure that patients and their families are able to access and comply with appropriate medical care.

Bibliography

Aldarondo, E. & Mederos, F., Editors (2002) *Programs for Men Who Batter: Intervention and Prevention Strategies in a Diverse Society.* Civic Research Institute, Inc., Kingston, NJ.

Bancroft, L. & Silverman, J., (2002) *The Batterer as Parent: Addressing the Impact of Domestic Violence on Family Dynamics.* Sage Publications, Inc. Thousand Oaks, California.

Binder, Arnold, and Meeker, James W. (1993) "Implications of the Failure to Replicate the Minneapolis Experiment Findings." *American Sociological Review* 57 : 698–708.

Buzawa, Eves., and Buzawa, Carl G. (1992) *Domestic Violence: The Changing Criminal Justice Response.* Beverly Hills, Calif. : Sage.

Daly, Martin, and Wilson, Margo. (1988) *Homicide.* Aldine de Gruyter.

Davies, Jill. (1998) *Safety Planning with Battered Women: Complex Lives/Difficult Choices.*

Dutton, Donald G., with Golant, Susan K. (1995) *The Batterer: A Psychological Profile.* New York: Basic Books.

Edelson, Jefferey L. (1992) *Intervention for Men Who Batter: An Ecological Approach.* Beverly Hills, Calif.: Sage.

Edleson, J. & Williams, O. editors. (2007) *Parenting by Men Who Batter: New Directions for Assessment and Intervention.* Oxford University Press, New York, NY.

Edleson, J. (1999) *The Overlap Between Child Maltreatment and Woman Abuse.* Minnesota School of Social Work. This paper has now been published in Violence Against Women, 5(2), pp. 134-154.

Family Violence Prevention Fund & World Childhood Foundation. (2005). *Turning Pain into Power: Trafficking Survivors' Perspectives on Early Intervention Strategies.* San Fransisco.

Ferraro, Kathleen J., and Boychuck, Tascha. (1992) "The Court's Response to Interpersonal Violence: A Comparison of Intimate and Nonintimate Assault." In *Domestic Violence: The Changing Criminal Justice Response.* Edited by Eve S. Buzawa and Carl G. Buzawa. Beverly Hills, Calif.: Sage,. Pages 209ff.

Fineman, Martha, and Mykiyiuk, Roxanne, eds. (1994) *The Public Nature of Private Violence.* New York: Routledge.

Gelles, Richard, and Loseke, Donileen R., eds. (1992) *Current Controversies on Family Violence.* Beverly Hills, Calif.: Sage.

Goldfarb, Sally. (1996) "Describing Without Circumscribing: Questioning the Construct of Gender in the Discourse of Intimate Violence." *George Washington Law Review* U.S. Department of Justice. 64: 582–631.

Gondolf, Edward W. (1980) "Who Are Those Guys? Toward a Behavioral Typology of Batterers." *Violence & Victims* 3: 187.

Greenfield, Lawrence, et al. (1998) "Violence by Intimates: Analysis of Data on Crimes By Current or Former Spouses, Boyfriends, and Girlfriends." Washington, D.C.: U.S. Department of Justice, Bureau of Justice Statistics.

Hanna, Cheryl. (1996) "No Right to Choose: Mandated Victim Participation in Domestic Violence Prosecutions." *Harvard Law Review* 109 : 1849–1910.

Healy, Kerry; Smith, Kristen; and O'Sullivan, Chris. (1998) *Batterer Intervention: Program Approaches and Criminal Justice Strategies* (NCJ 168638). Washington, D.C.: U.S. Department of Justice.

Hilton, N. Zoe, ed. (1993) *Legal Responses to Wife Assault.* Beverly Hills, Calif.: Sage.

Holzworth-Munroe, Amy, and Stuart, Gregory L. (1994) "Typology of Male Batterers: Three Subtypes and the Differences Among Them." *Psychological Bulletin* 116: 476–497.

Knudsen, Deand D., and Miller, Joann L., eds. (1991) *Abused and Battered.* New York: A. de Gruyter.

Moroz, K. J. (2005, August 26). *Understanding the current mental health needs of children experiencing domestic violence in Vermont: Recommendations for enhancing and improving responses.*

National Resource Center on Domestic Violence (1999, July). *Getting the Word Out...Domestic Violence in Rural Communities by the West Virginia Coalition Against Domestic Violence.*

National Resource Center on Domestic Violence (2002, March). *Children exposed to intimate partner violence.*

O'Keefe, M. (2005, April). *Teen Dating violence: A review of risk factors and prevention efforts.*

Peacock, D., & Rothman, E. (2001, November). *Working with young men who batter: Current strategies and new directions.*

Pence, Ellen, and Paymar, Michael. (1993) *Education Groups for Men Who Batter: The Duluth Model.* New York: Springer.

Rosenfeld, Barry D. (1992) "Court Ordered Treatment of Spouse Abuse." *Clinical Psychology Review* vol. 12 : 205–226.

Schneider, Elizabeth M. (1992) "Particularity & Generality: Challenges of Feminist Theory and Practice in Work on Woman Abuse." *New York University Law Review* 67: 520–568.

Sherman, Lawrence. (1992) *Policing Domestic Violence: Experiments and Dilemmas.* New York: Free Press.

Smuts, Barbara. (1996) "Male Aggression Against Women: An Evolutionary Perspective." In *Sex, Power, Conflict.* Edited by David M. Buss and Neil Malamuth. New York: Oxford University Press. Pages 231–268.

Spears, L. (2000, February). *Building Bridges between Domestic Violence Organizations and Child Protective Services by Linda Spears.*

Steinman, Michael, ed. (1991) *Woman Battering: Policy Responses.* Highland Heights, Ky.: Academy of Criminal Justice Sciences, Northern Kentucky University.

Straus, Murray, and Gelles Richard, eds. (1990) *Physical Violence in American Families: Risk Factors and Adaptations to Violence in 8,145 Families.* New Brunswick, N.J.: Transaction.

Vann, A. A. (2003). *Developing culturally-relevant responses to domestic abuse: Asha Family Services, Inc.*

West, Angela. (1992) "Prosecutorial Activism: Confronting Heterosexism in a Lesbian Battering Case." *Harvard Women's Law Journal* 15 : 249–271.

Yllo, Kerti, A., and Bogard, Michele, eds. (1998) *Feminist Perspectives on Wife Abuse.* Beverly Hills, Calif.: Sage.

Zorza, Joan. (1994) "Must We Stop Arresting Batterers? Analysis and Policy Implications of New Police Domestic Violence Studies." *New England Law Review* 28: 929–990.

INDEX